THE ART OF THE CHASE

Amanda Lockhart

THE ART OF THE CHASE

Amanda Lockhart

Introduction by Robin Lane Fox

Adelphi Publishers

Soft, fleecy clouds were sailing,
Across the vault of blue;
A fairer hunting morning,
No huntsman ever knew.

All nature seemed rejoicing,
That glorious morn to see;
All seemed to breathe a fresher life –
Beast, insect, bird and tree.

But sound and sight of beauty
Fell dull on eye and ear;
The huntsman's heart was heavy,
His brow oppressed with care.

High in his stirrups raised he stood,
And long he gazed around;
And breathlessly and anxiously,
He listened for a sound.

But nought he heard save song of bird,
Or jay's discordant cry;
Or when among the tree tops,
The wind went murmuring by.

No voice of hound, or sound of horn,
The woods around were mute,
As though the earth had swallowed up,
His comrades – man and brute.

He thought, I must essay to find,
My hounds at any cost;
A huntsman who has lost his hounds
Is but a huntsman lost.

Then round he turned his horse's head,
And shook his bridle free,
When he was struck by an aged fox,
That sat beneath a tree.

He raised his eyes in glad surprise,
That huntsman keen and bold;
But there was in that fox's look
That made his blood run cold.

He raised his hand to touch his horn,
And shout a 'Tally-Ho!'
But, mastered by that fox's eye,
His lips refused to blow.

For he was grim and gaunt of limb,
With age all silvered o'er;
He might have been an Arctic fox,
Escaped from Greenland's shore.

But age and vigour had not tamed,
Nor dimm'd his sparkling eye,
Which shone with an unearthly fire –
A fire could never die.

And thus the huntsman he addressed,
In tones distinct and clear,
Who heard as they who in a dream,
The fairies' music hear.

'Huntsman,' he said – a sudden thrill,
Through all the listener ran,
To hear a creature of the wood,
Speak like a Christian man-

'Last of my race, to me 'tis given
The future to unfold
To speak the words which never yet
Spake fox of mortal mould.

'Then print my words upon your heart,
And stamp them on your brain,
That you to others may impart
My prophecy again.

'Strong life is yours in manhood's prime,
Your cheek with heat is red,
Time has not laid his finger yet
In earnest on your head.

'But ere your limbs are bent with age,
And ere you locks are grey,
The sport that you have loved so well
Shall long have passed away.

'In vain shall generous Colmore
Your hunt consent to keep;
In vain the Rendcombe baronet
With gold your stores shall heap.

'In vain Sir Alexander,
And Watson keep in vain,
O'er the pleasant Cotswold Hills
The joyous sport maintain.

'Vain all their efforts; spite of all
Draws nigh the fatal morn,
When the last Cotswold fox shall hear
The latest huntsman's horn.

'Yet think not, huntsman, I rejoice
To see the end so near;
Nor think the sound of horn and hound
To me a sound of fear.

'In my strong youth which numbers now
Full many a winter back,
How scornfully I shook my brush
Before the Berkeley Pack.

'How oft from Painswick Hill I've seen
The morning mist uncurl,
When Harry Ayres blew the horn
Before the wrathful Earl.

'How oft I've heard the Cotswold's cry,
As Turner cheered the pack,
And laughed to see his baffled hounds,
Hang vainly on my track.

'Then think not that I speak in fear,
Or prophesy in hate;
Too well I know the doom reserved,
For all my tribe by fate.

'Too well I know, by wisdom taught,
The existence of my race
O'er all wide England's green domain,
Is bound up with the Chase.

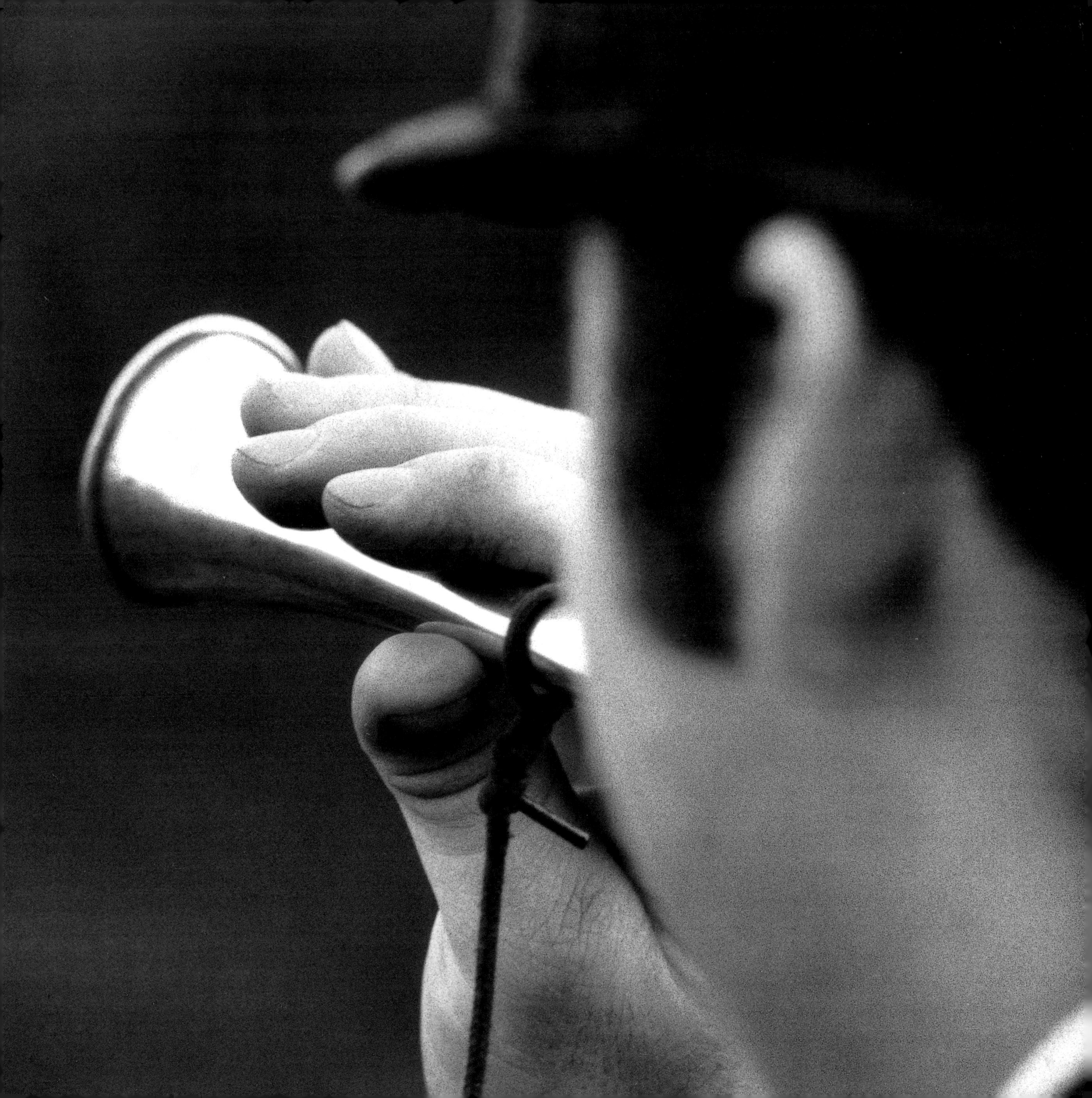

Foreword Amanda Lockhart

There are many people, too countless to mention, without whose help this book would not have been possible. In particular, together with Adelphi Publishers, I would like to thank the following very much for their generous support:

The Duke of Bedford

Mr and Mrs Dick Burchnall

Anthony Burrell

Hugo de Ferranti

Roddy Fleming

Mr and Mrs Piers Hillier

The Earl and Countess of Hopetoun

Mr and Mrs James Inglis

Tom Kenyon-Slaney

The Countess of Lichfield

The Duke of Marlborough

Rudolf Freiherr von Mentzingen

Mark Miller-Mundy

Lord Neidpath

Mr and Mrs Hugh Pinney

The Marquess of Salisbury

The Duke of Westminster

Preface   Robin Lane Fox

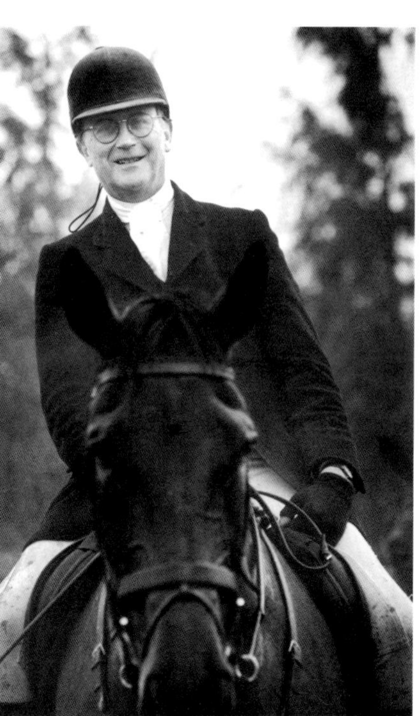

Robin out with the Heythrop

"Everyone who has loved hunting," wrote that ancient lover of the sport, Xenophon, "has been a good man." He was writing more than two thousand years ago and although we now have excellent hunting women too and one or two hunting rascals on and off the field, he catches what we still think. It will take more than one government in thrall to its backbenchers to change that fact or our pursuit. Hunting with dogs will be restored and quite probably hedged about with heritage legislation to protect it. Nobody will waste so much government time and money trying to ban it again. The sport will have gone through what used to occur in good T.V. programmes: a short intermission. In this case it will be shorter than the one which interrupted it between 1939 and 1945 and left our coverts teeming with foxes when hunting resumed. And for ever after, hounds will be hounds, not 'dogs'.

Five years ago, Amanda Lockhart decided to capture fox-hunting on camera, from Scotland to Devon. It was, she admits, a labour of love, and these superb black and white photographs are proof that facts become art through love. She had hunted as a girl in the daunting Wynnstay country, and after four years at Oxford University, she ended up hunting again, but this time with the camera-lens which has become her livelihood. Her aim, brilliantly realised, was to catch the enduring look of hunting across more than a hundred years. After these pictures have hit home by showing what you recognise and value, take another look and you will see how carefully she has chosen the view which is free of telegraph-poles or that curse of the twentieth century, barbed wire. If there is plenty of plough, it is there not only because we all have to live with it nowadays, even in the Vale of Belvoir, but also because it was there more than a century ago, in the 1870's, before the farming recession increased the empire of English grass. To catch that hound on the heights of the Blencathra, Amanda had to be quick and patient, after so many false starts. It may have been easier to snap some Wynnstay ladies doing up their horses' girths, but such photographs could only be taken by someone who knows from the inside those character-istic little skills and manoeuvres which become second nature to anyone who hunts. Only when we train a young fox-hunter in the next generation do we come to realize how many of these tricks have become a knack for us, though they are hard for outsiders to imitate, from tying a stock in the mornings to flicking open a gate-catch, from knowing not to canter on the concrete surface of a farmyard to facing hounds head-on and not showing off by trying to call them, as if they would ever obey a mere follower.

Amanda's photographs bring out the social diversity of those who love hunting. They are certainly not snooty or the 'toffs' whom backbenchers love to invent. Hunting is not a cheap sport for those who live in a classy four-day a week country and choose to farm out their horses at livery. But there are many others who look after their own horses too, quite apart from the valiant mothers who help children with ponies, those farmers who keep horses on their own land and the vast number of foot-followers. Those who contribute the most are part of a shared enterprise which Amanda has memorialised so beautifully for us. Whether it is John Hughes shoeing horses in the Malpas in Cheshire, experts making hats, wind-ruffled foot-followers with a view (perhaps the wrong one) of where 'the' fox went, her photographs set us thinking of these and a hundred other mental snapshots of our own hunting days. So many of us are tied to our own well-loved hunt country that it is fun to zoom north, with her camera, to Scotland just before the legal muddles began there or to go right down to mid-Devon and imagine ourselves in those green hills, with sideways glances at woodlands in the Cotswolds or a stretch of single file round the edge of a field of seeds.

Above all, she evokes hounds and houndwork, the living heart of the sport which opponents simply ignore. It has taken more than two centuries of skill and breeding to make our foxhounds the pride of the world. By 1800, the blood-lines of the Meynell's Gusman and the Beaufort's brood-bitch Gladsome were famous far and wide. By 1918, rough-coated Welsh hounds were being introduced into English hunts against a barrage of criticism which has never quite gone away. Are they too individual or even, as the late Lord Daresbury of the Belvoir dismissed them, just "barking dogs"? It is still such a thrill to hunt with the tan-coloured Belvoir pack, the nobility of old English foxhounds with their branch-line over in Ireland's Limerick and their kin in the Brocklesby or the Percy. In the 1860's, the Master of the Meynell was already dismissing the Belvoir as "a very beautiful summer pack." But they have given me two of the most memorable days of my hunting life, going away from Clawson Thorns in a vintage year when I had an unspeakably lazy young pupil from Leicestershire whose parents rewarded me for their son's lack of effort in Oxford by offering me a free away day in the Belvoir's best country. At the same time, the sport in my own home patch, the Bicester, was incomparably improved by the decision of Ian Farquhar, early in his great career, to introduce woolly Welsh hounds who would cope with the growing tide of heavy ploughland.

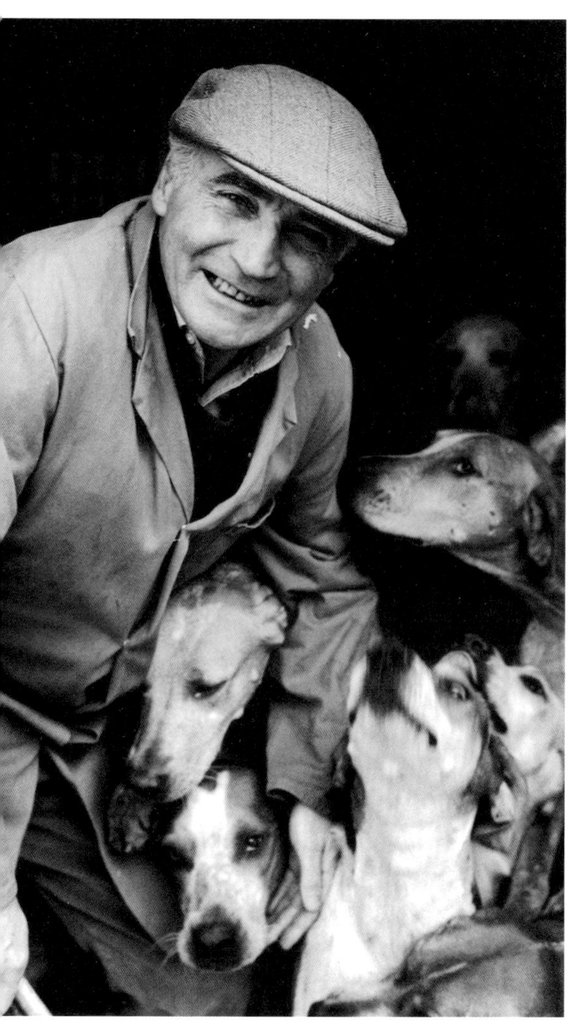

Ian Farquhar and the Beaufort hounds

In parts of France and Italy, local priests bless the hounds who are brought up to the altar by their puppy-walkers at the start of each season. Hounds in Amanda's 'overview' photographs deserve a blessing of some sort, and I would not be alone in blessing the co-ordination and self-direction of the present-day Beaufort, Farquhar's masterpiece. In the early 1800's, an English master of hounds found himself living for reasons of economy in France and bringing ten couple of hounds over for *chasse à cheval*. His French followers were horrified that these fine hounds would not chase and kill rabbits as well as foxes, and when the field *à cheval* deliberately headed the first fox straight back into the pack, a *Monsieur* rode up to the huntsman, took off his hat and congratulated him on "catching his fox so soon, and with so little trouble." Will the blood-lines of the Fernie or the Heythrop really be safe in exile in France if we have to sit out a few years of urban tyranny?

Amanda has some lovely shots of hounds puzzling the line out and hunting for themselves. Everywhere, the country has become so much more difficult nowadays, while the soaring costs of livery and subscriptions mean that sport must be shown, or fabricated. Some of our huntsmen have such fox-sense that they seem able to think for their hounds and draw them brilliantly down a line which they have recognised. I side with those who prefer to see hounds, head-down, puzzling out the fox's direction in a bunch so compact that you could mentally throw a pocket-handkerchief over them. In bad scenting years, hounds who work out the answers do show steadier sport. In his excellent observations *On Foxhunting*, Colonel John Cook (famous as an Essex Master) already deplored in the 1820's how "the moment hounds come to a check," in many admired countries, "their heads are up and they are ready to start with the huntsman wherever his genius might direct. In consequence, they never put their noses down…" In our globally-warming winters, patchy scenting does no favours to frequently-lifted packs.

There is no such thing, we are all taught, as a bad day's hunting. For me, nonetheless, there are 'best bits', in the early morning and the early evening. Early mornings are cub-hunting time, when Octobers can be spectacularly beautiful, time in the saddle is being burgled from time in a traffic-jam on the way to work and most of our younger huntsmen let their hounds go from early October onwards as fast as ever again in the year. Over the thorn hedges and miles of wet cattle-pasture between Bicester and Aylesbury, those early mornings are when I have struck up long relationships with the horses which have then carried me, never changing, for full days and an average of ten completely sound seasons. Cub-hunting has settled them, and focussed their excitement while scaring me in the process. The hunting scenes in Sassoon's *Memoirs* tend to be rather tame, but I treasure him on cub-hunting. "The mornings I most remember were those which took us up onto the chalk downs. To watch the day breaking from purple to dazzling gold while we trotted up a deep-rutted lane to inhale the early freshness and to gaze back at the low country with its cock-crowing farms and mist-cooled waterways – to be riding out with a sense of discovery – was it not something stolen from the luckless city-workers? – even though it ended in nothing more than the killing of a brace of foxcubs (for whom, to tell the truth, I felt an uncon-fessed sympathy)?"

There have been great mornings, when even a great Leicestershire pack has stopped by 1:30 p.m., the hounds exhausted, the horses far from home. But evenings, when the field has shrunk to twenty or less, are the supreme hunting moments, as the light sinks on a clearing horizon, frost is coming in on the air and there is such a concentrated stillness beside a famous covert. Hounds run like smoke and set our blood racing with their cry, when twenty minutes make up for all the mud and scrimmage of the previous four hours in a crowd. If it really does come to a last day of fox-hunting, at least for the next four or five years, remember how many fine huntsmen have gone out at the end of a final season with some of the greatest days of their career. Was there ever anything much better than Brian Fanshawe's last Christmas Eve in the Cottesmore (a nine-mile hunt in the morning, a fifteen mile hunt in the evening), Ian Farquhar's farewell day in March in the open north end of the Bicester country where he showed such exceptional sport, Jim Webster's last day with the Belvoir in spring 1983 when hounds flew for thirty minutes from the inimitable Hose Thorns, and reputedly 'the Best Season Ever' in 1883-4 when the Quorn were hunted by the legendary Tom Firr, then in his early forties (he "closely resembled a fox" in appearance and his hounds "obeyed the slightest wave of his hand") while his lynch-pin of a Master, the Liverpool ship-broker John Coupland, was leading the field for the last time? If there is to be that short intermission, Act One will end with the same sort of climax and by the time our nerves and memories have recovered it will be time for a renewed Act Two.

Robin Lane Fox

New Year, 2005

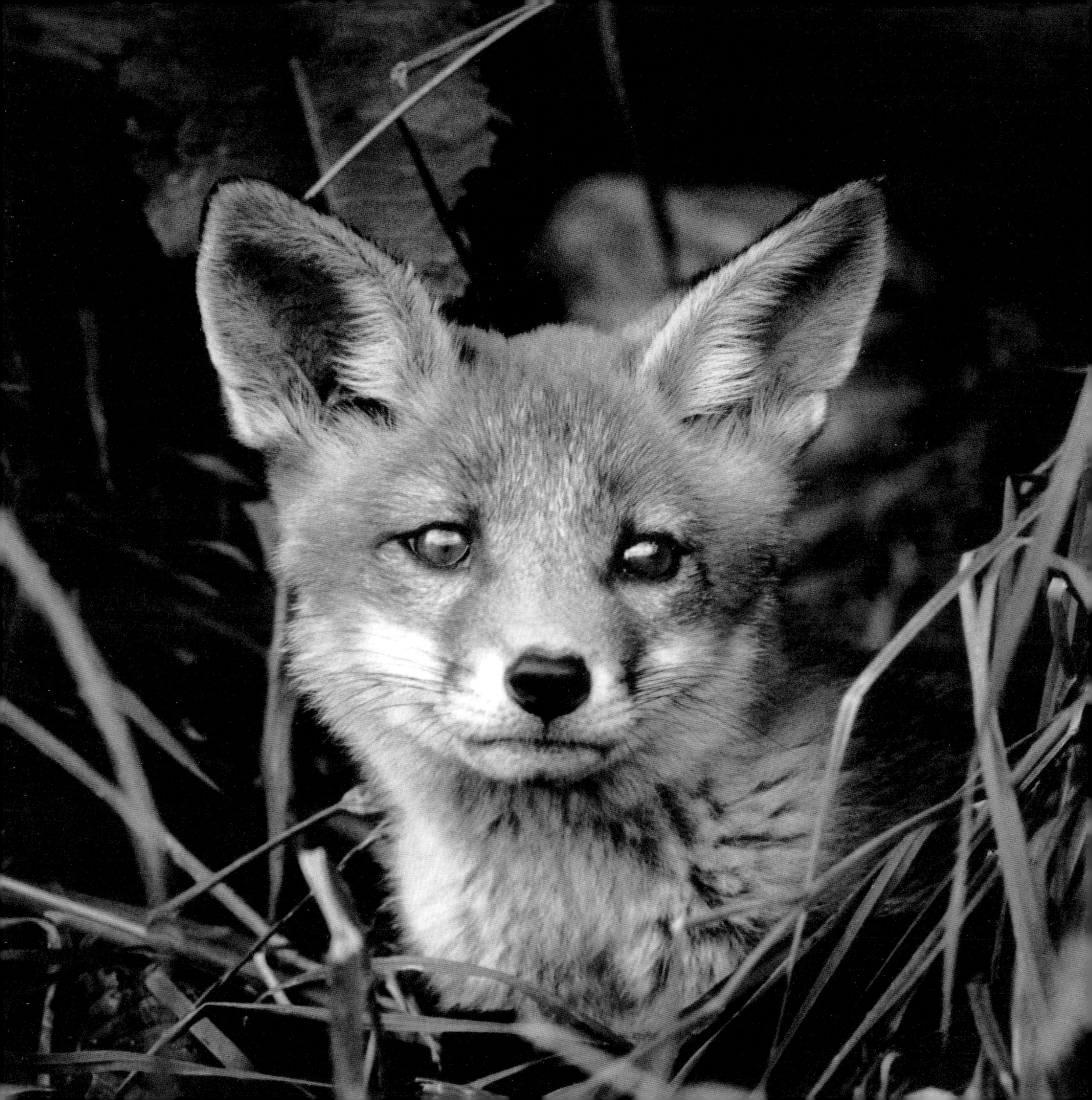

The Preparation

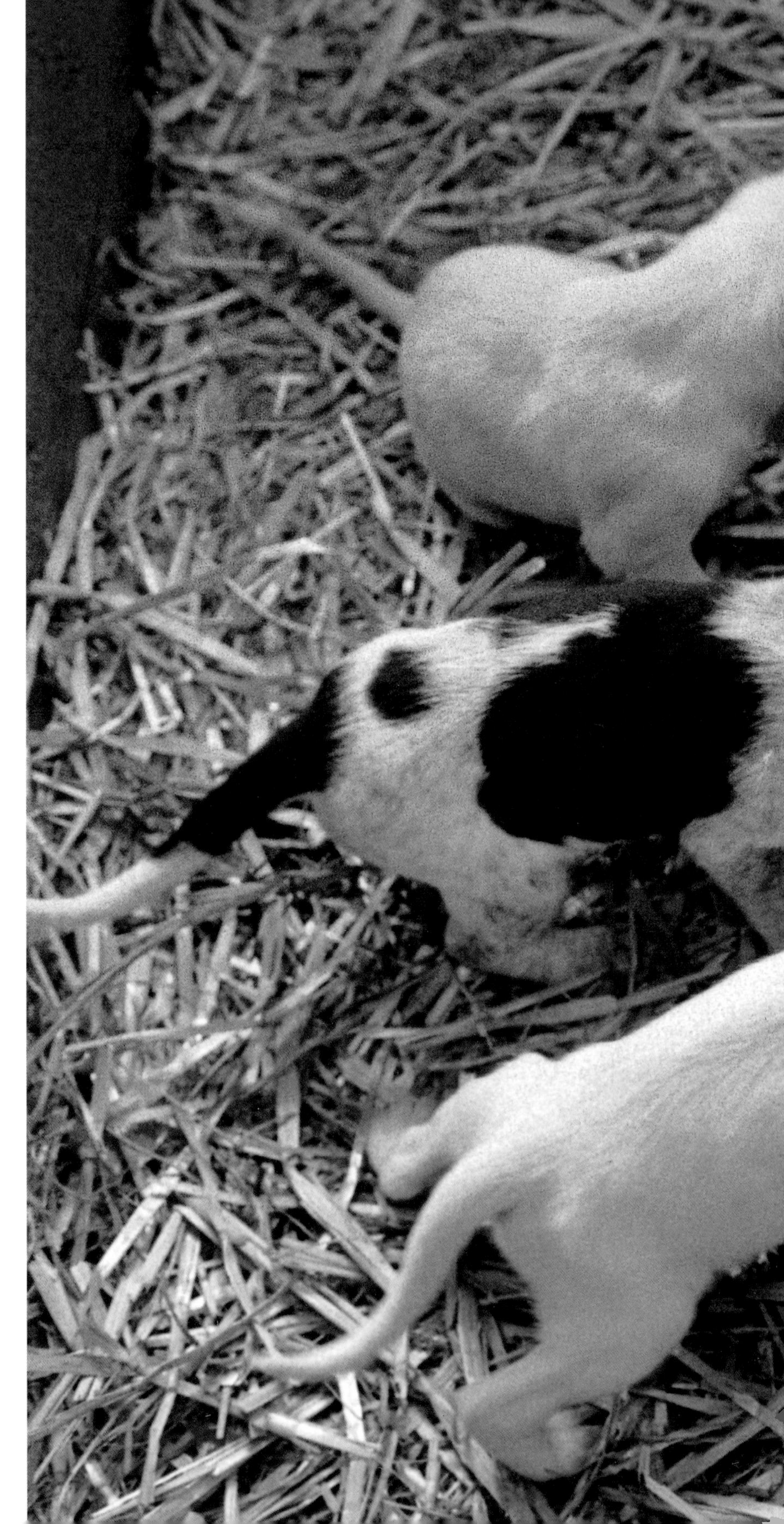

Beaufort Hunt puppies

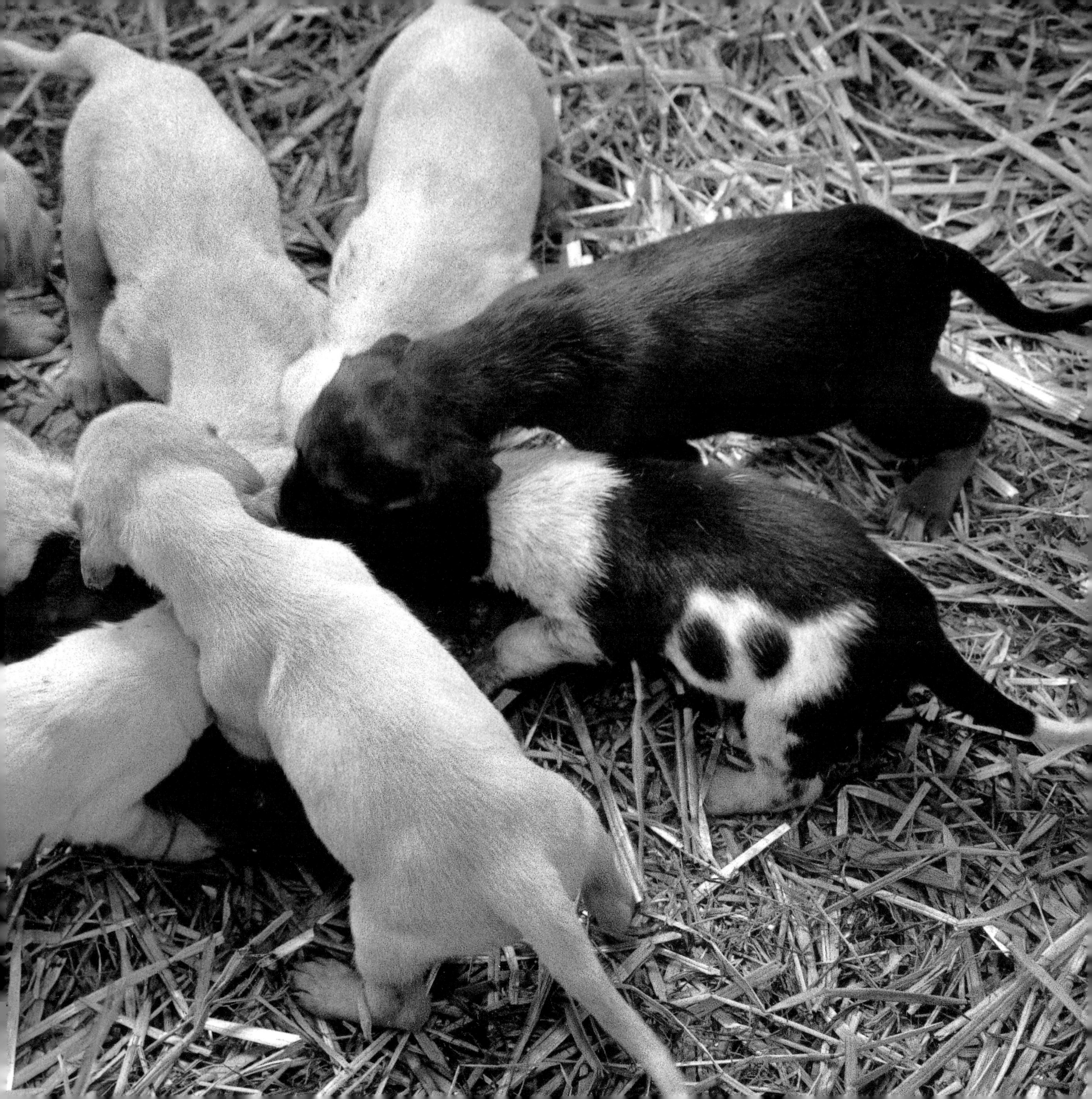

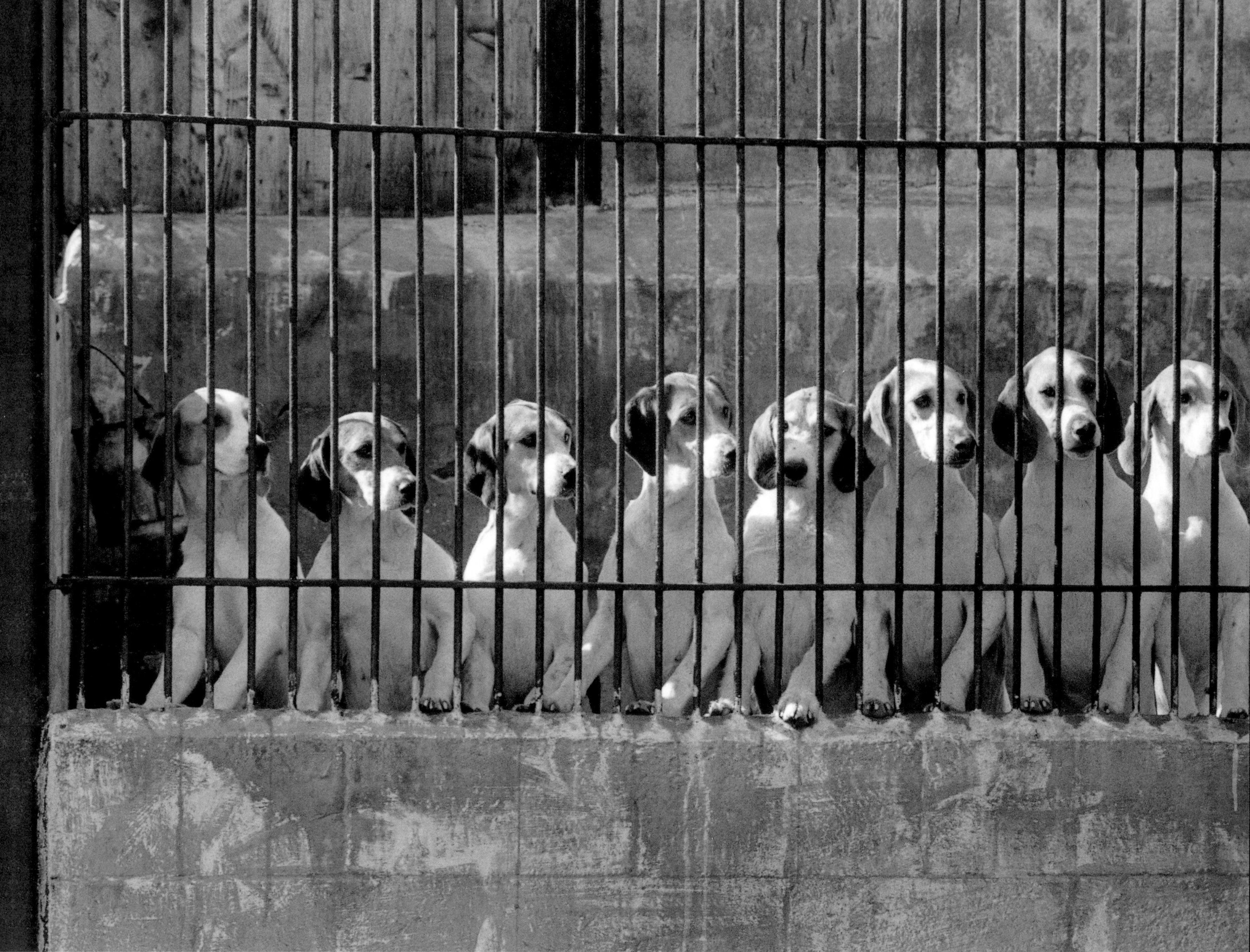

Liddesdale Kennels

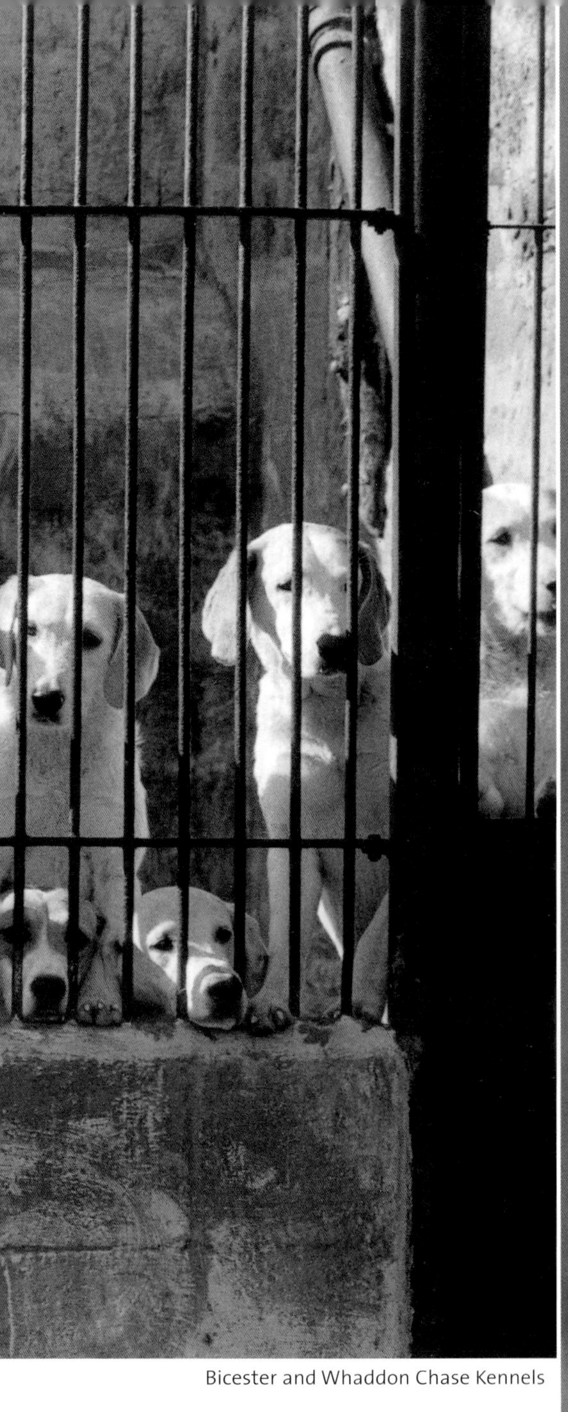

Bicester and Whaddon Chase Kennels

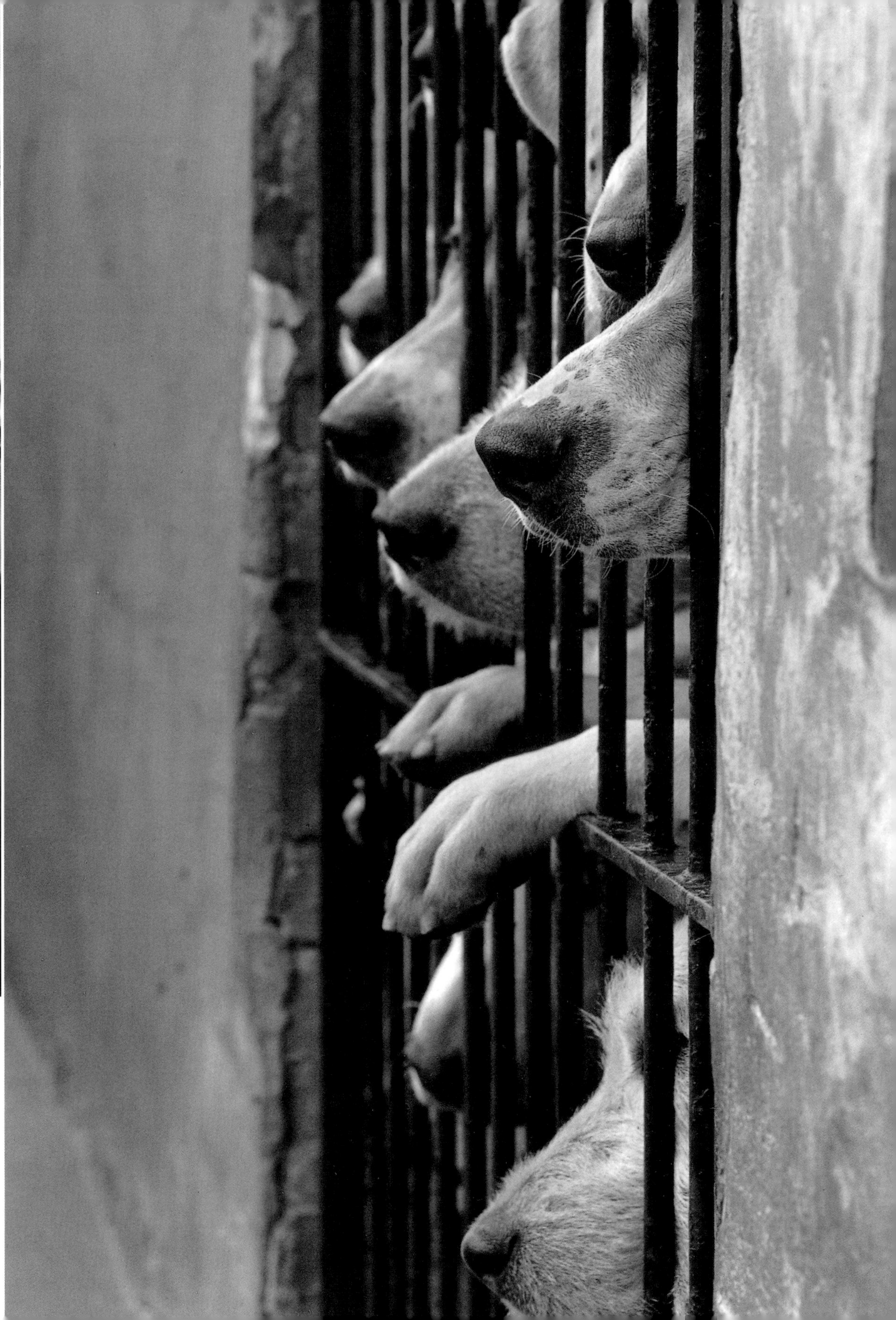

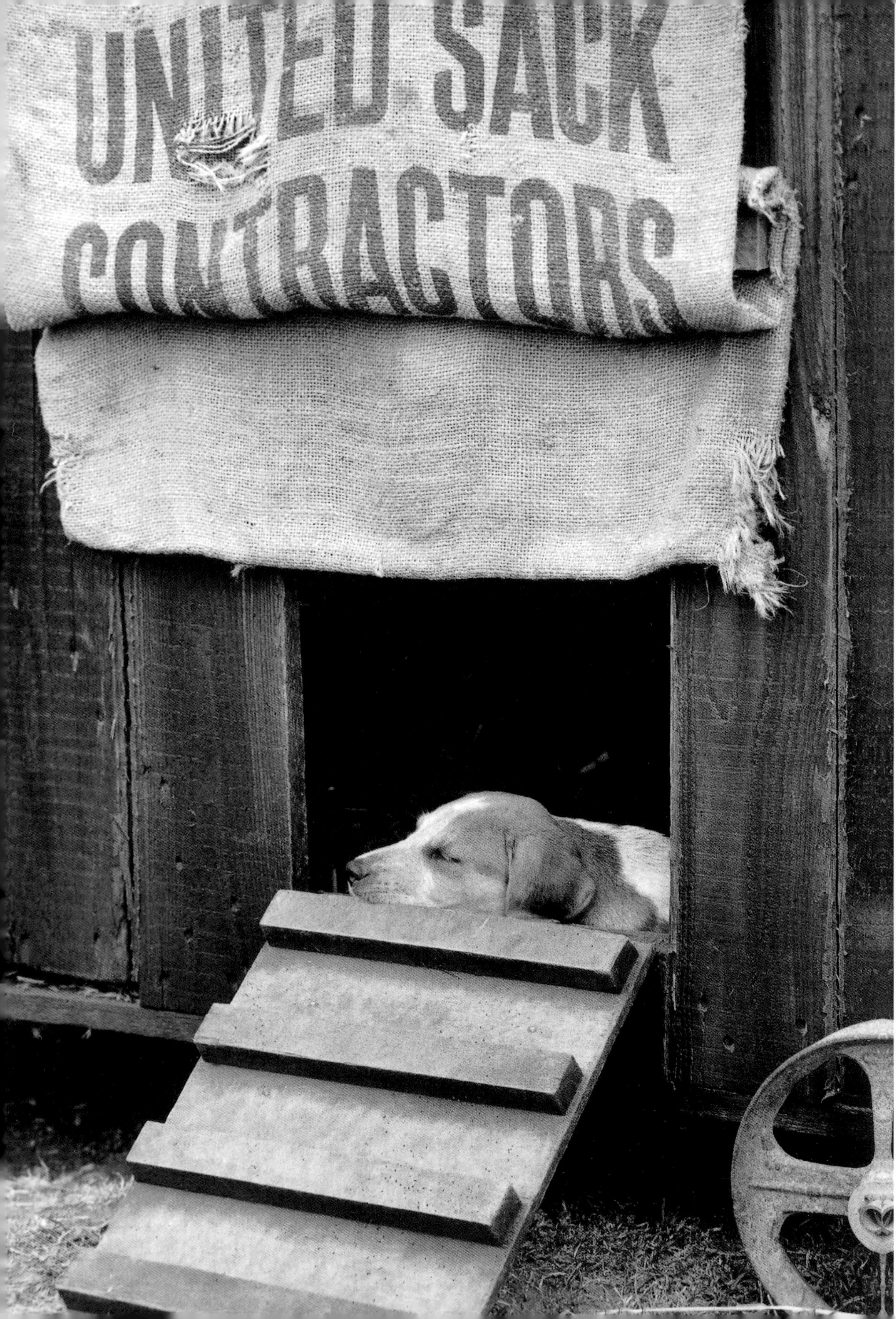

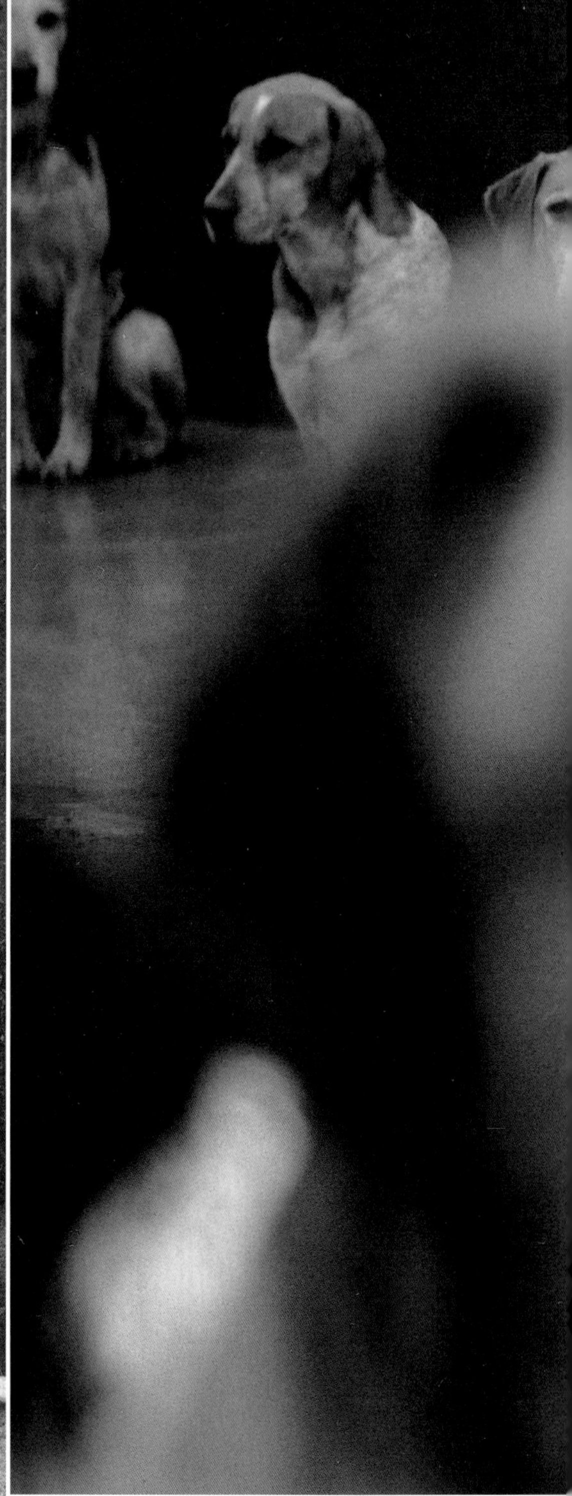

Cotswold hound puppy

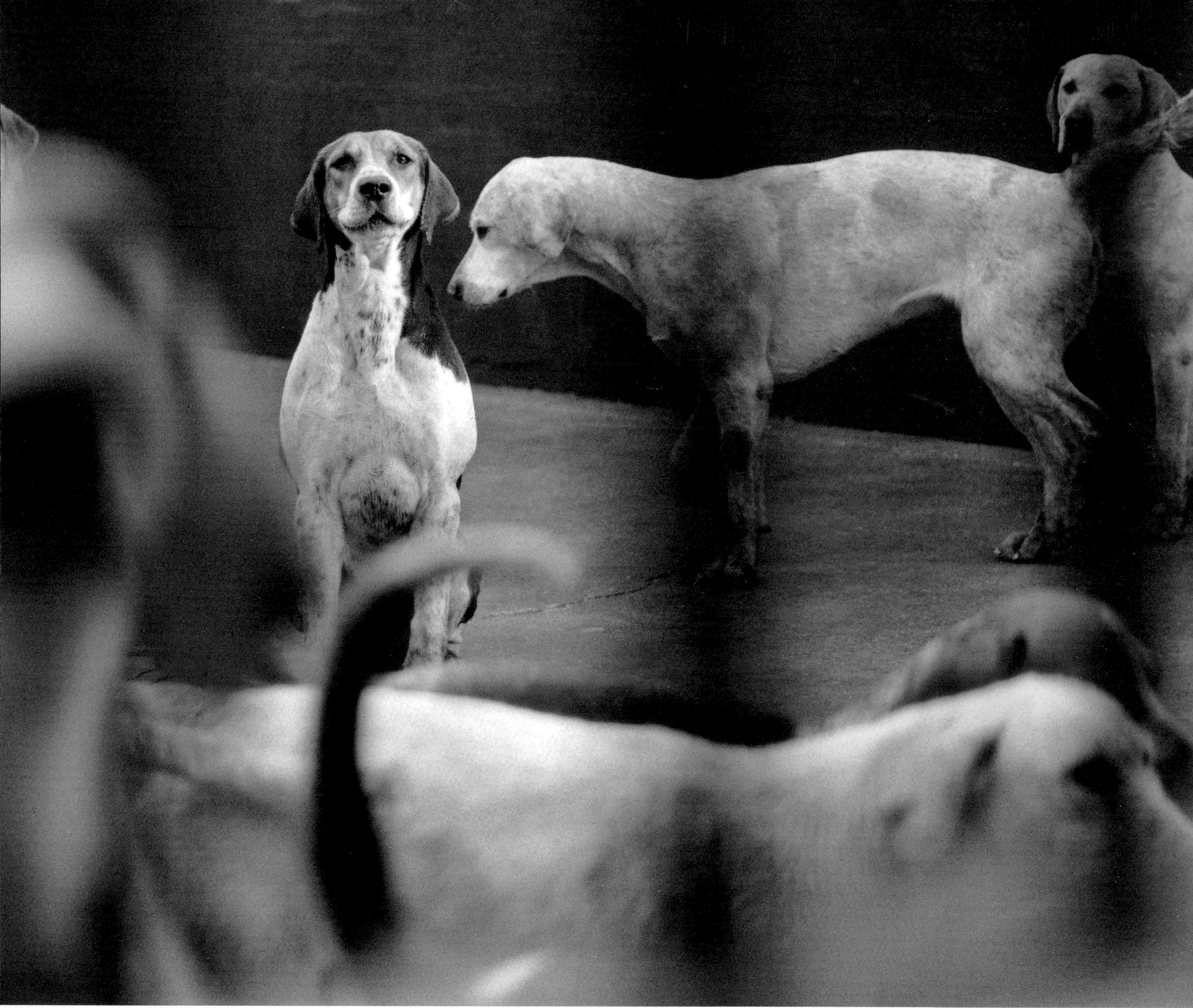

Blackmore and Sparkford Vale Kennels

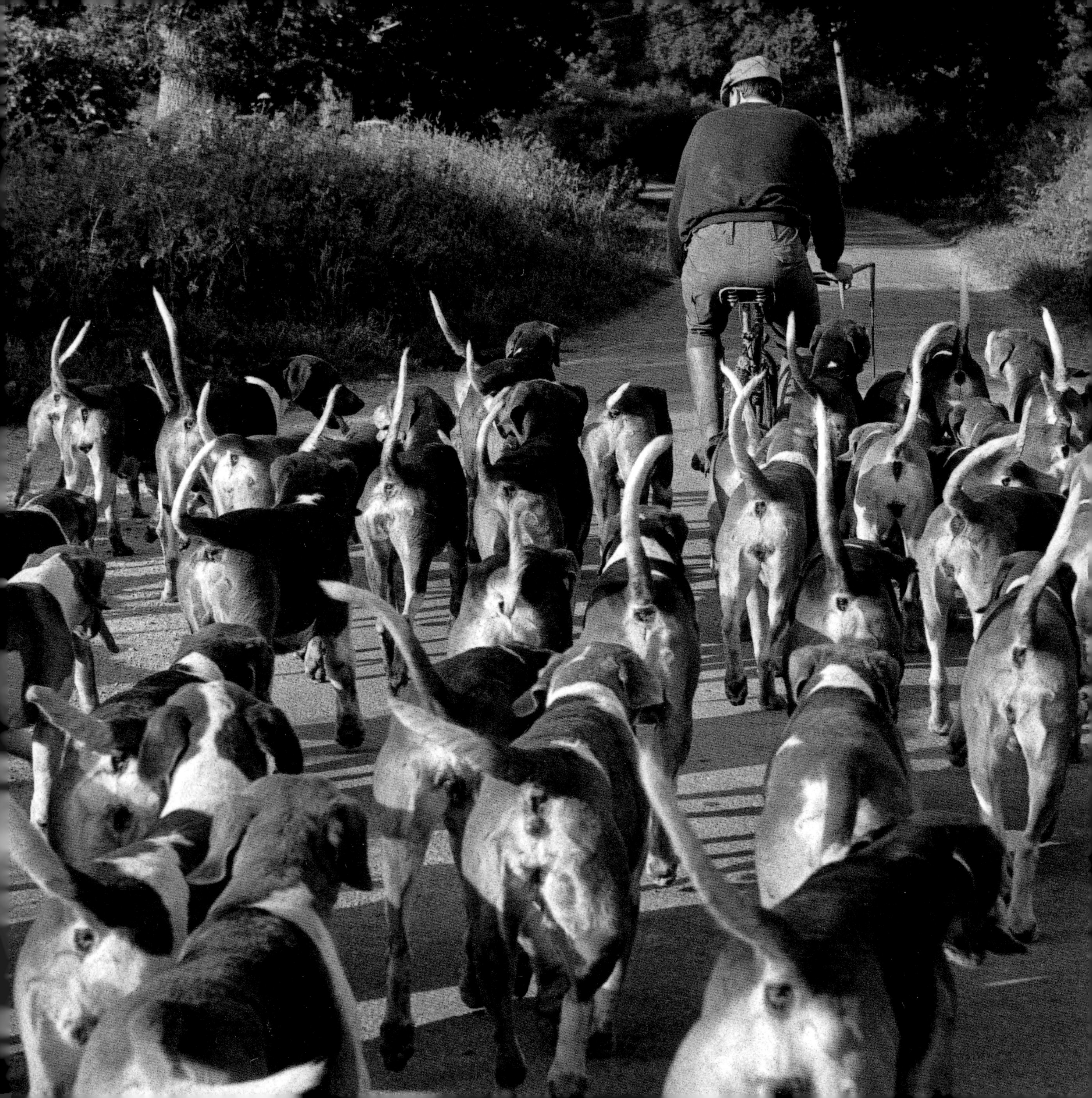

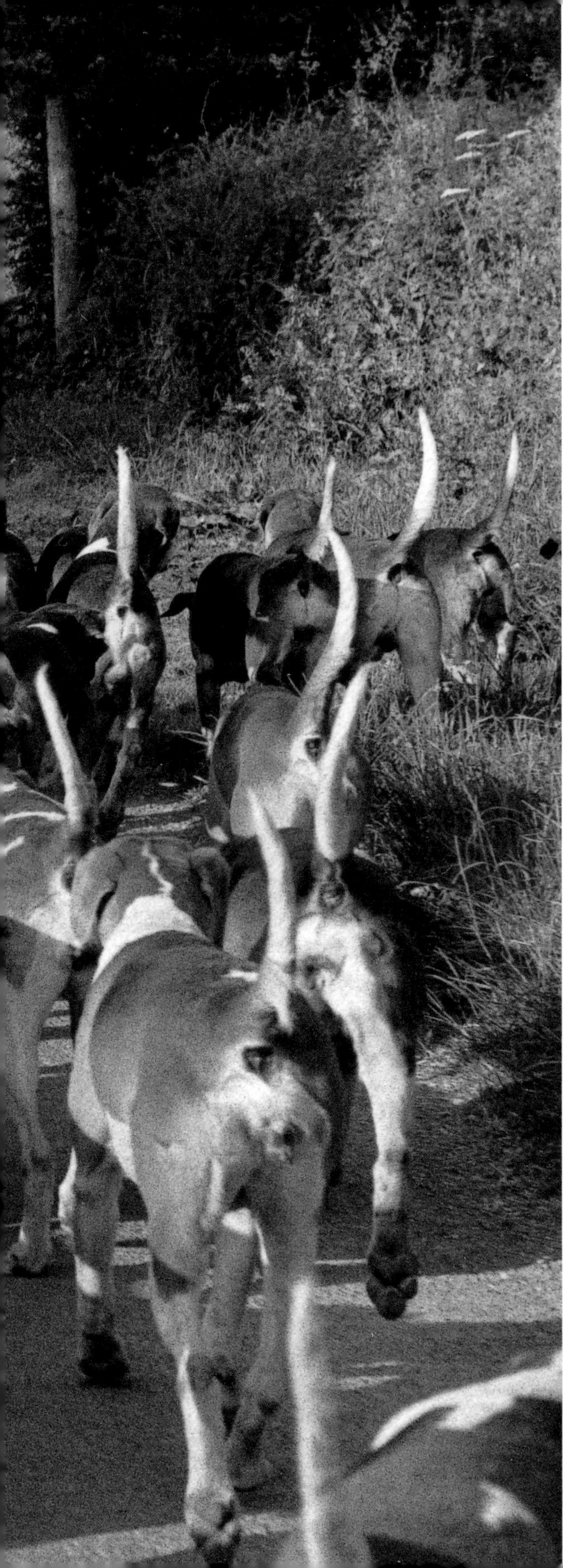

Wynnstay hound exercise

Bedale hound exercise

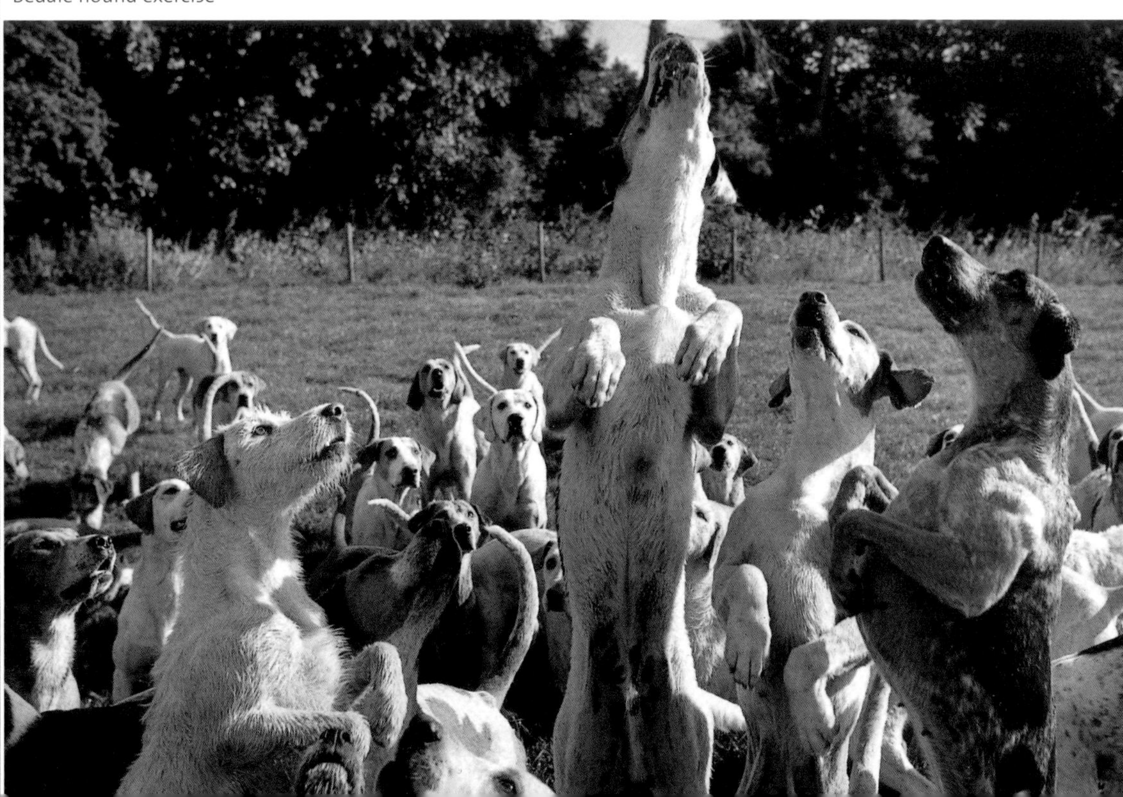

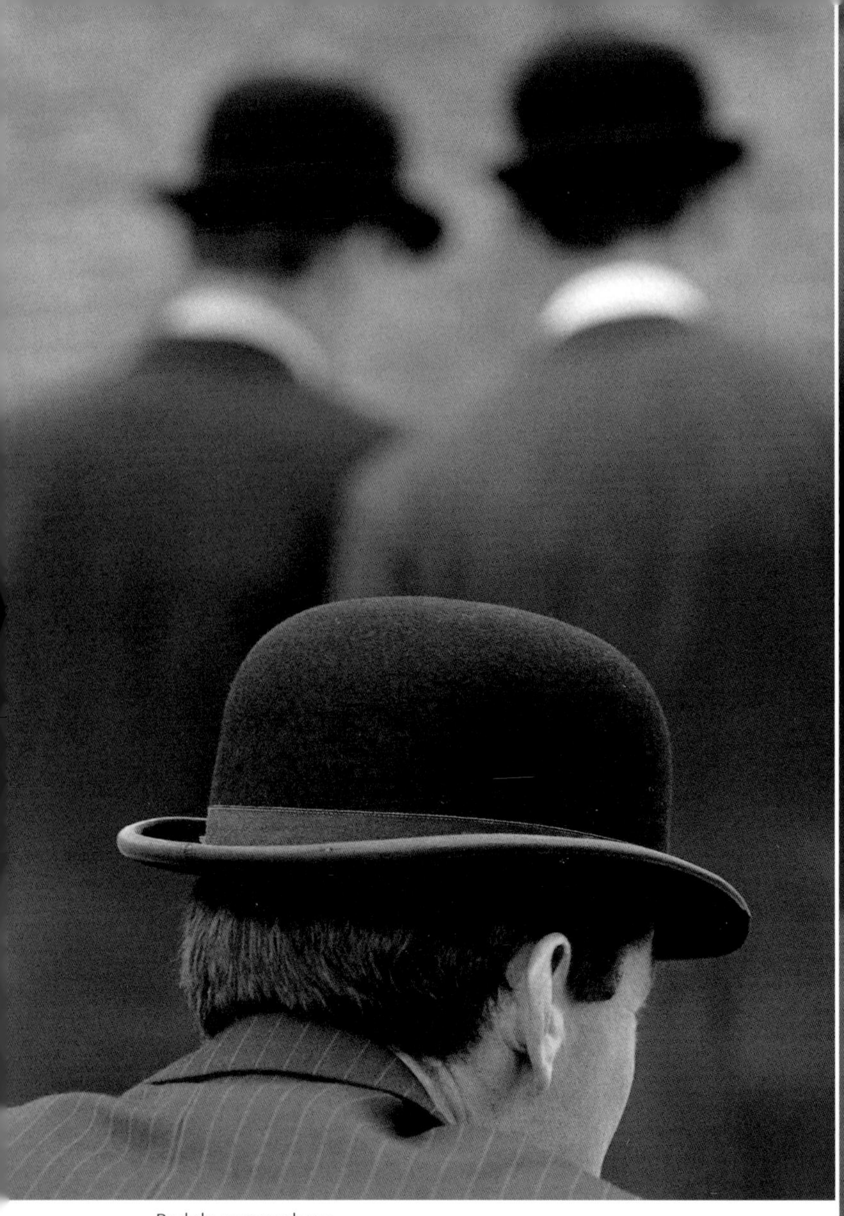

Bedale puppy show

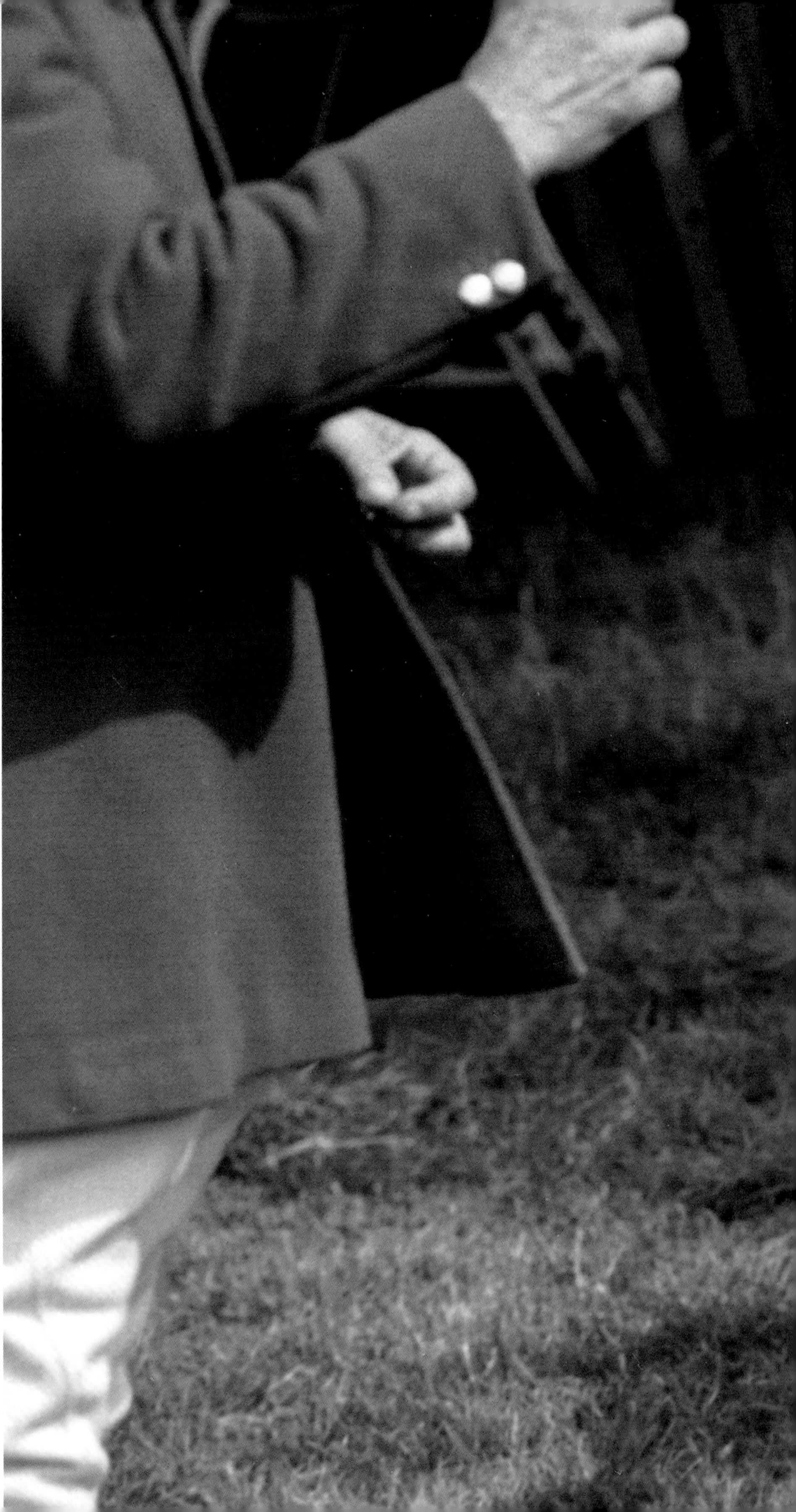

Lowther Show

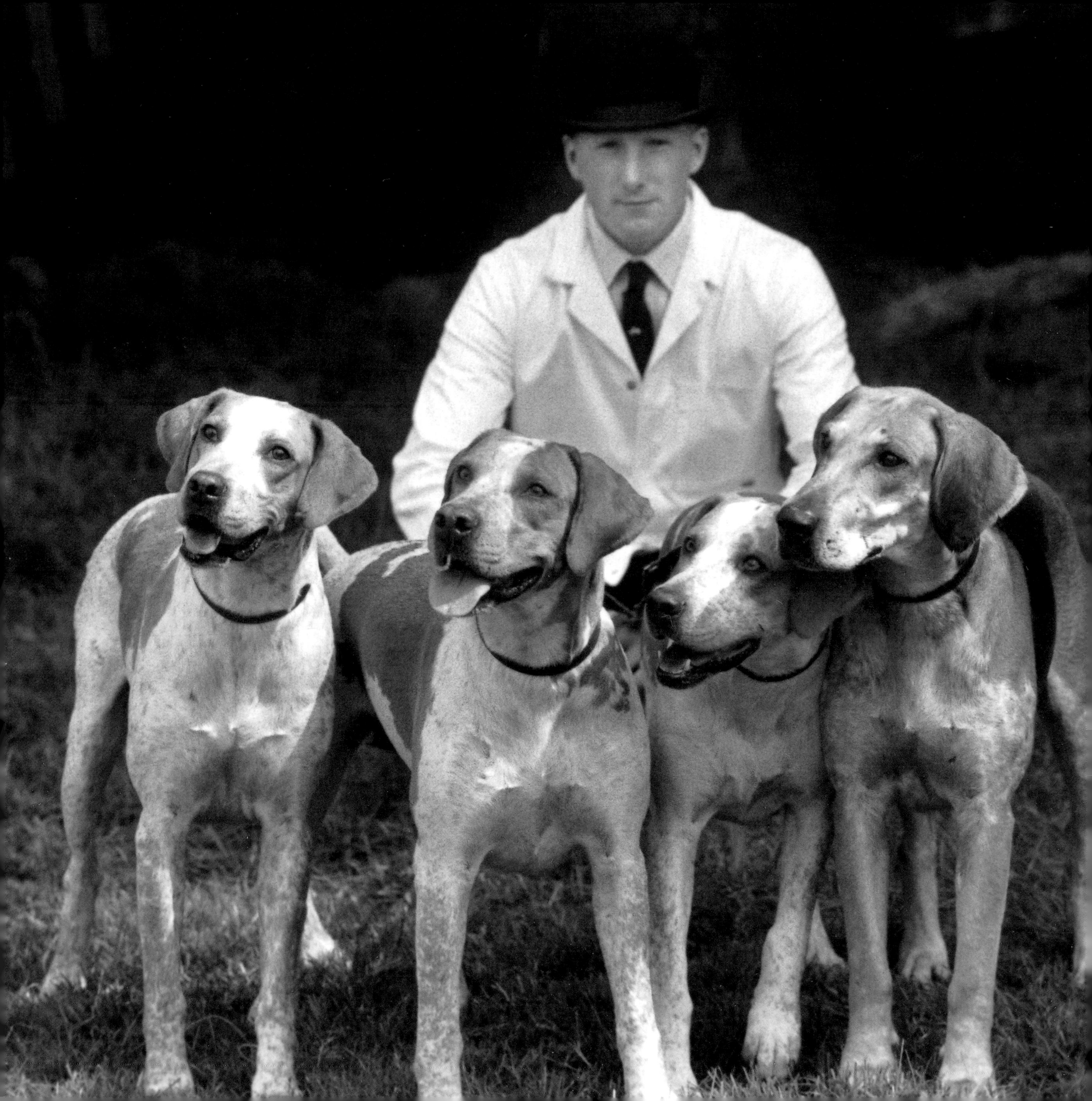

Lowther Show

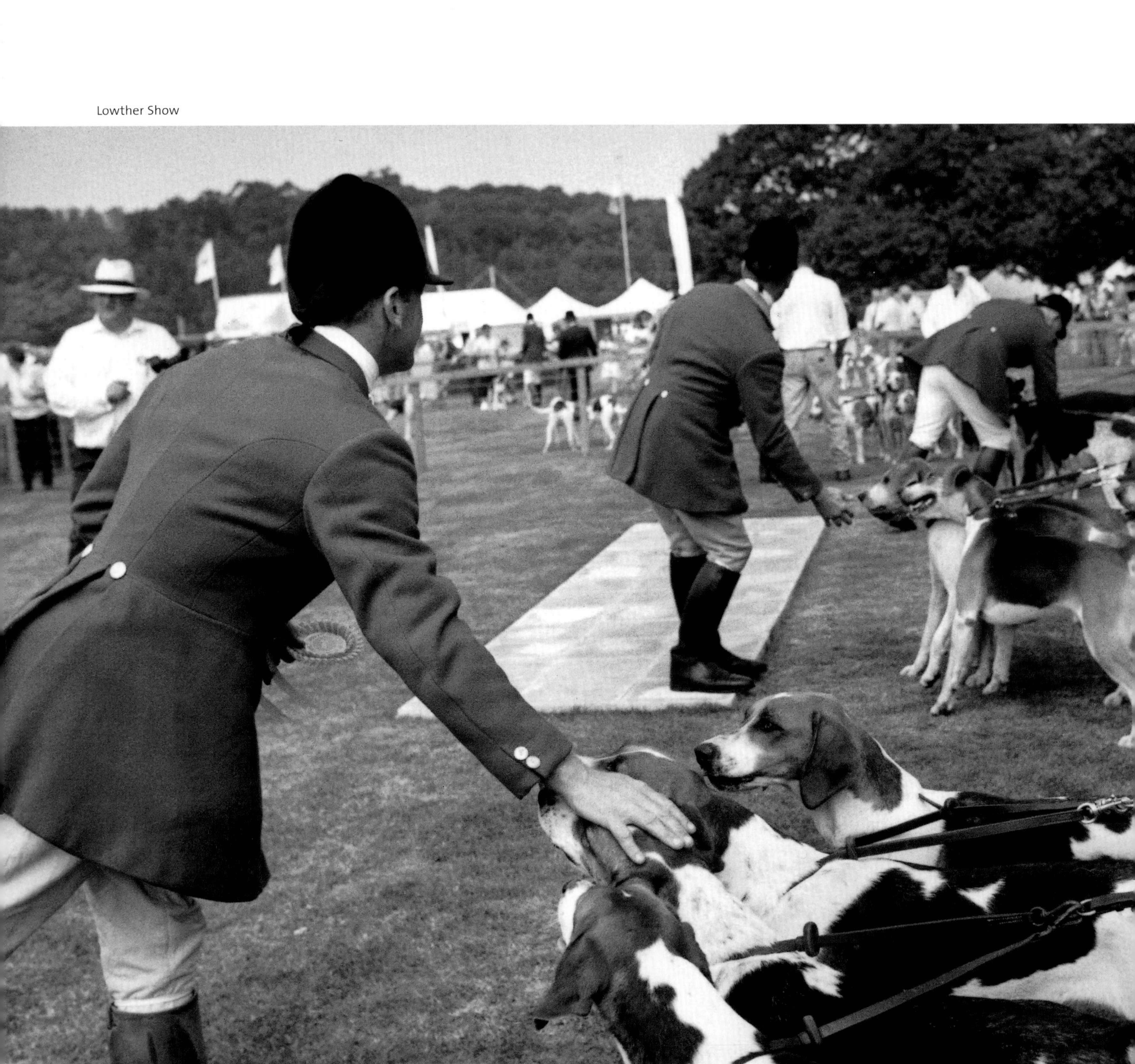

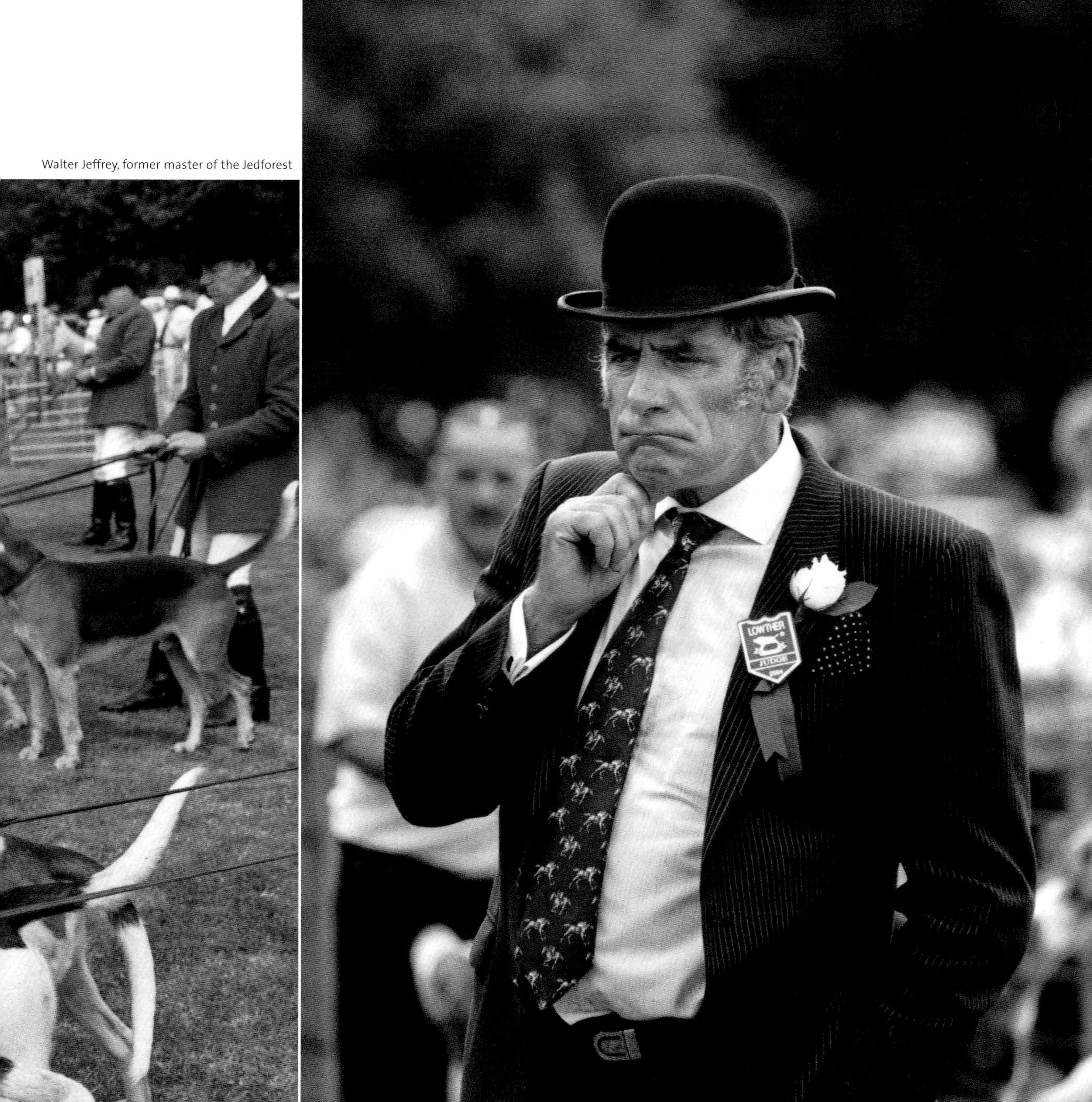

Walter Jeffrey, former master of the Jedforest

Edmund Porter, Eskdale and Ennerdale and Barry Todhunter, Blencathra

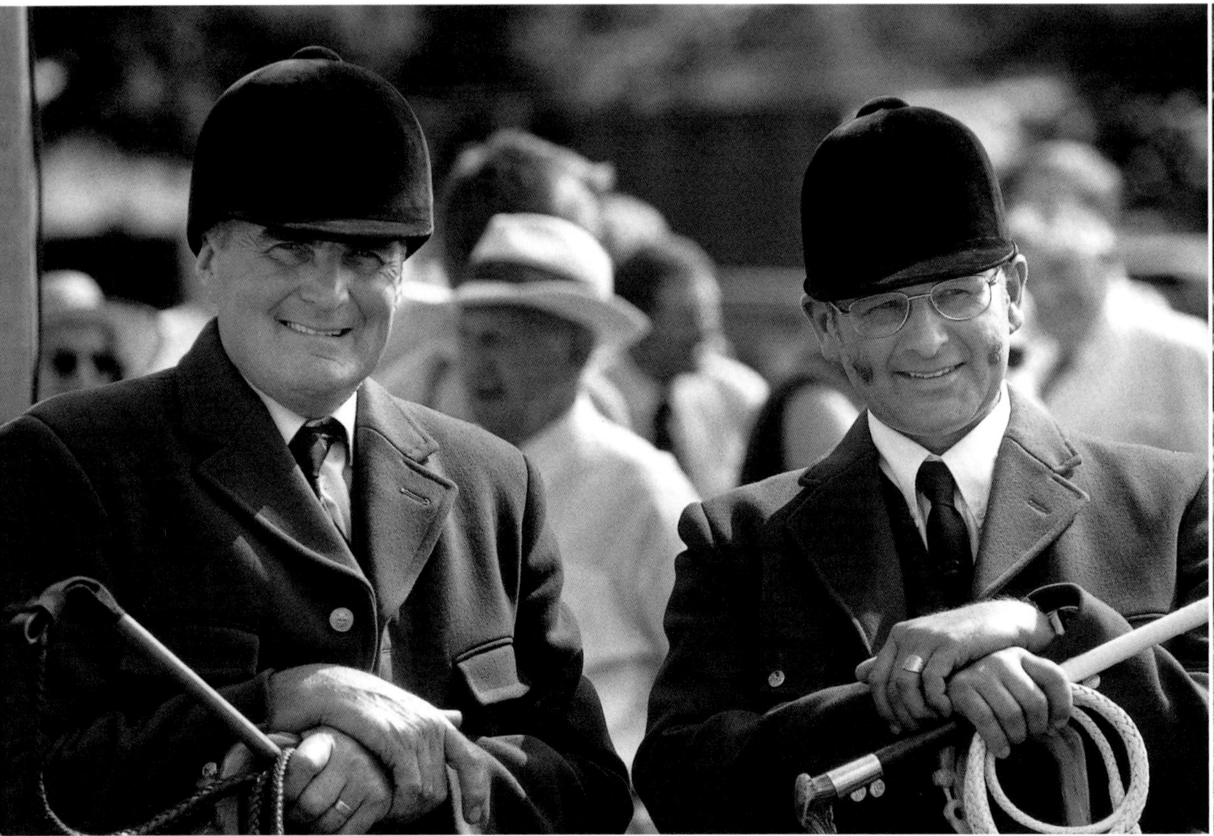

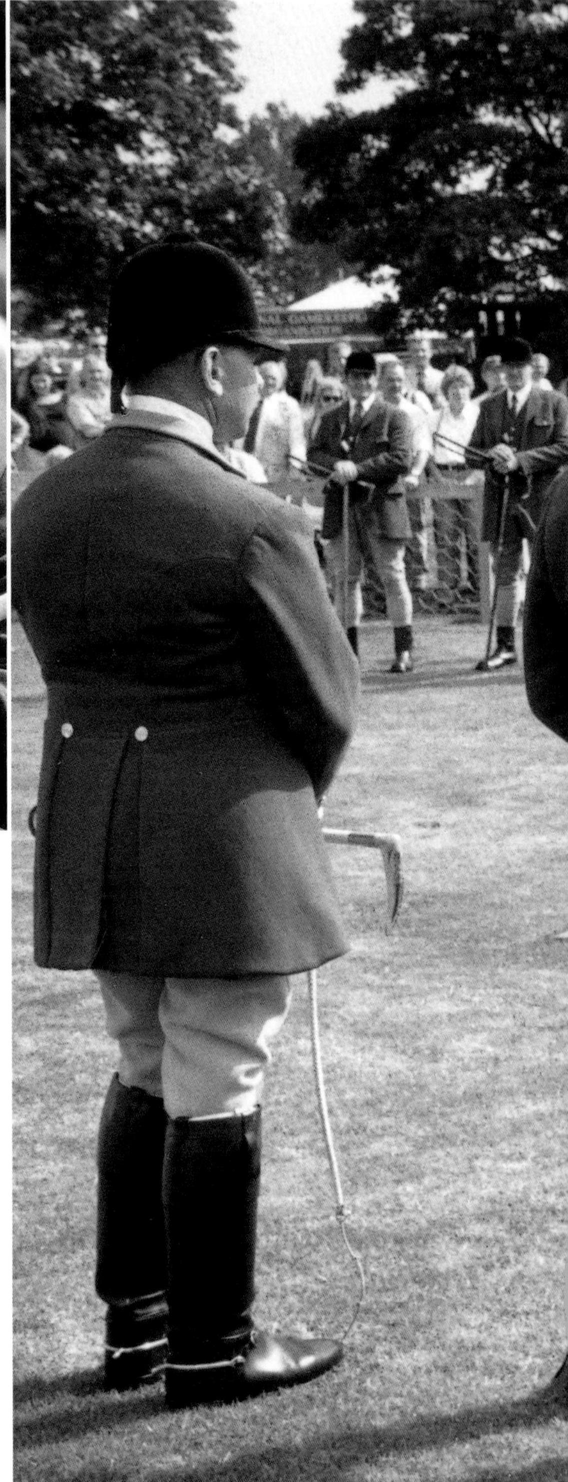

The Lowther Show Best Dressed Huntsman Competition

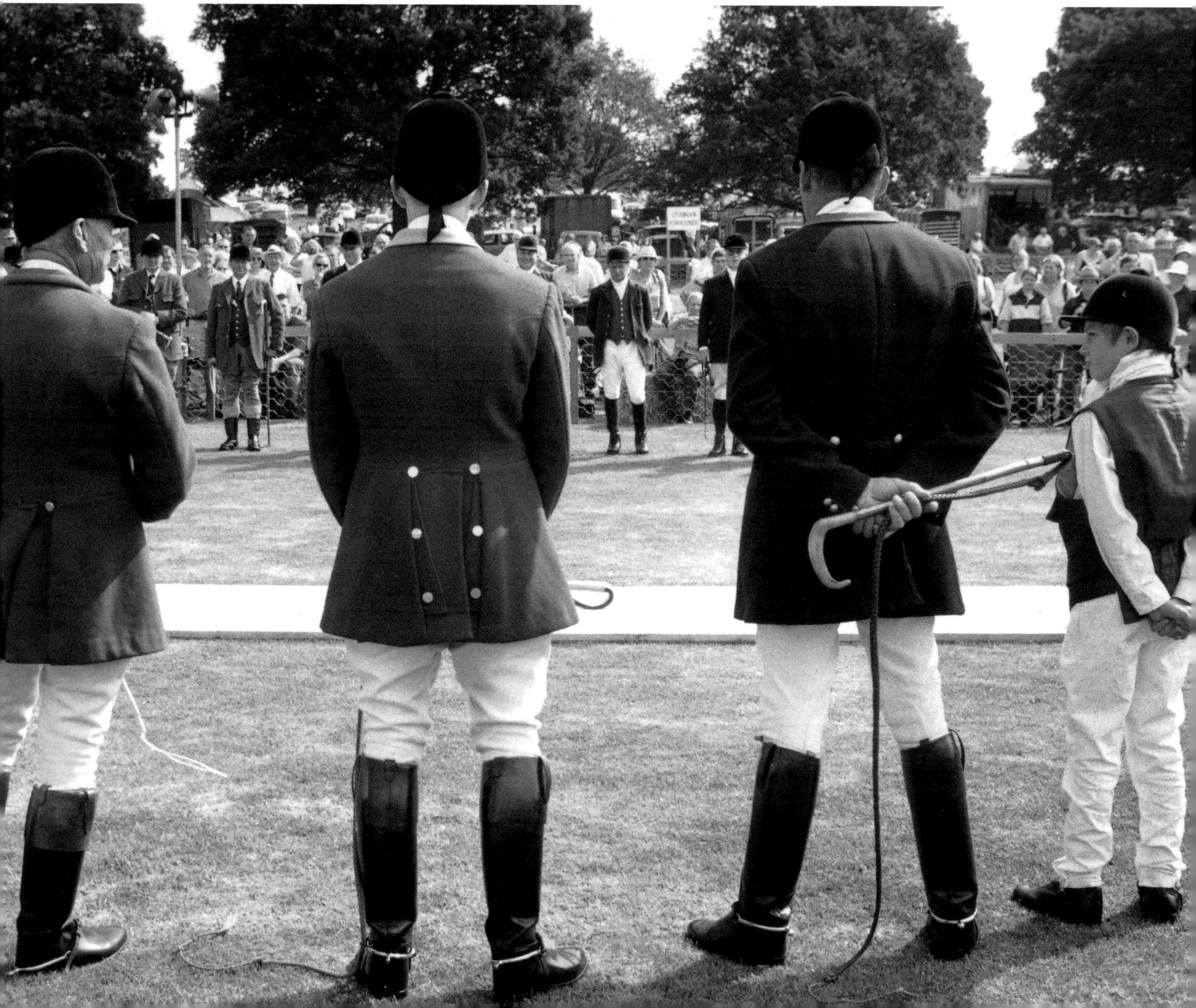

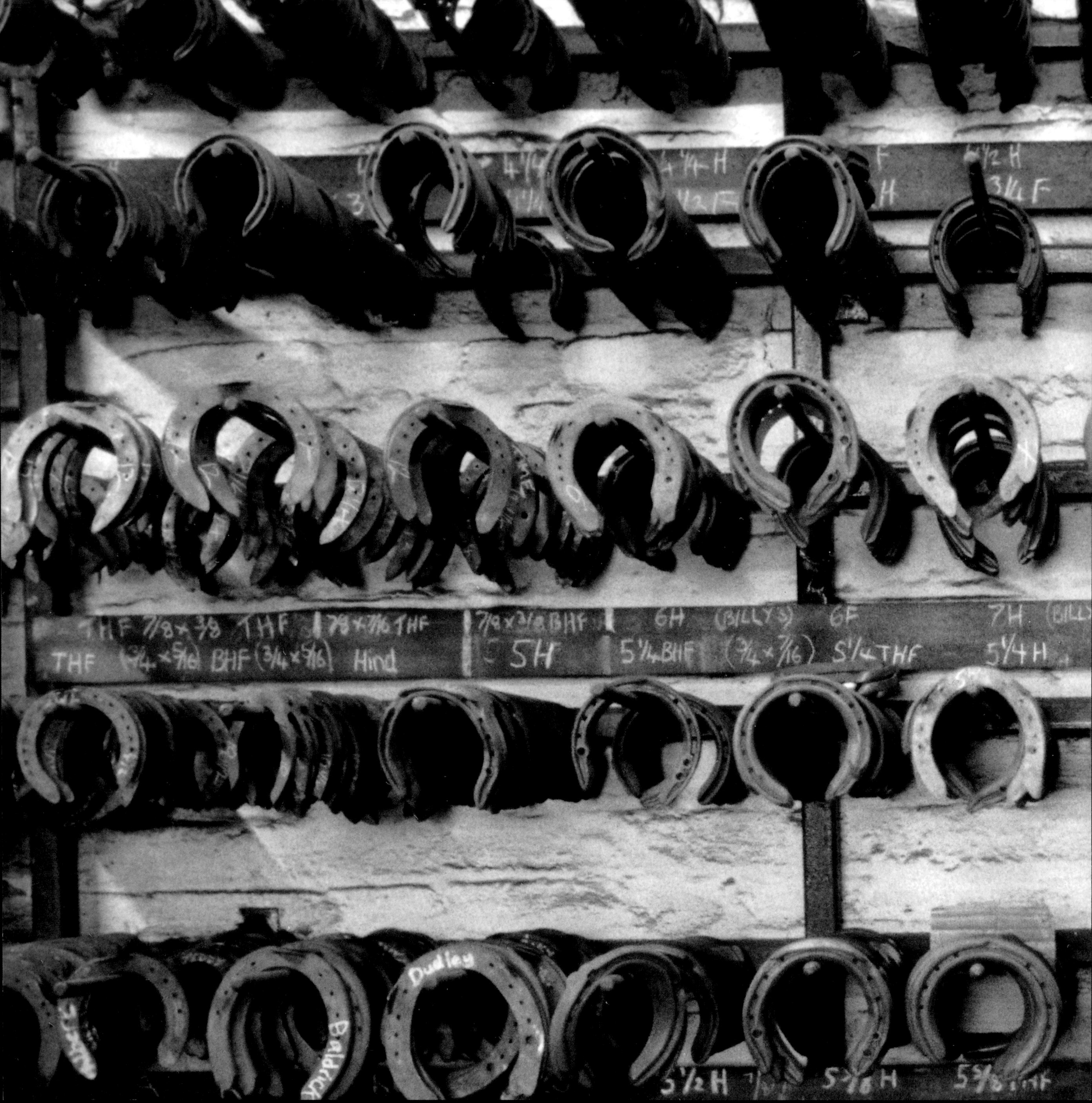

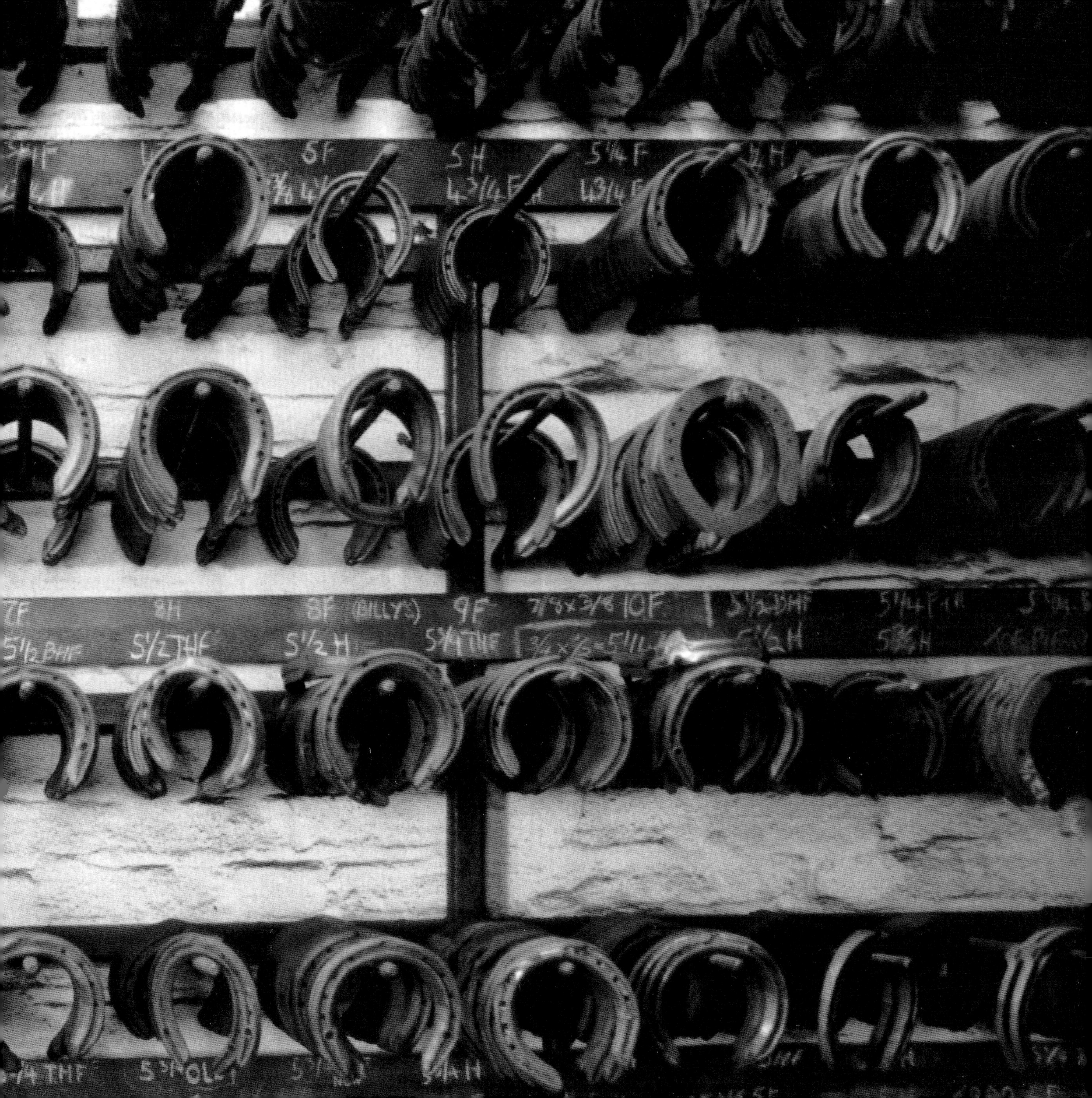

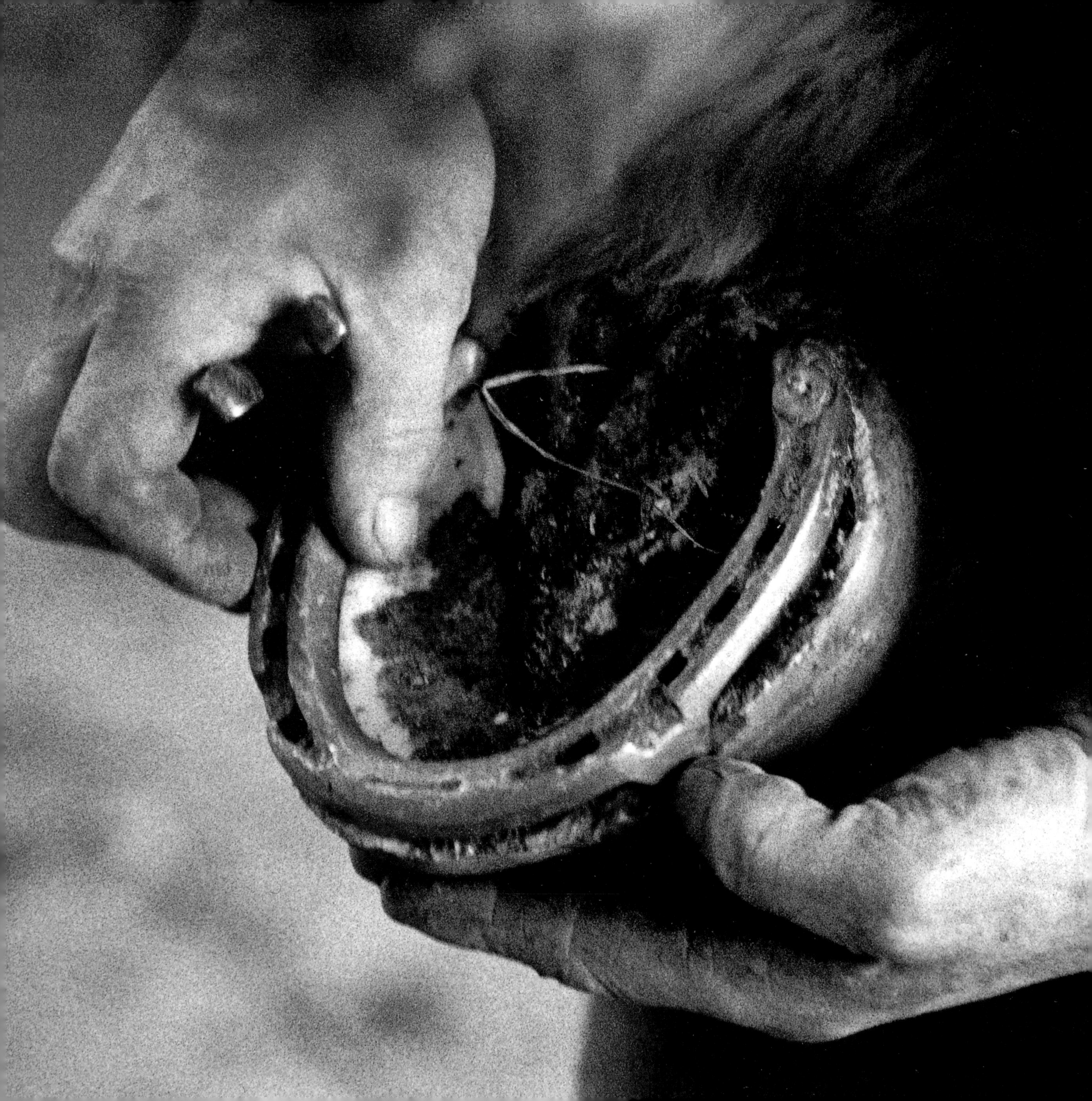

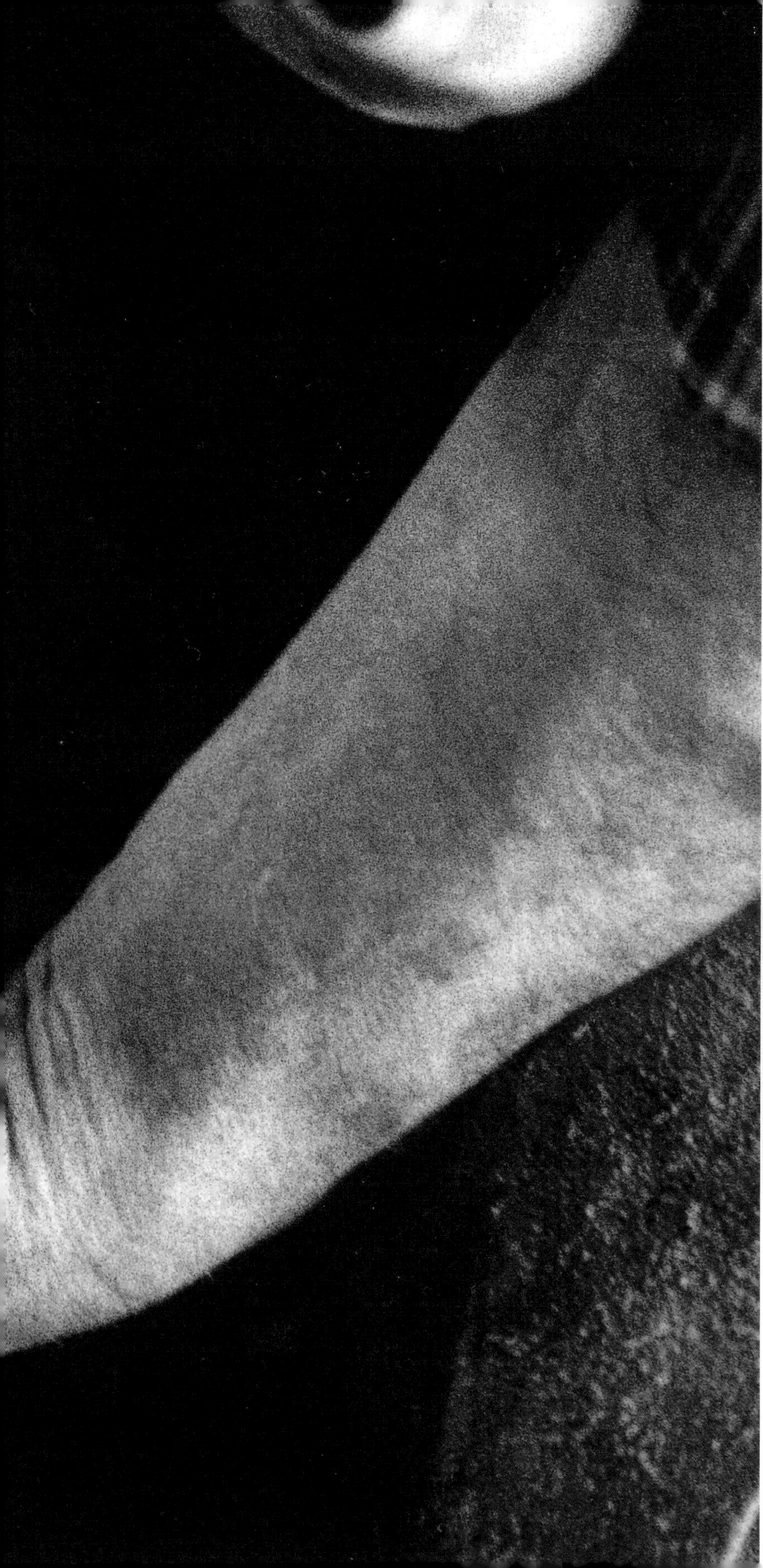

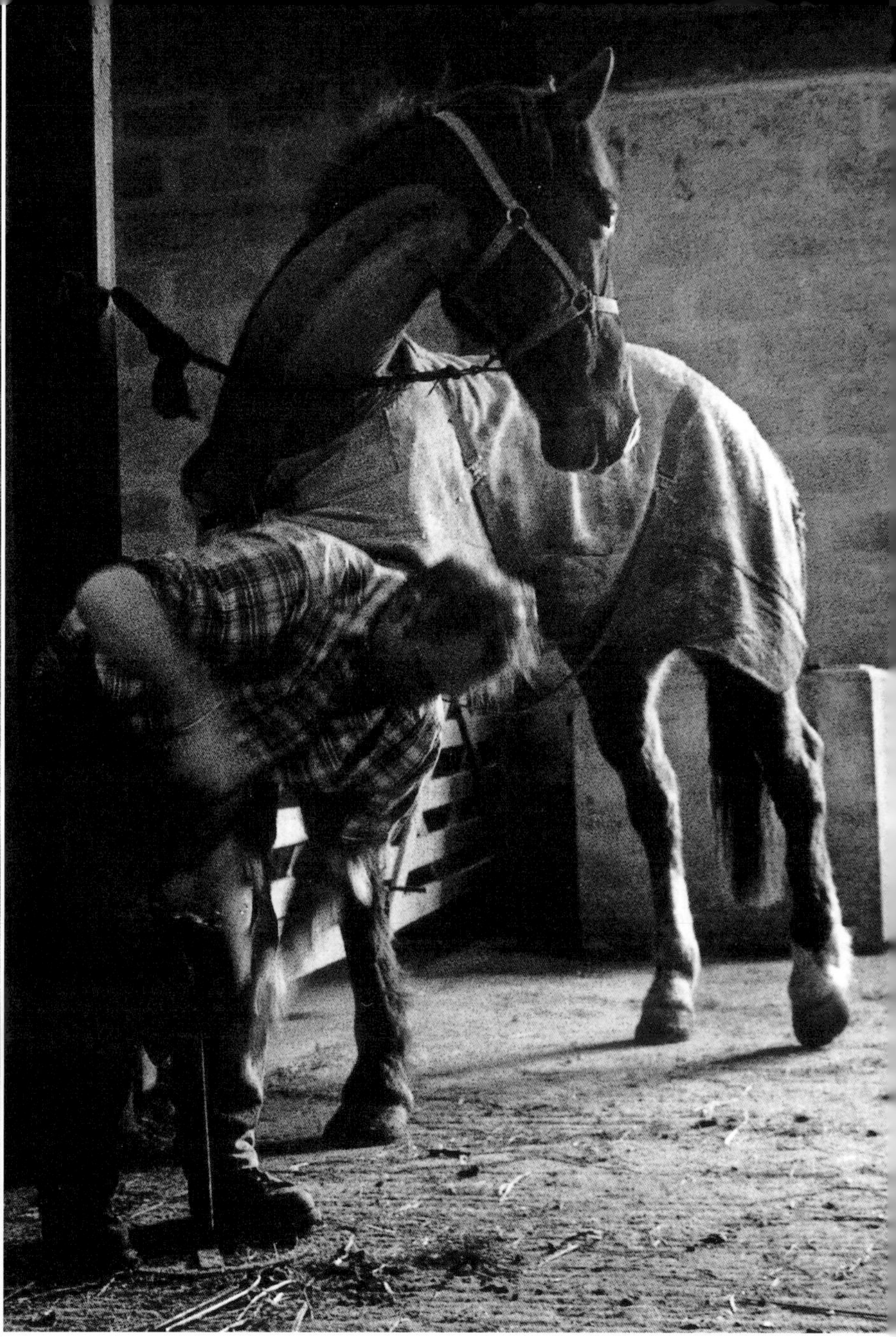

Dave Young, Buccleuch farrier

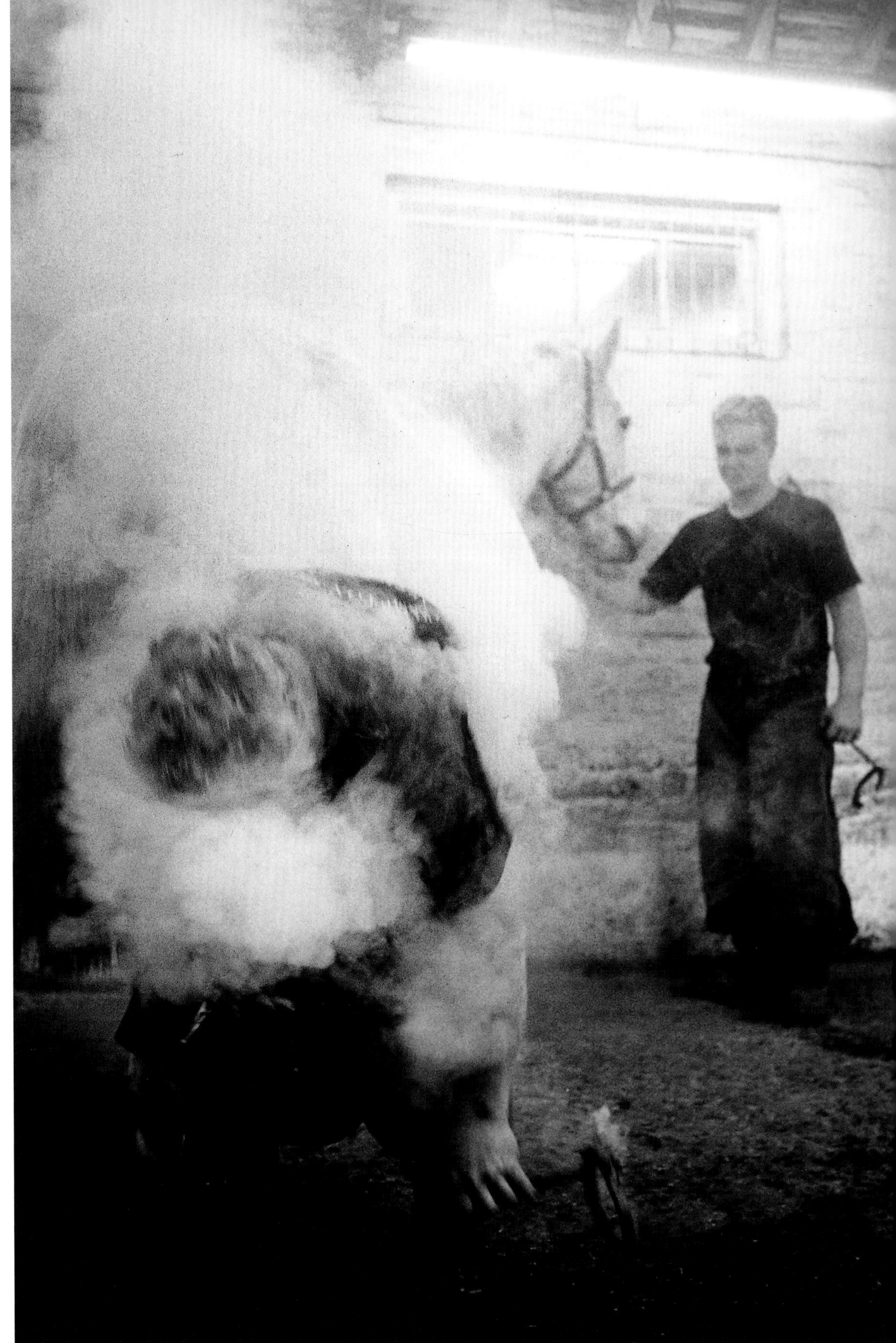

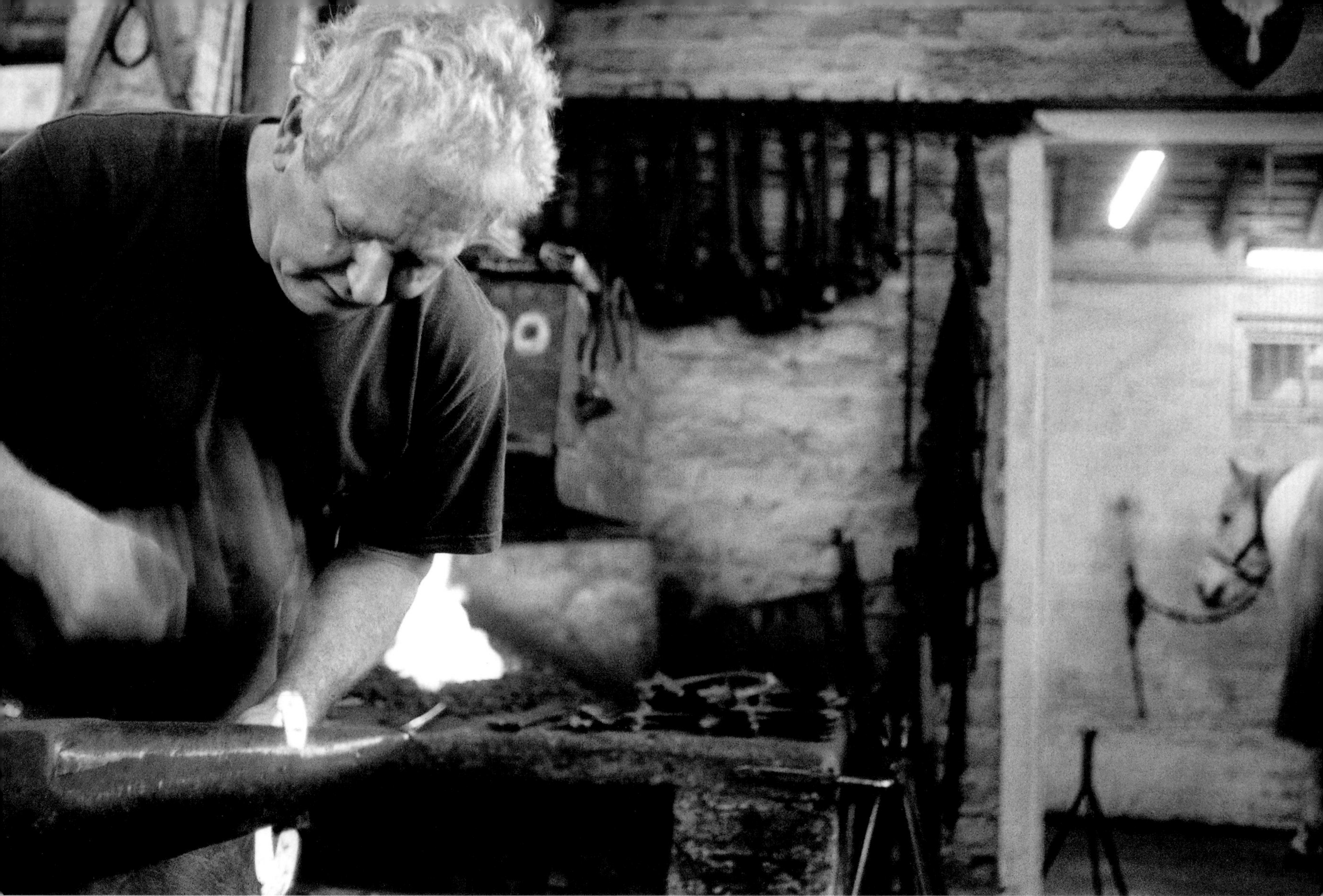

Wynnstay blacksmith John Hughes, with his son Charlie

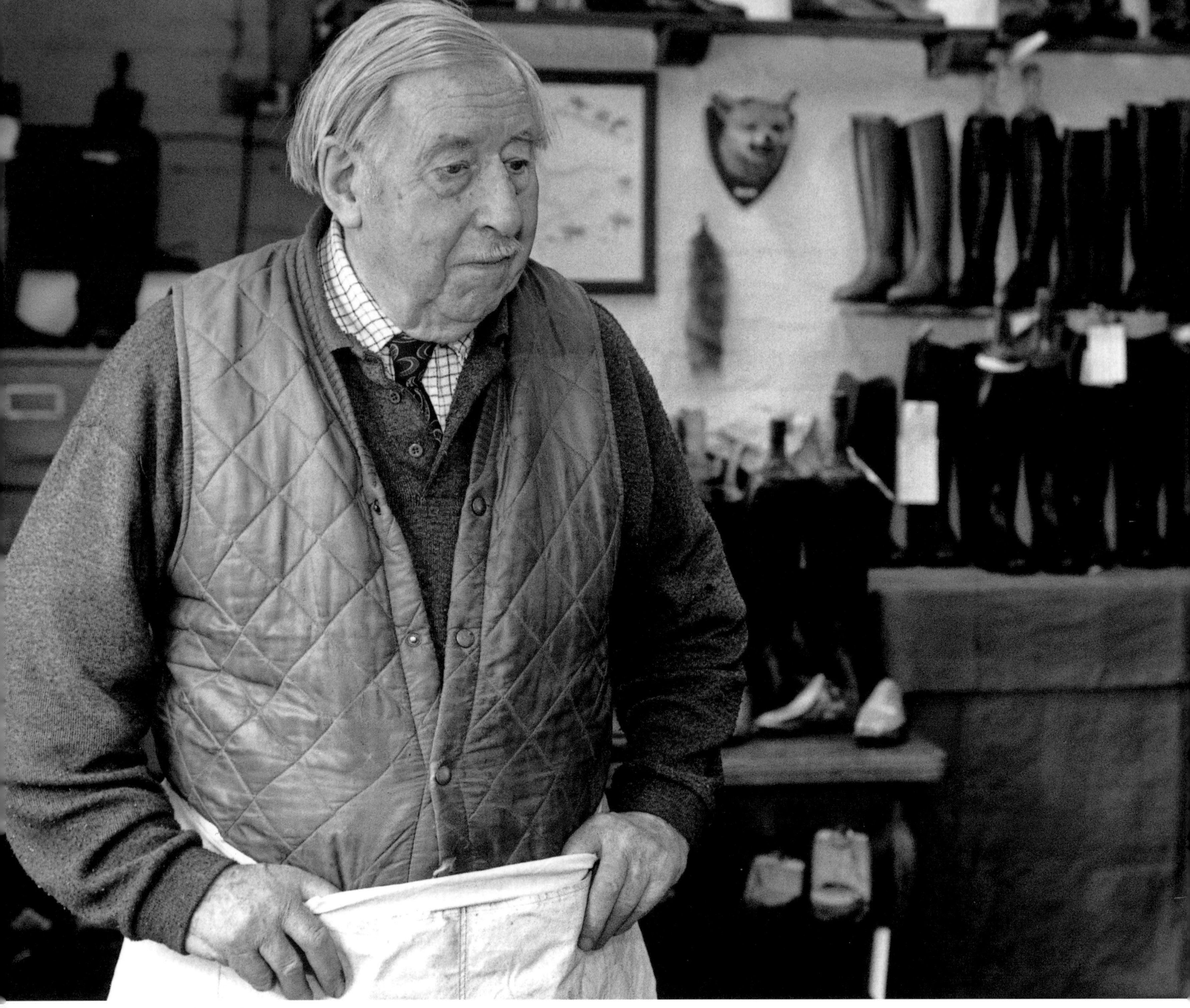

Horace Batten, bootmaker

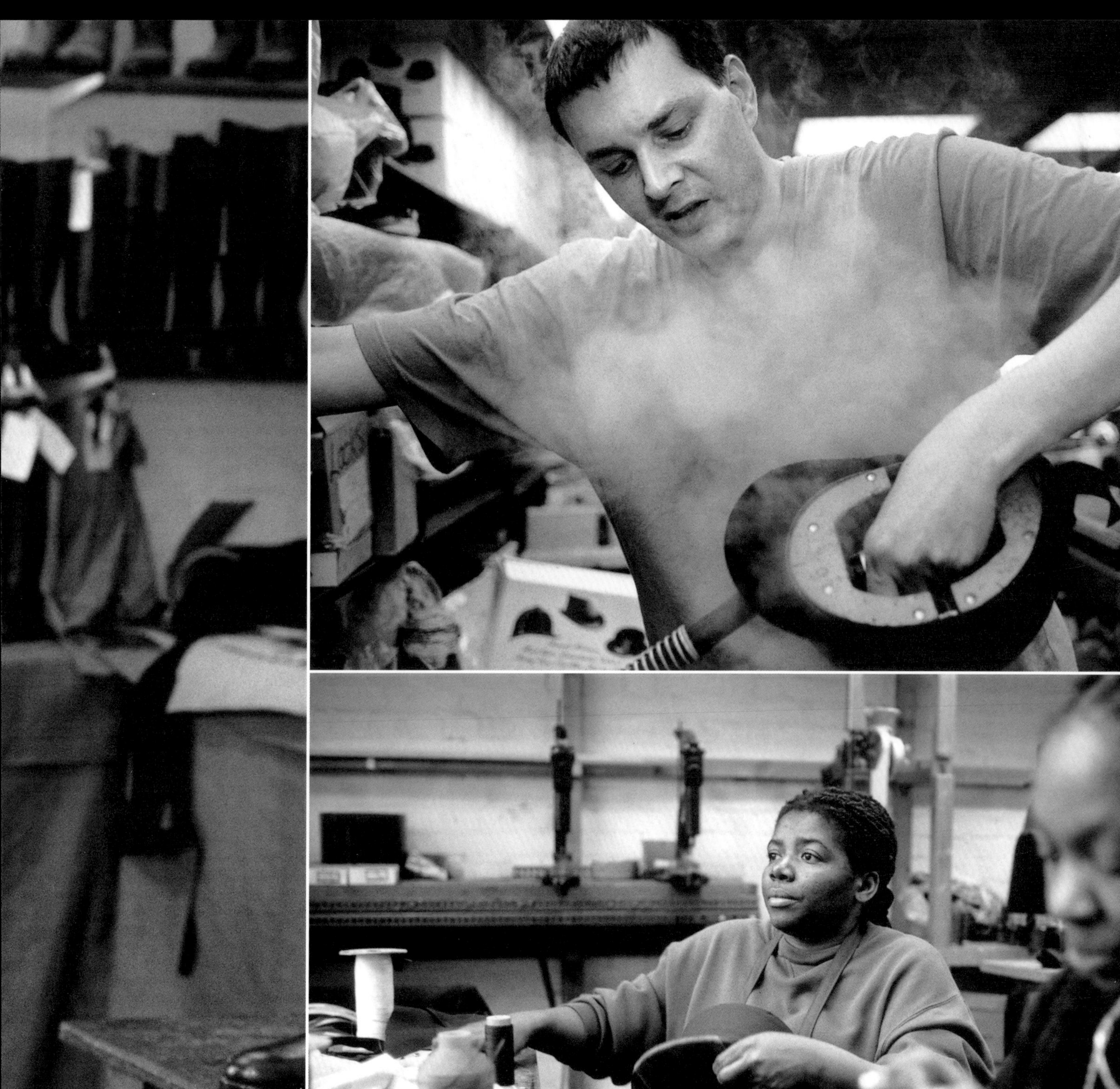

Stephen Cutts and Myrtle Taylor with her sister Evelyn, Patey's Hatters

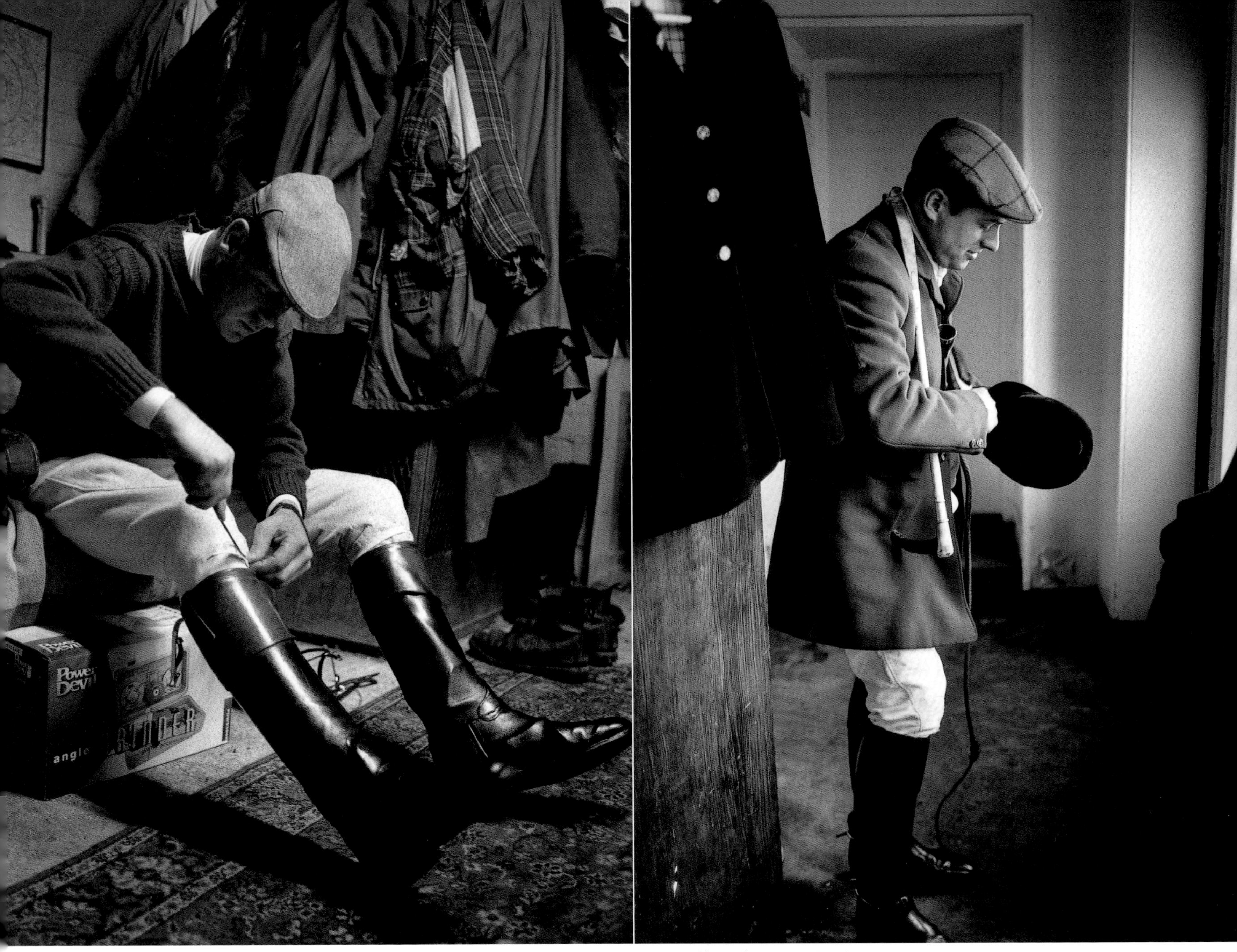

Cotswold huntsman, Julian Barnfield

Former Jedforest huntsman, Rory Innes

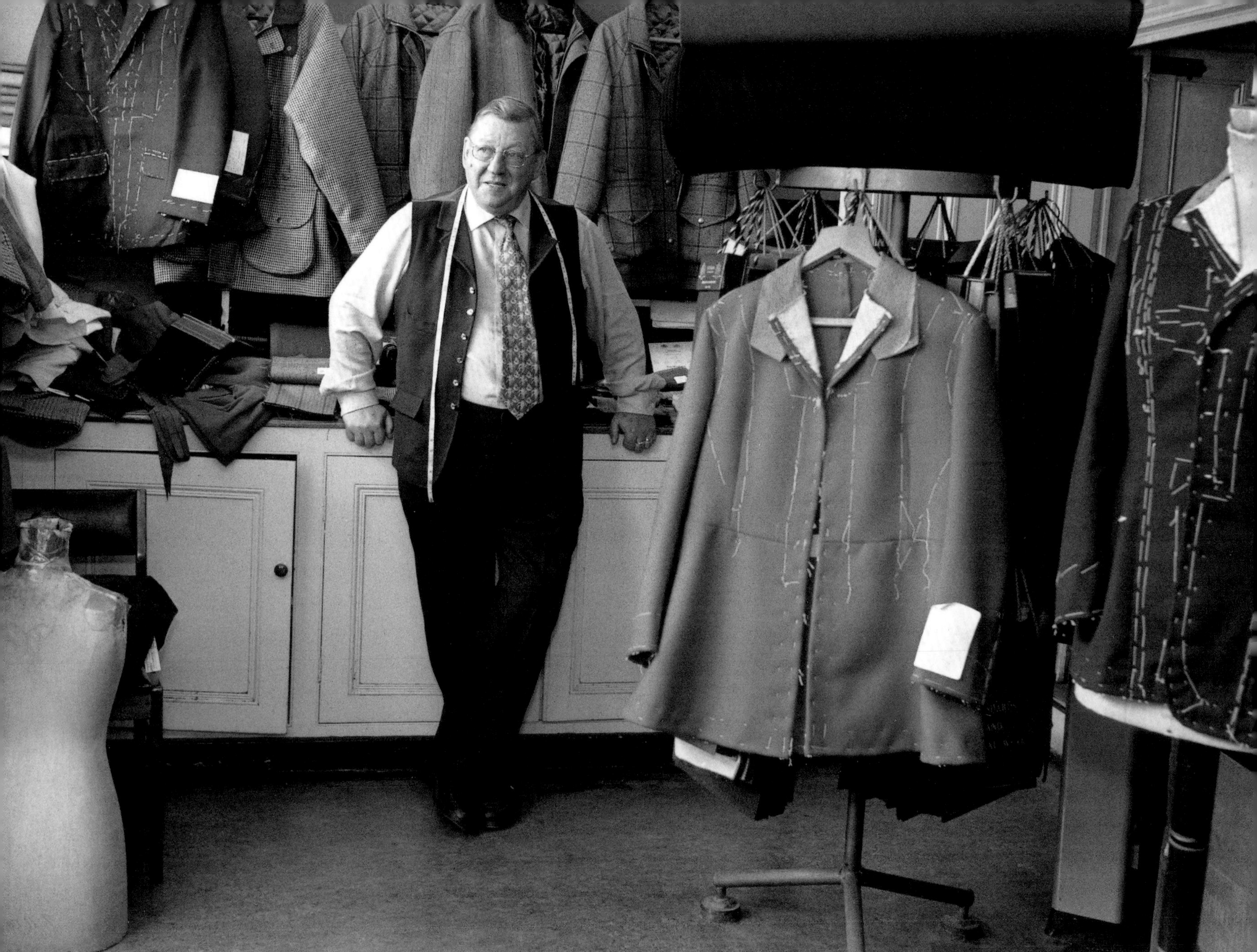

Peter Ripley of Frank Hall's tailors

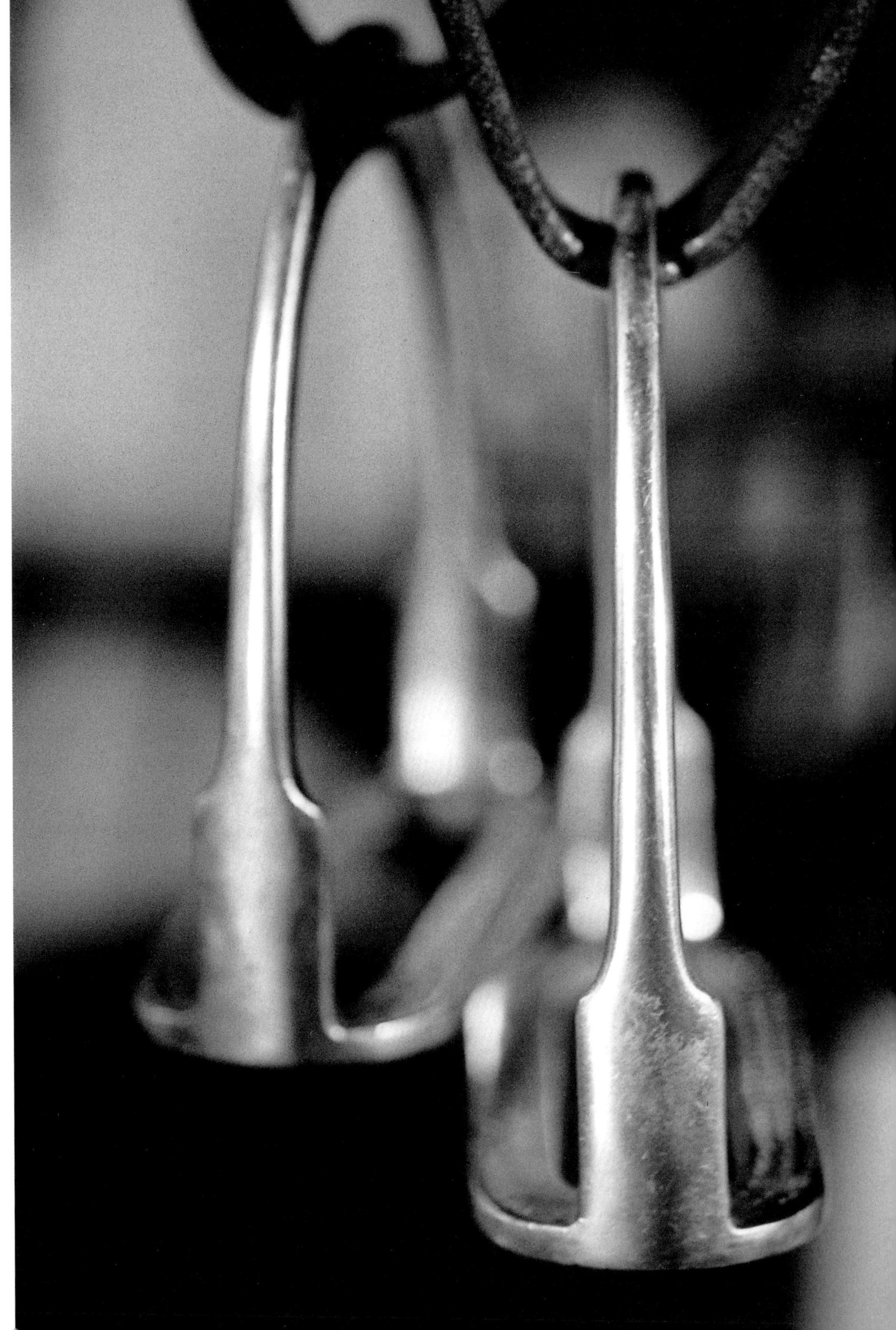

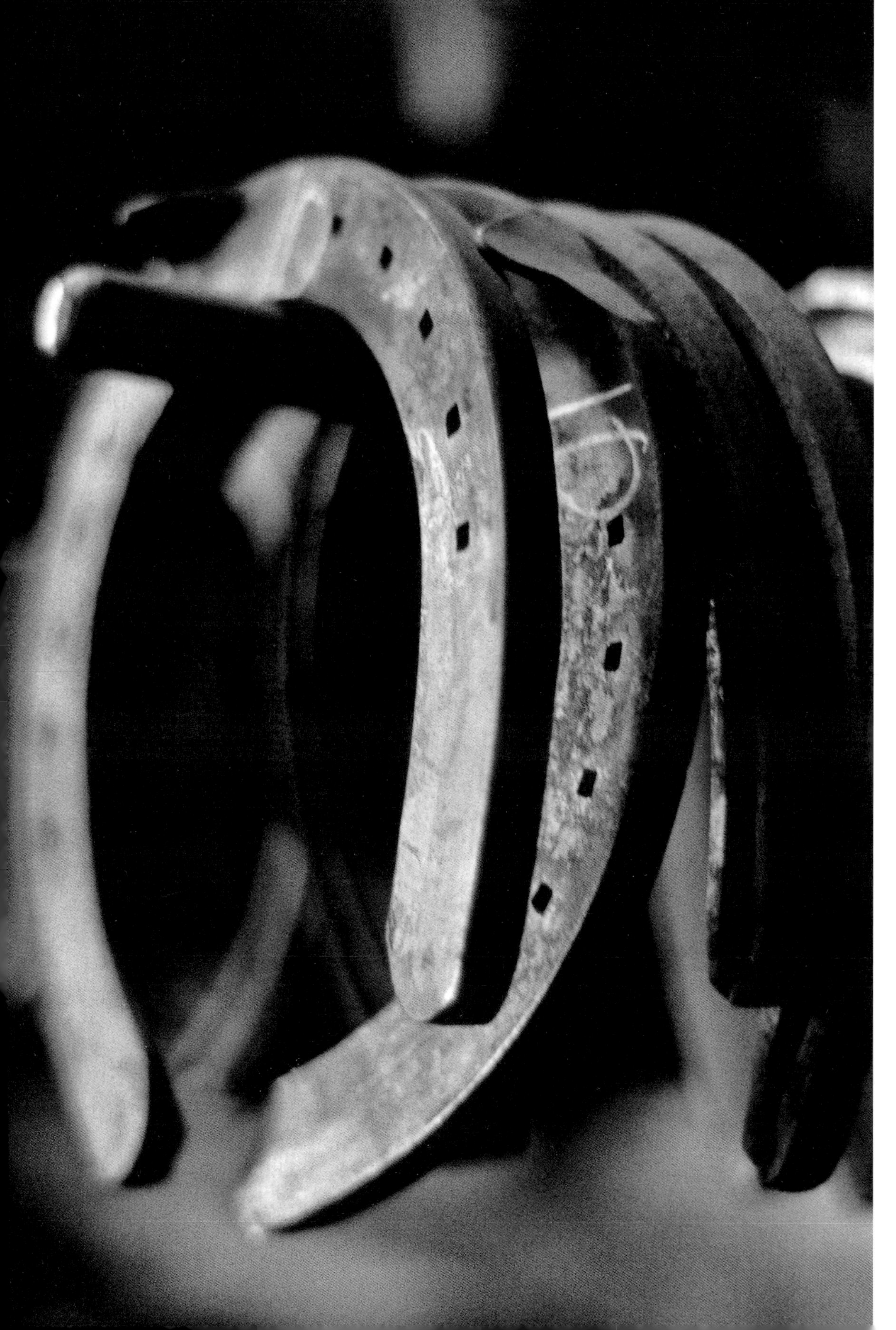

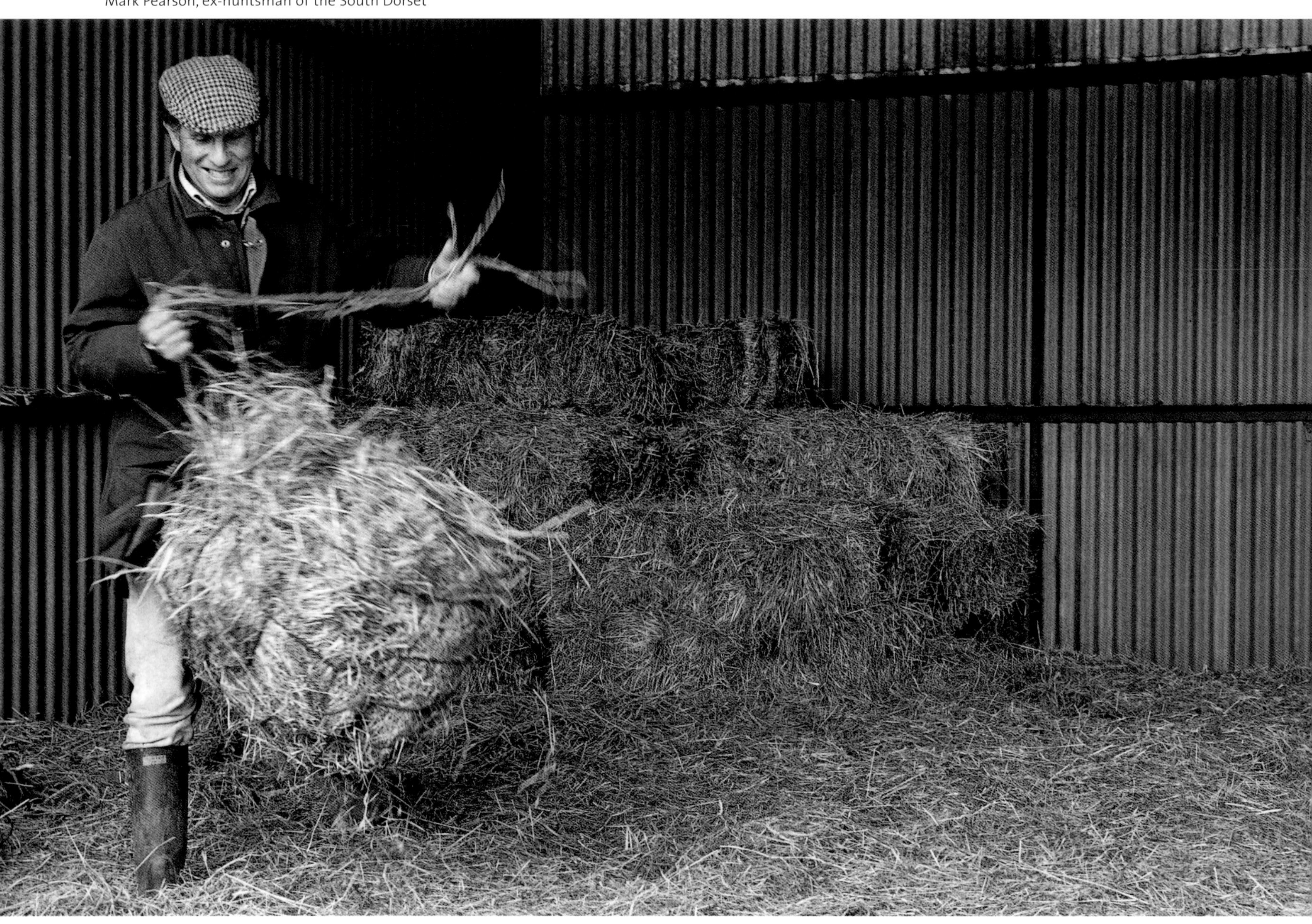
Mark Pearson, ex-huntsman of the South Dorset

Horses from the Ledbury country

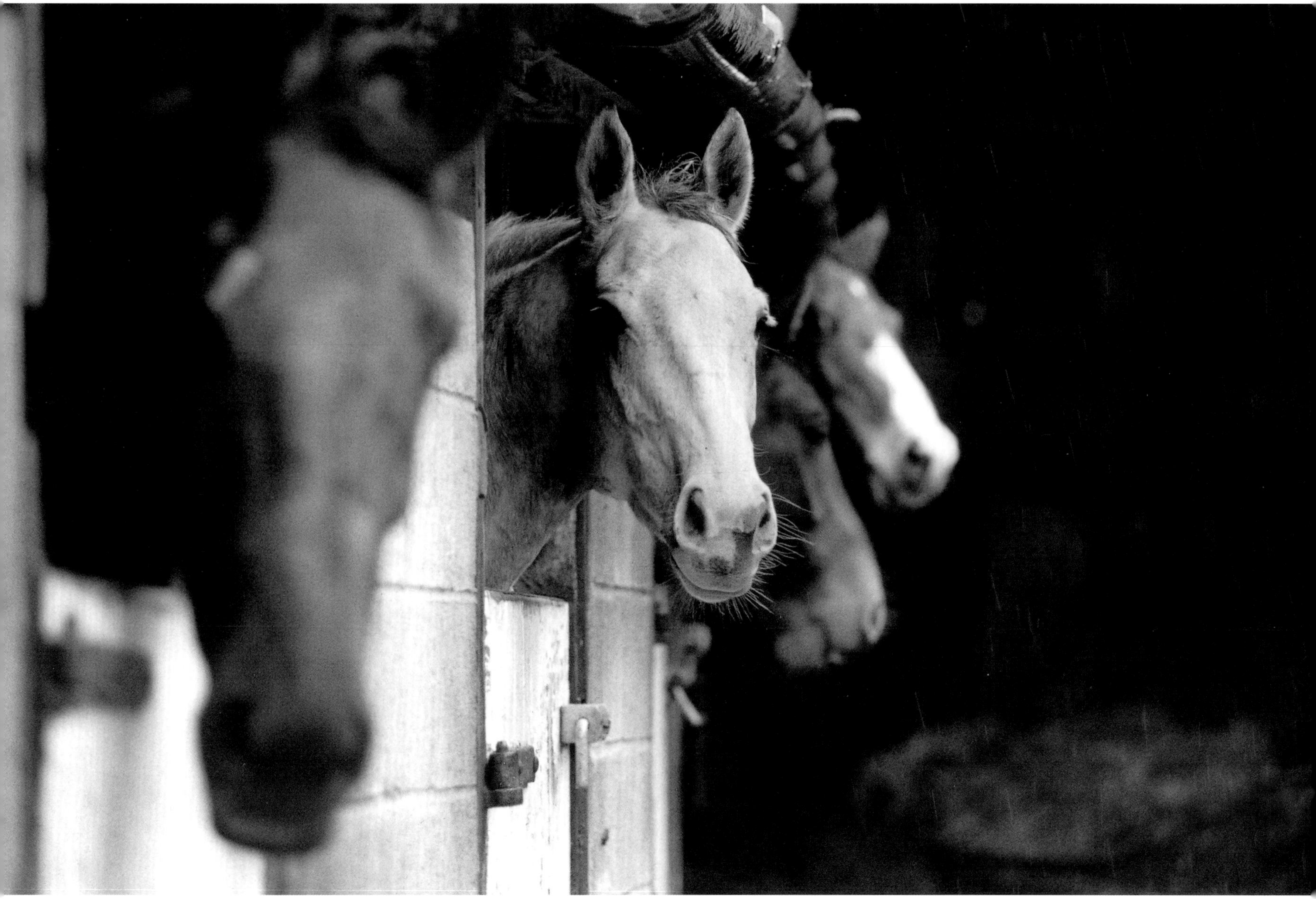

The Hunt

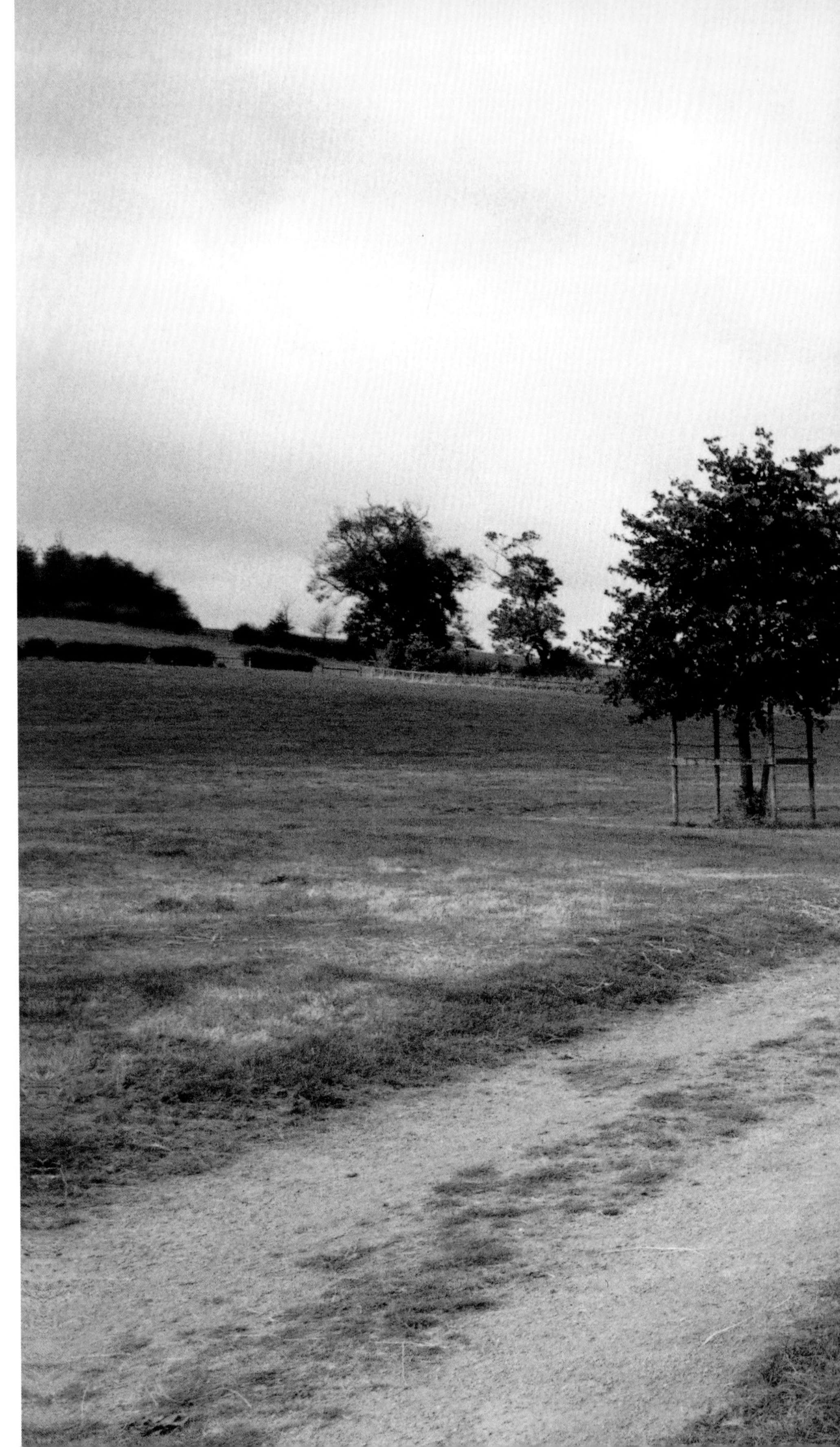
Bicester and Whaddon Chase meet

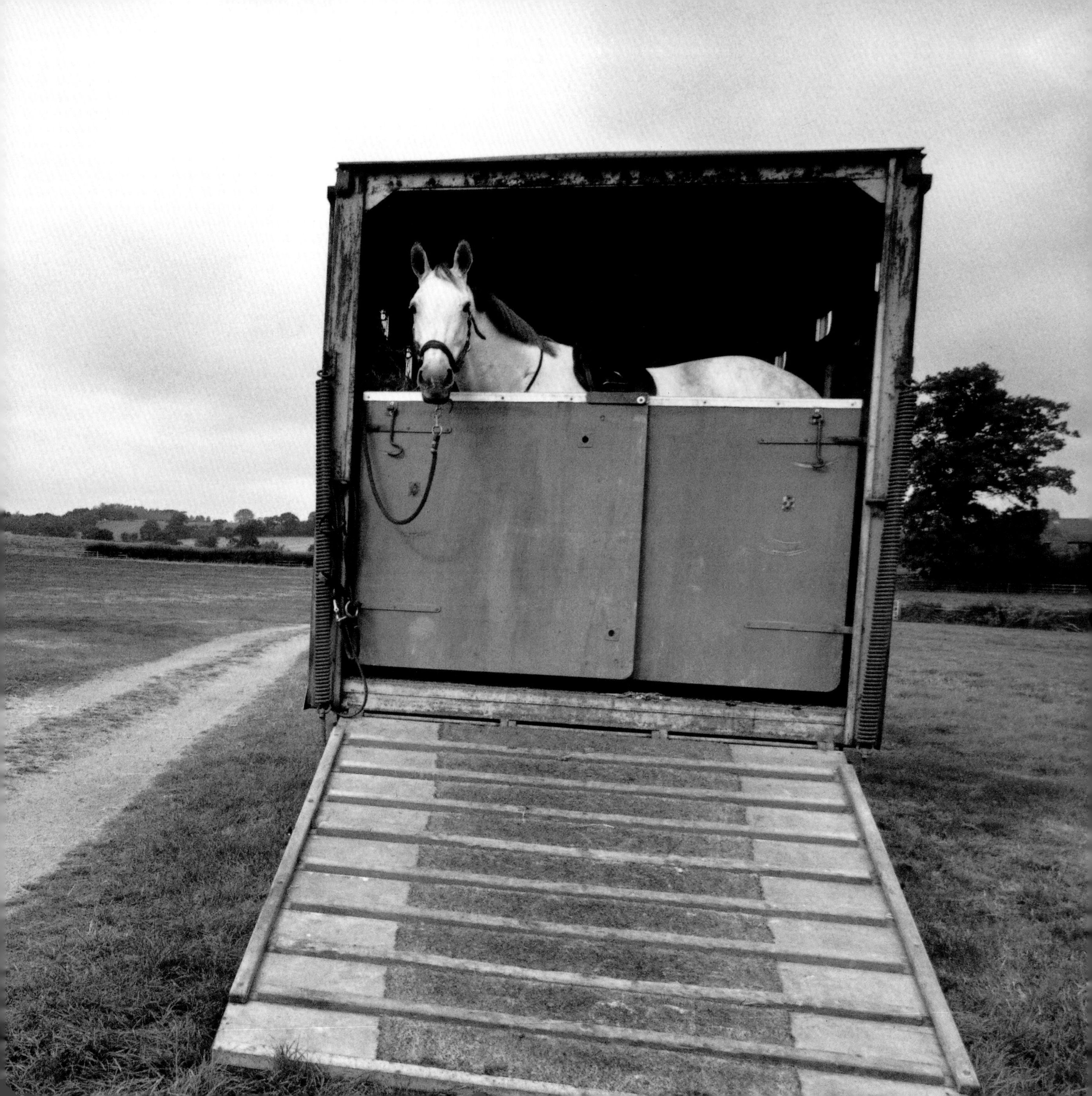

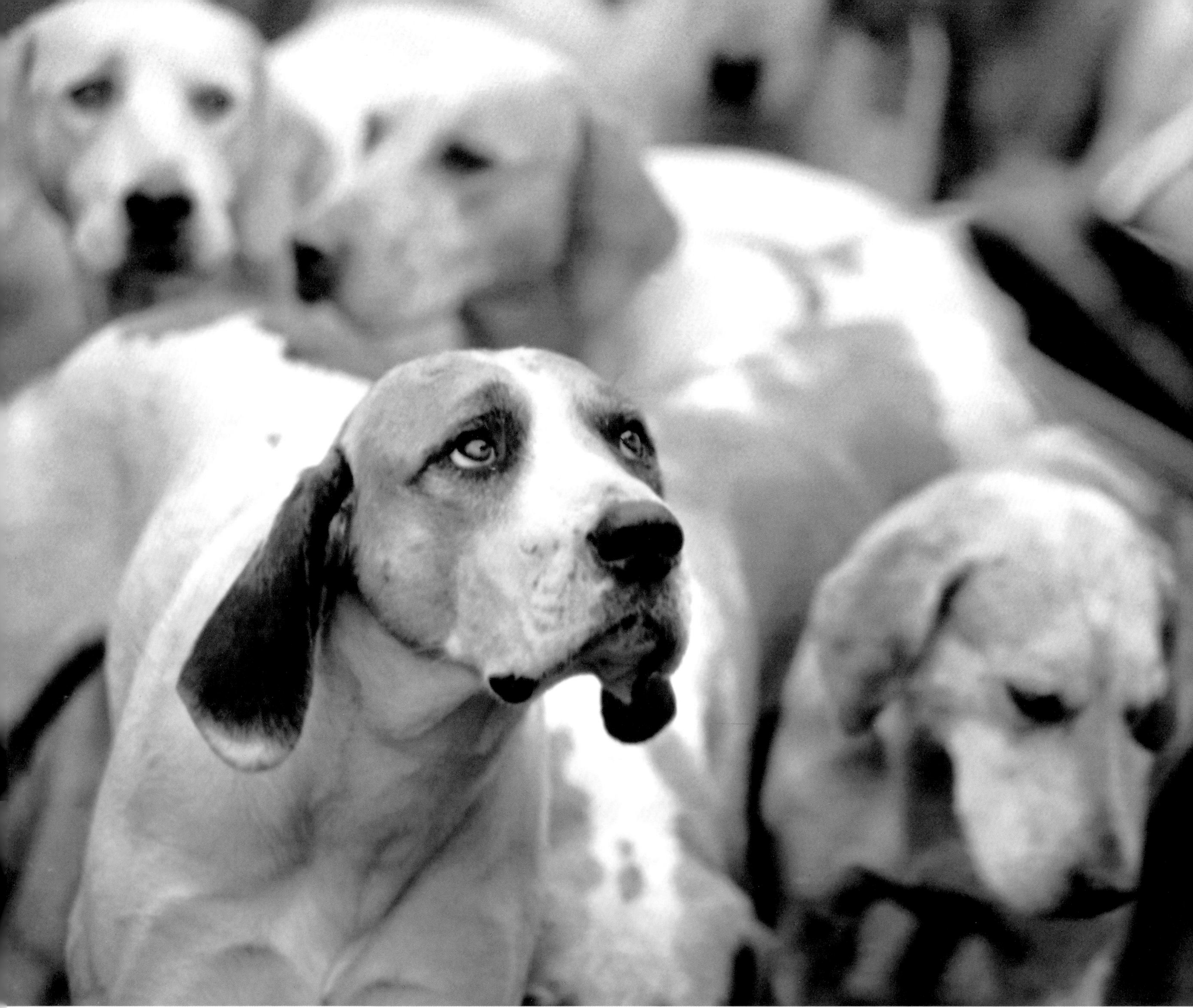

Cotswold meet

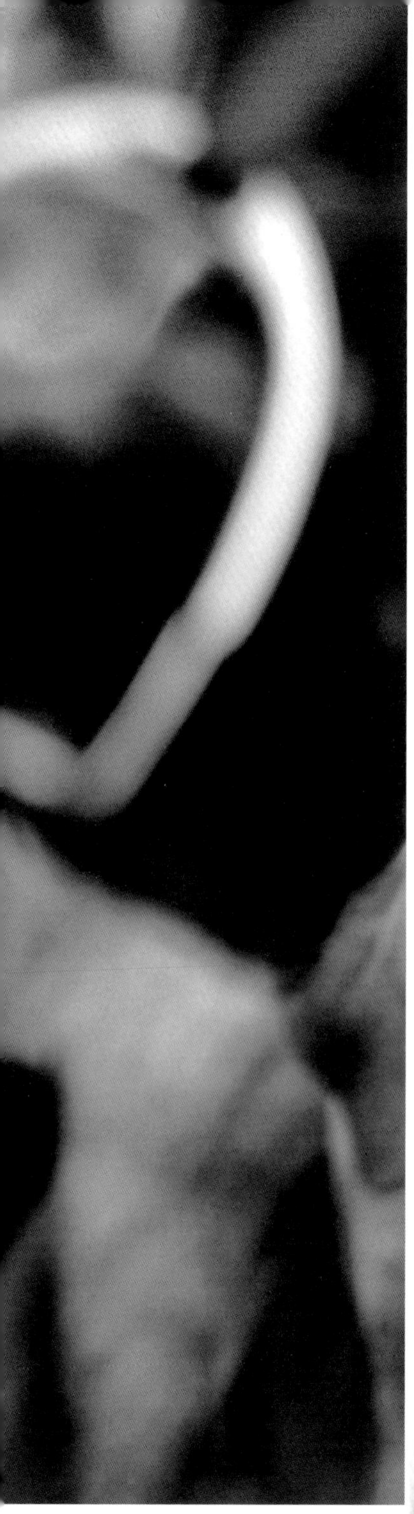

The Duke of Buccleuch's hounds

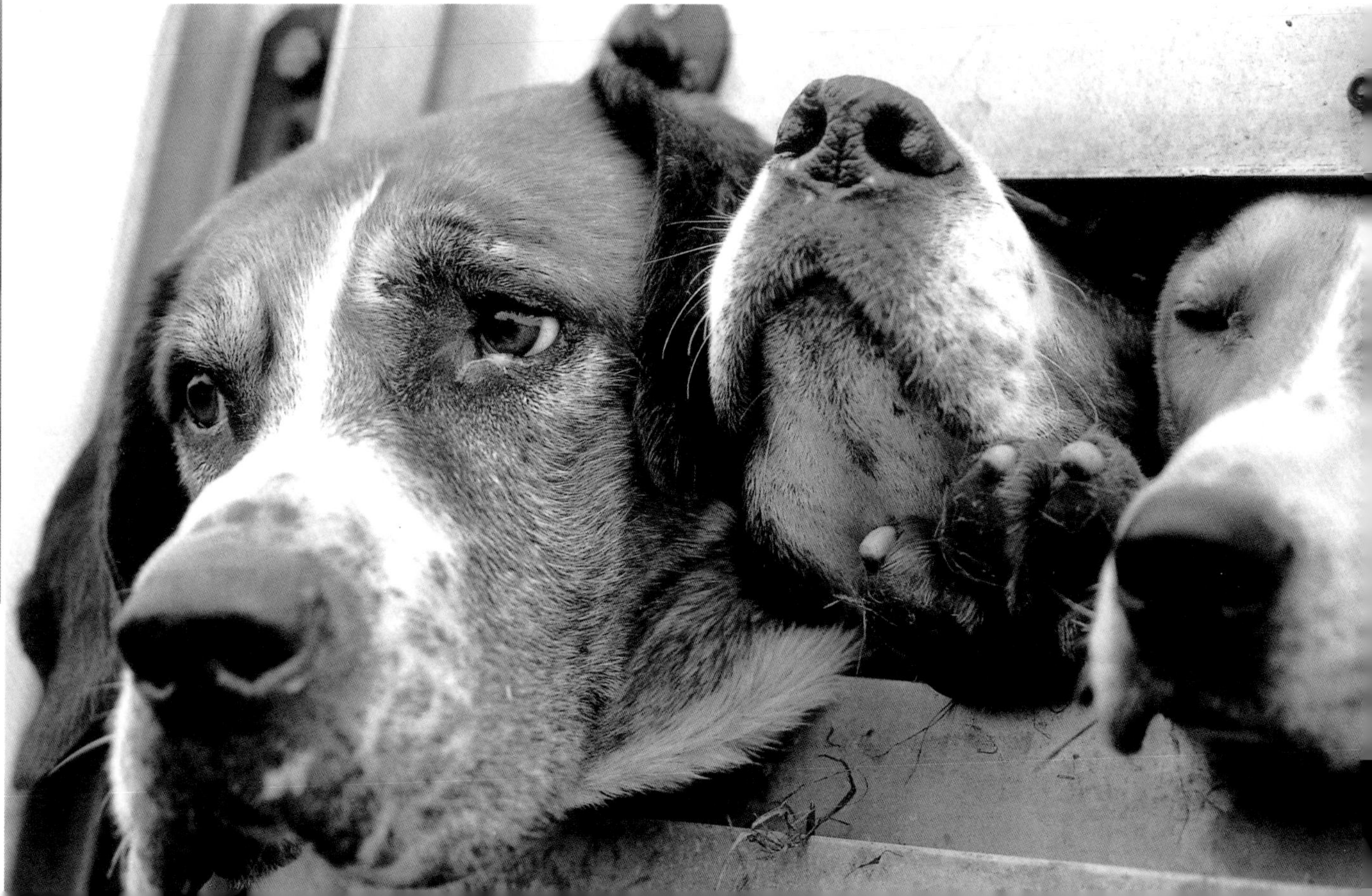

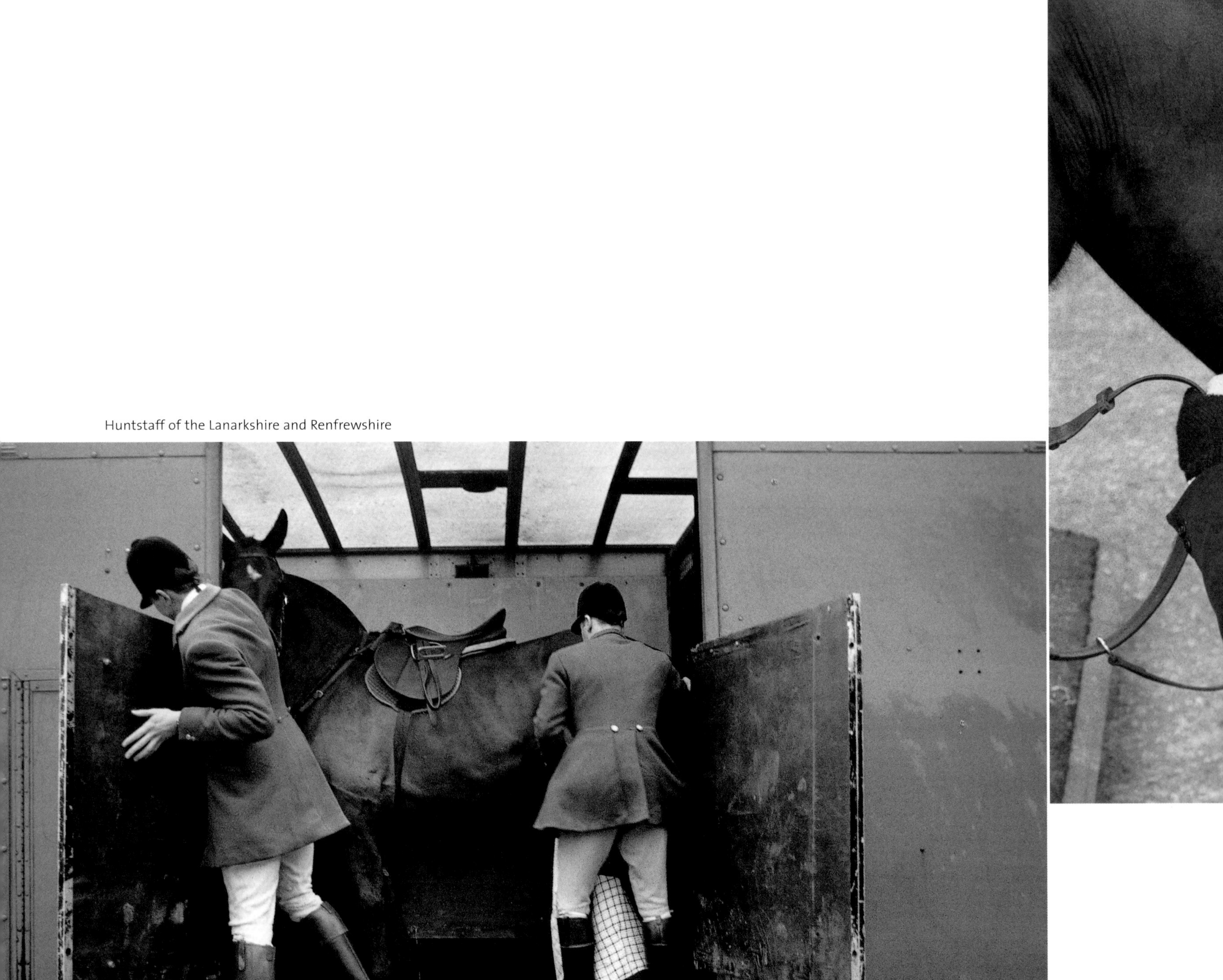

Huntstaff of the Lanarkshire and Renfrewshire

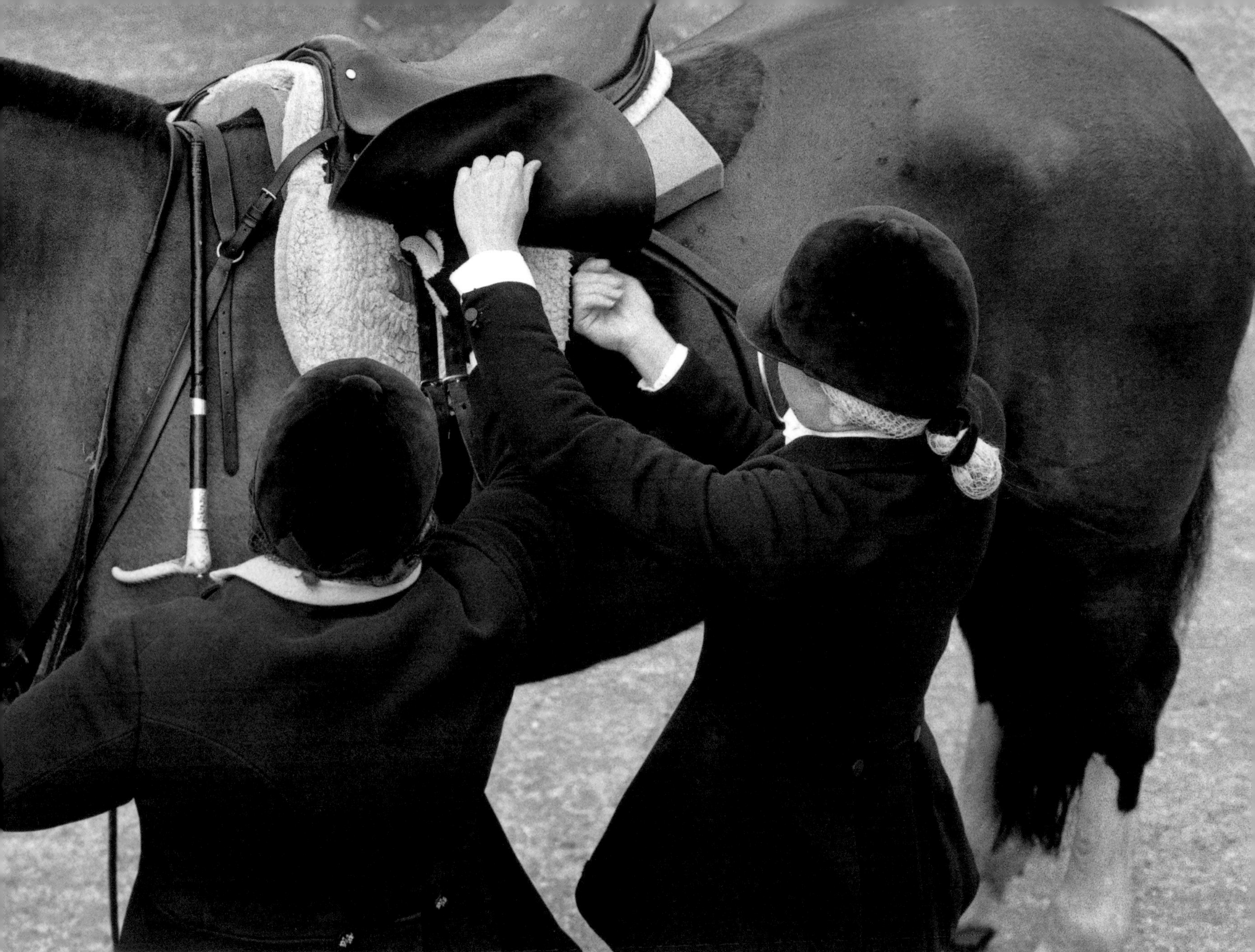

Wynnstay followers

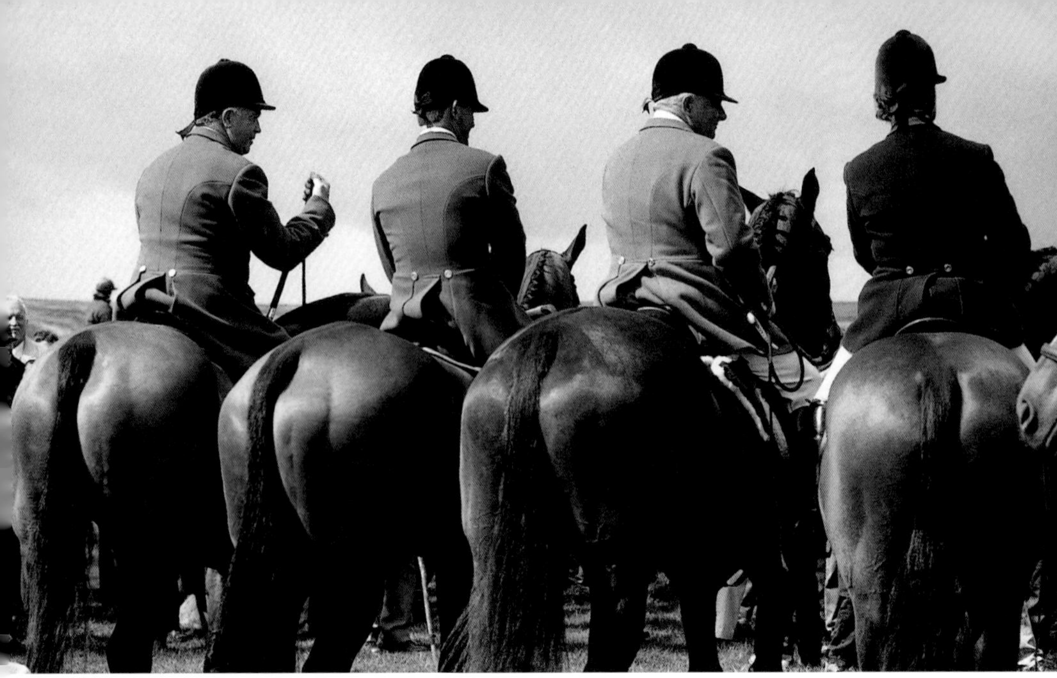

The mastership of the Devon and Somerset Staghounds

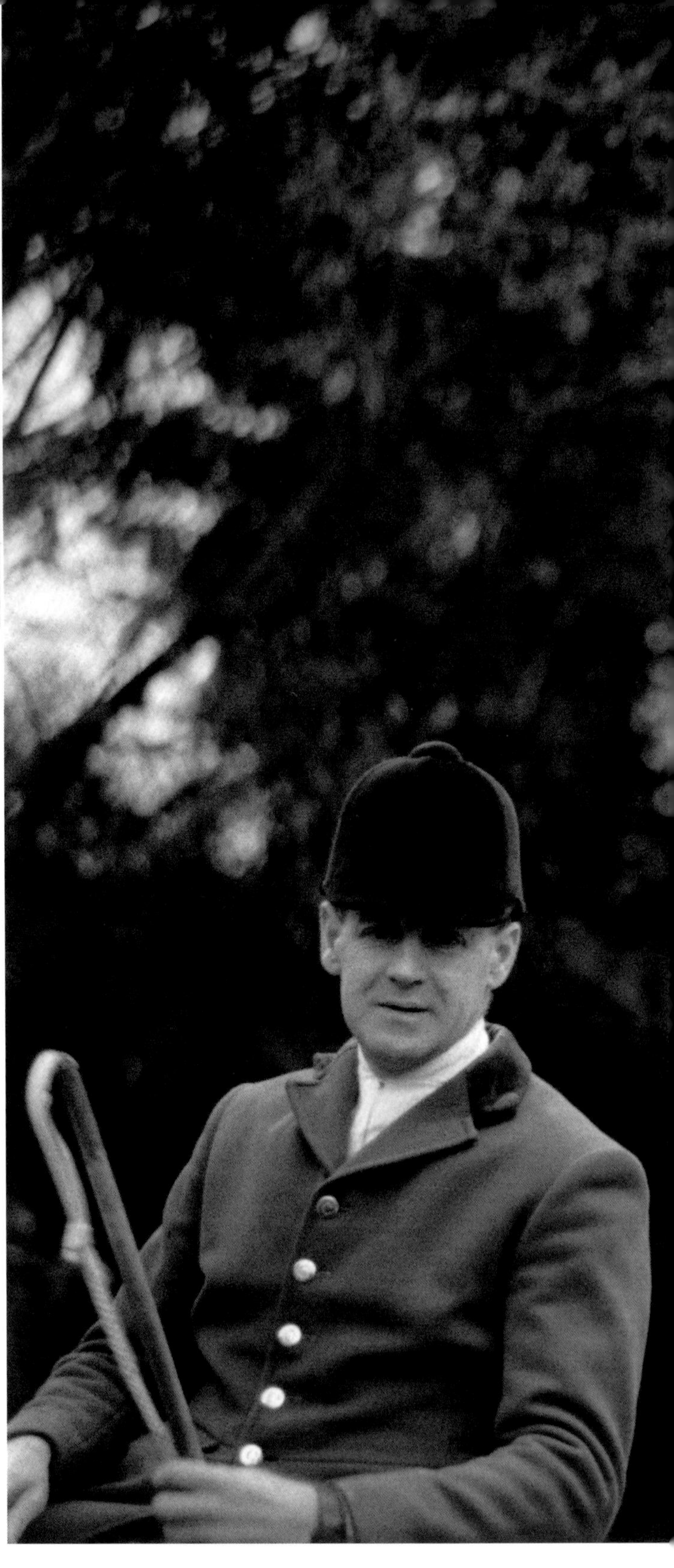

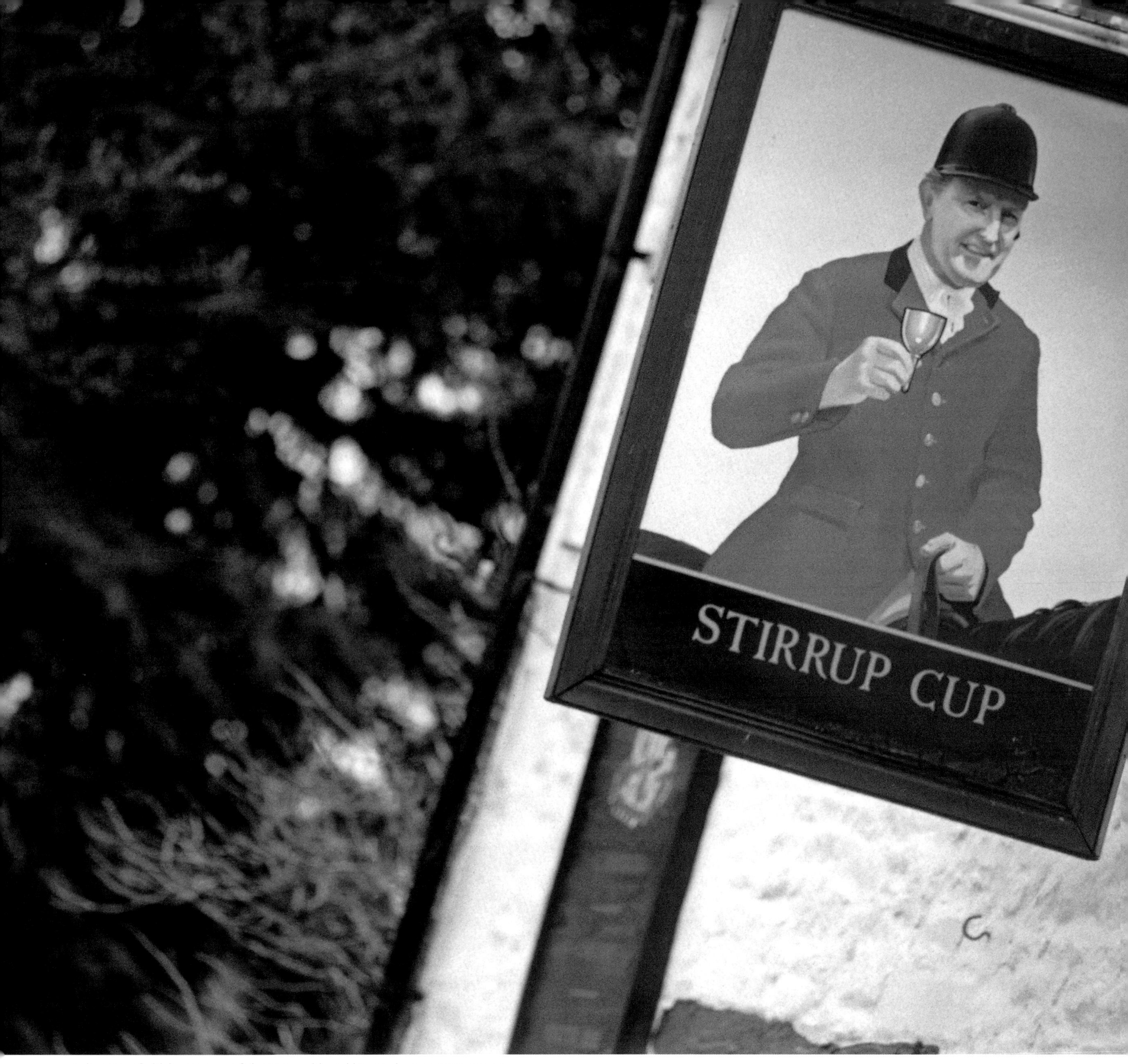

Julian Barnfield, huntsman of the Cotswold, and his predecessor Tim Unwin

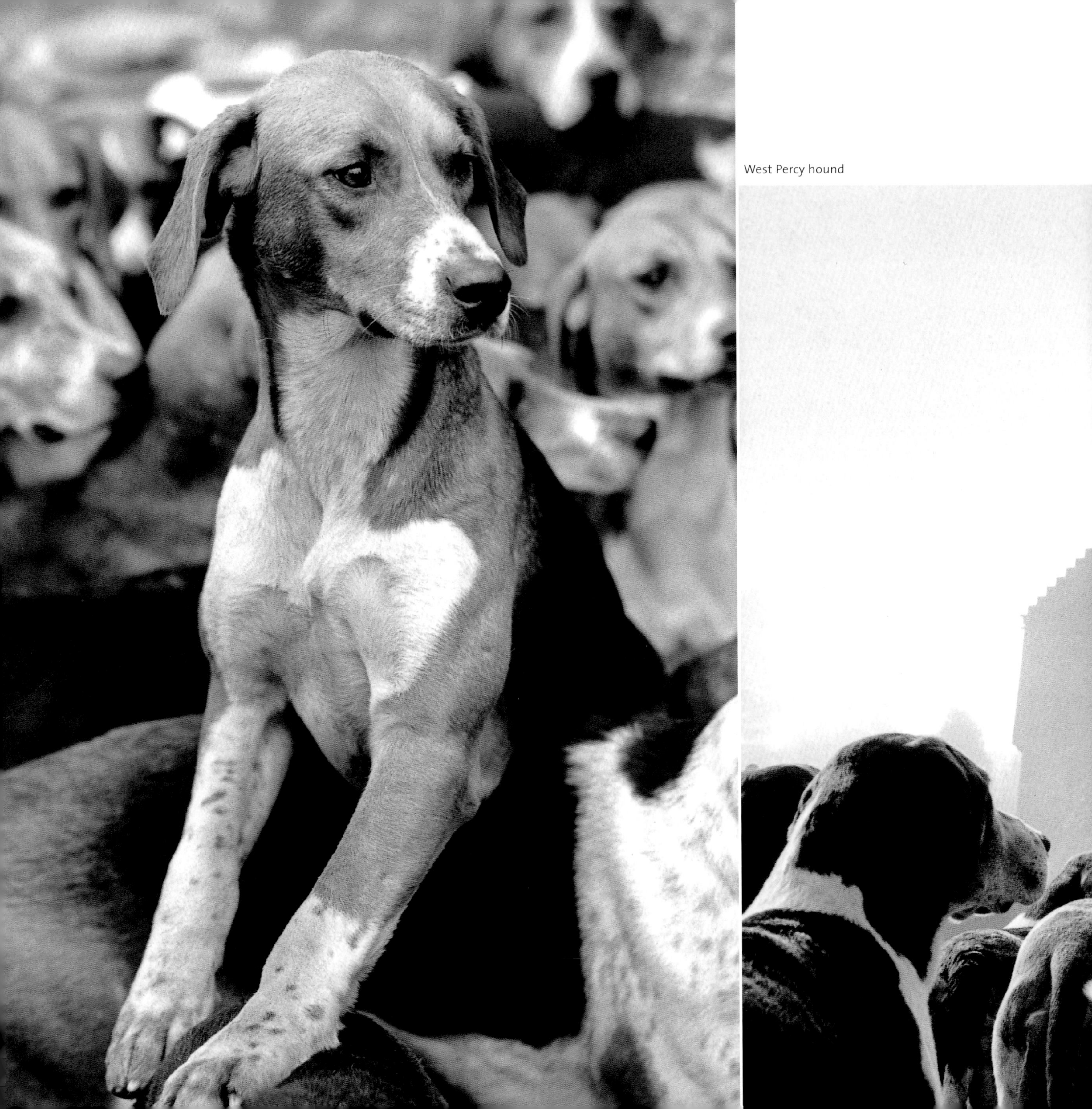

West Percy hound

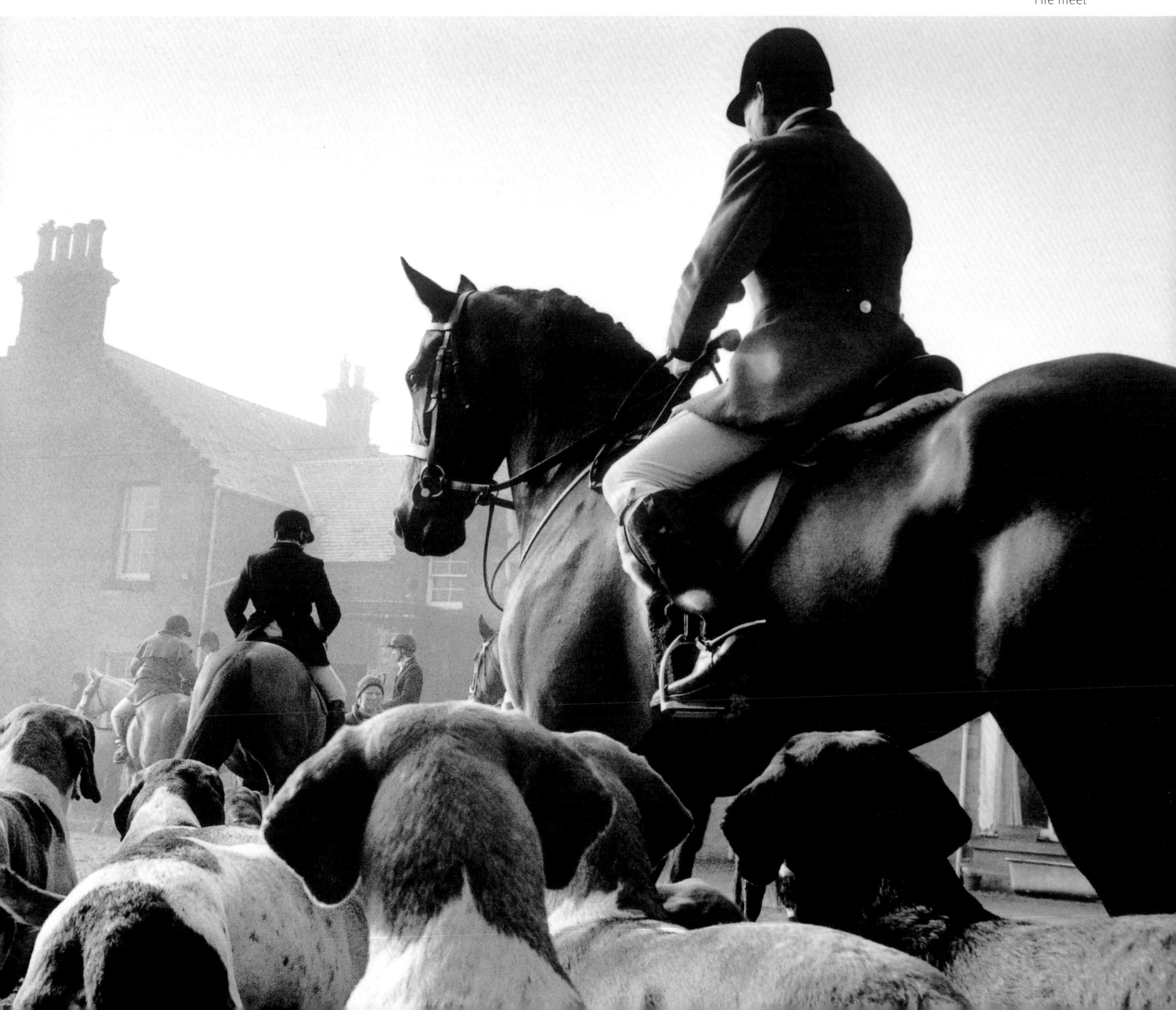

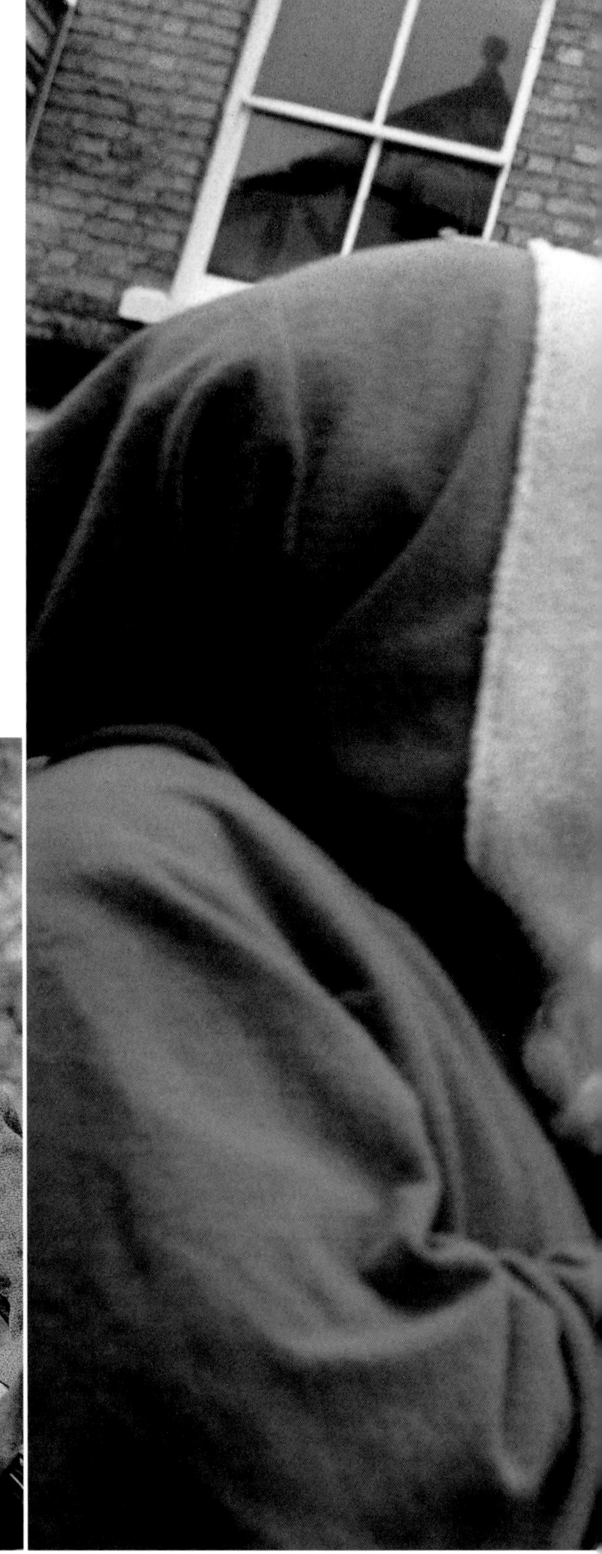

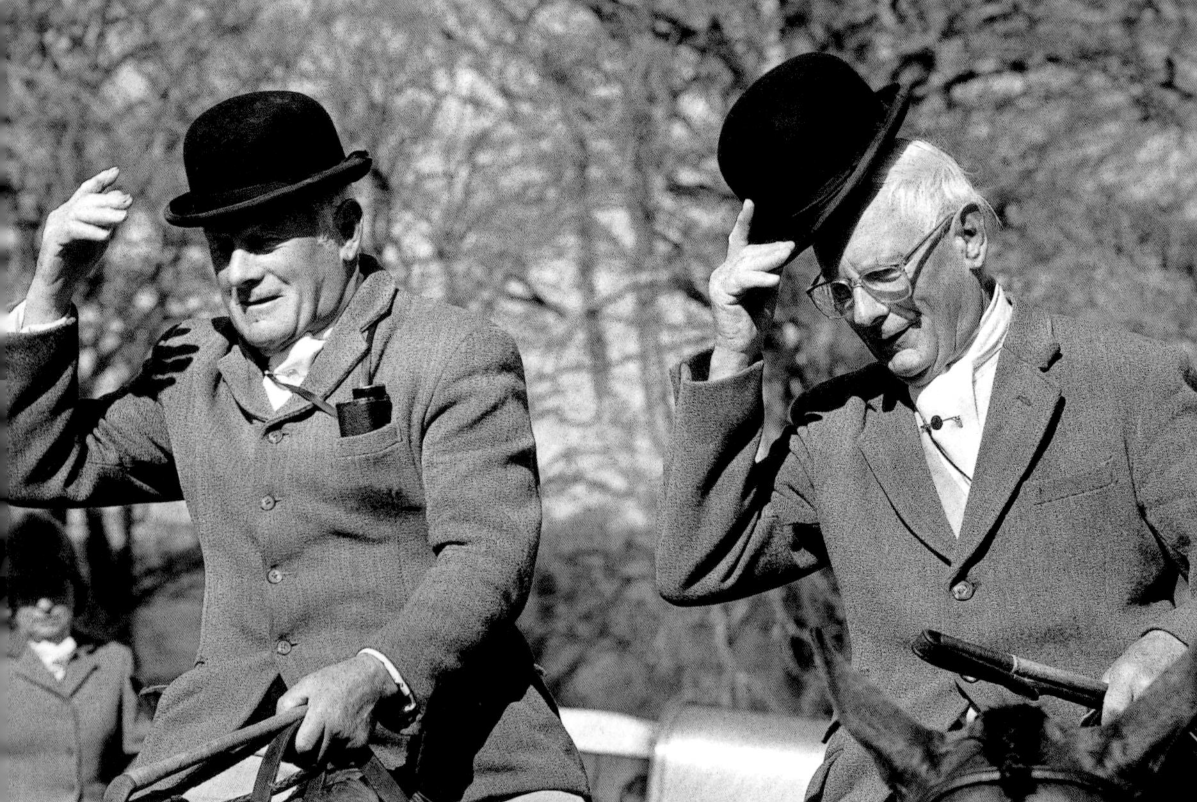

Dick and Pat Lloyd at a meet of the Devon and Somerset Staghounds

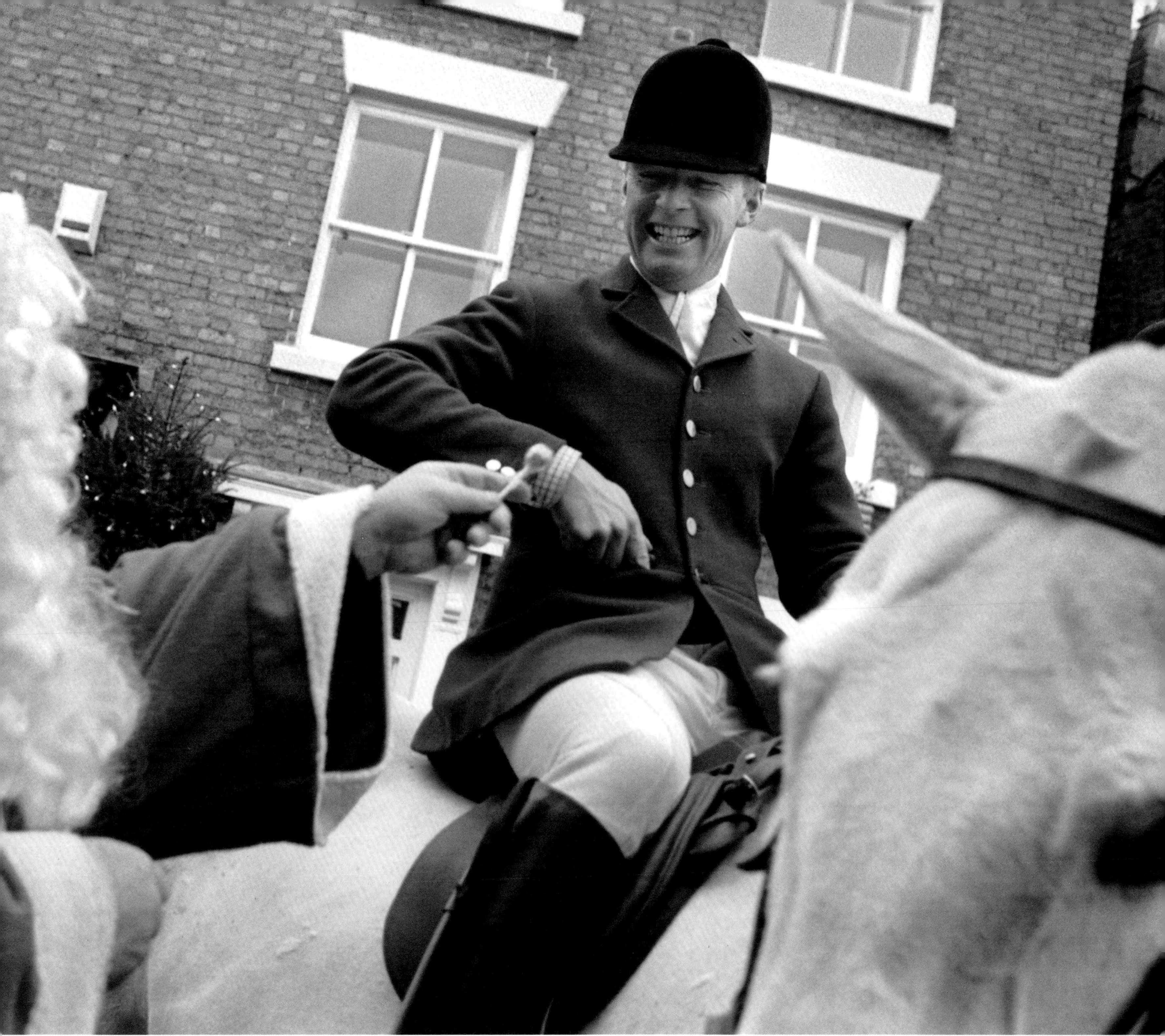

Bert Loud, Wynnstay kennel huntsman, and Santa

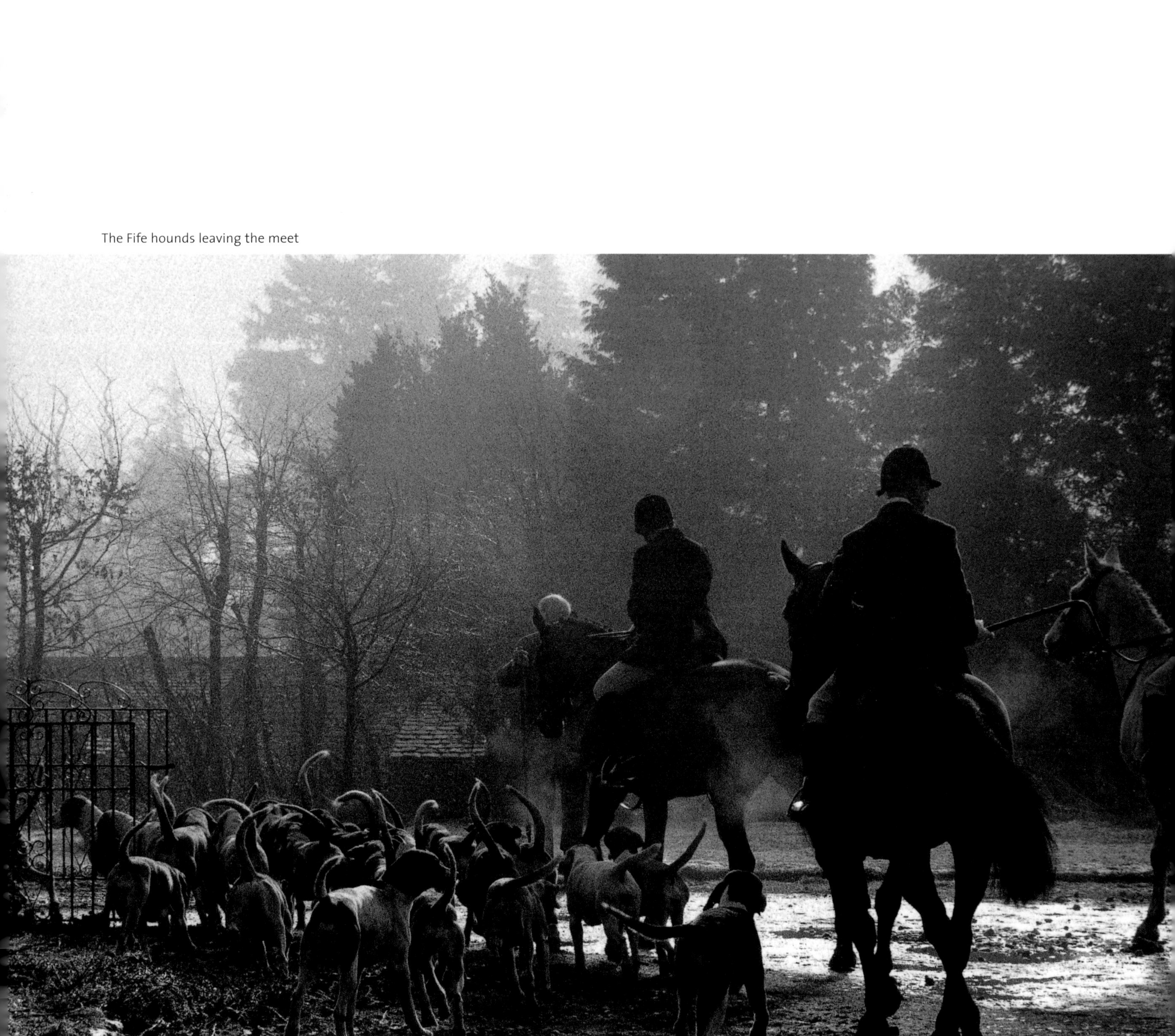

The Fife hounds leaving the meet

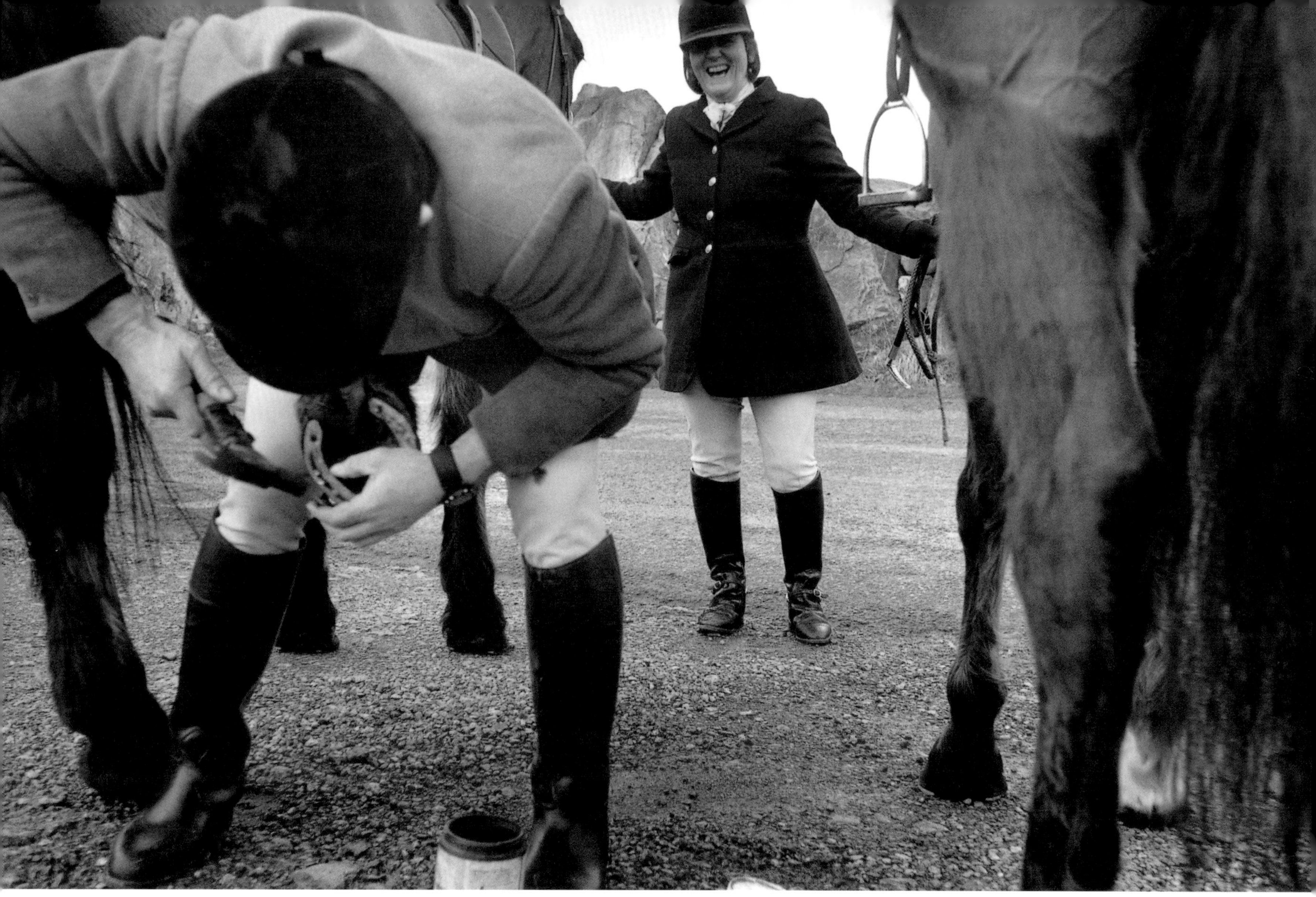

Members of the Galway Blazers

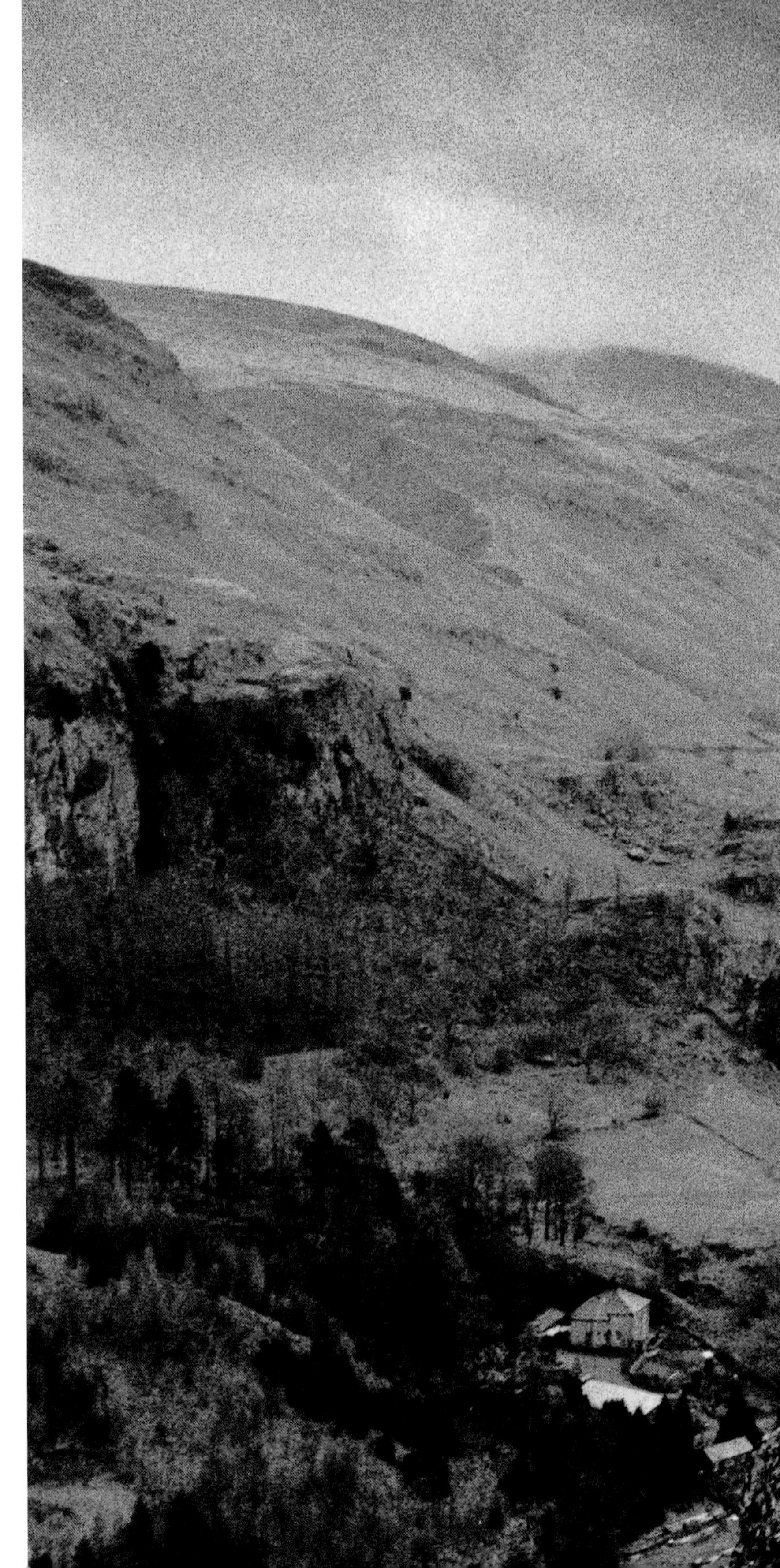

Blencathra hound

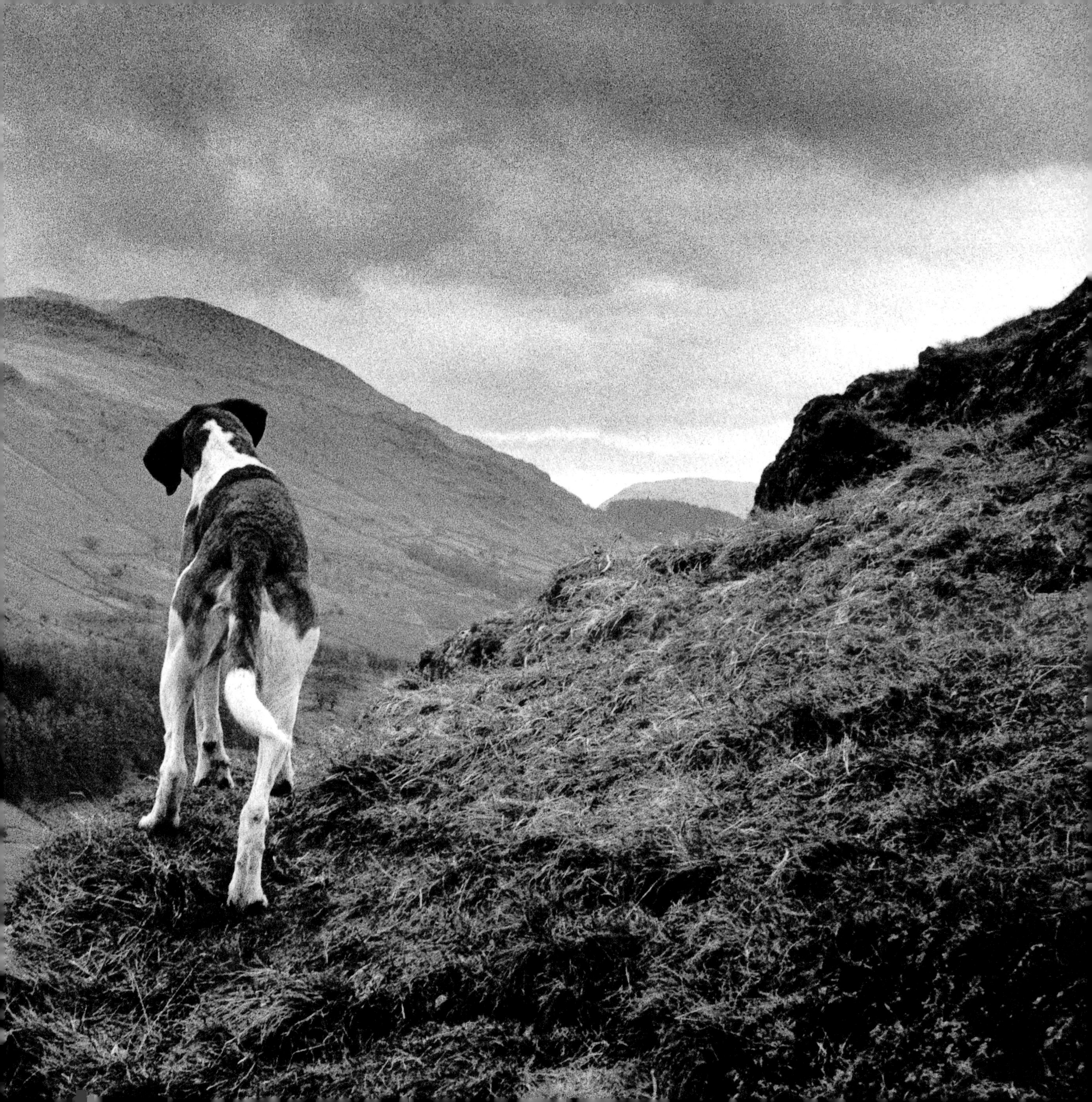

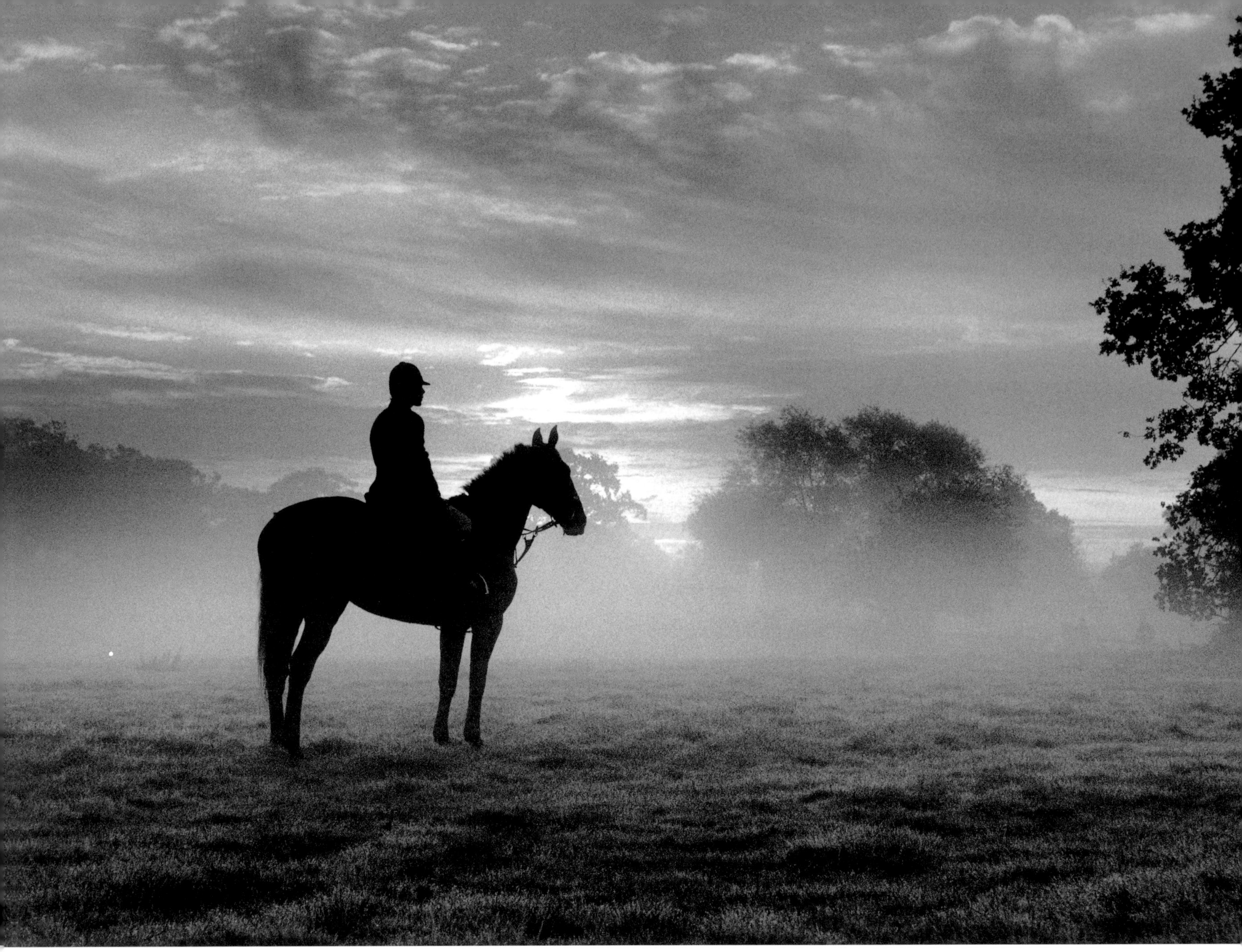

Wynnstay point

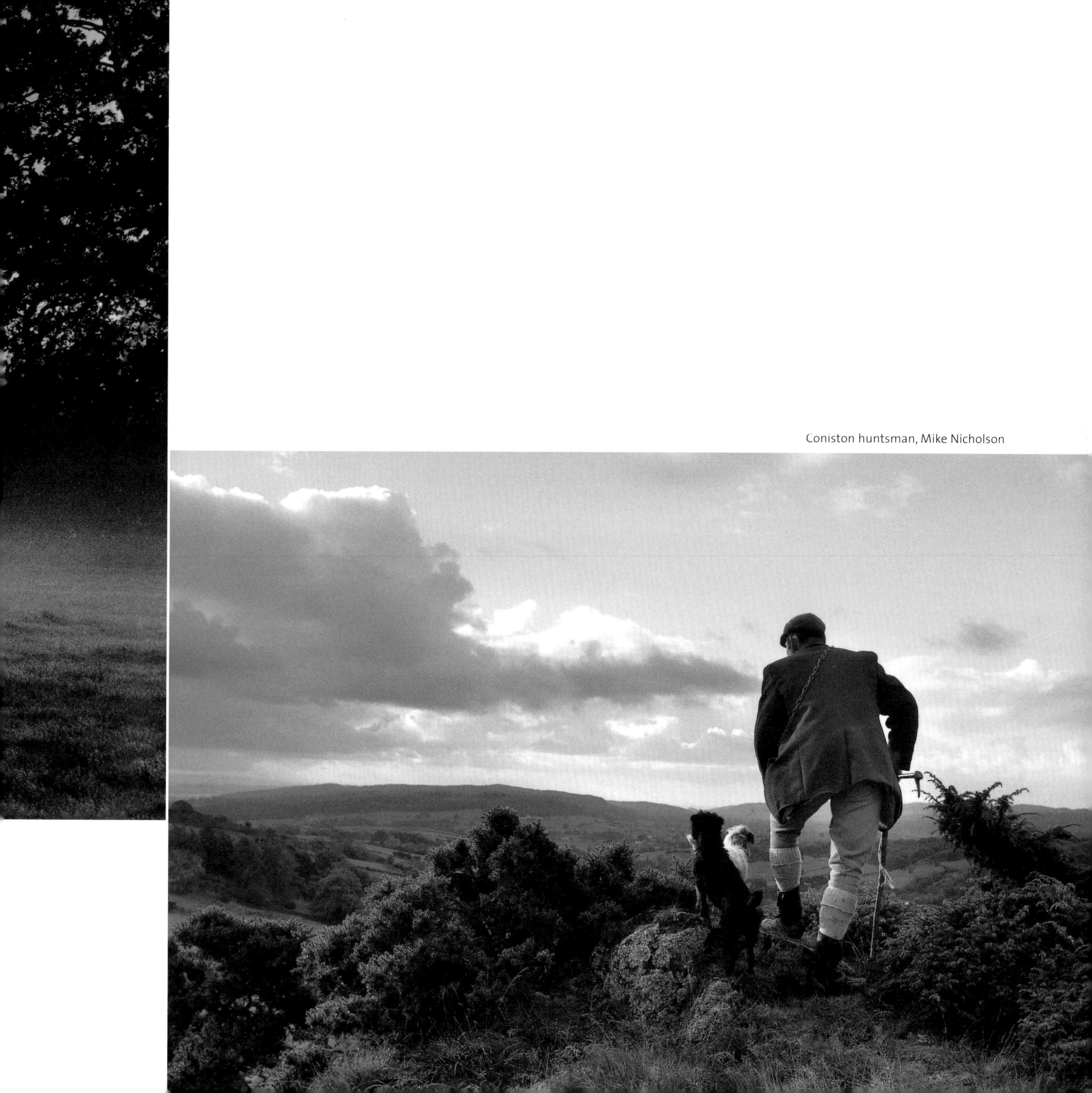

Coniston huntsman, Mike Nicholson

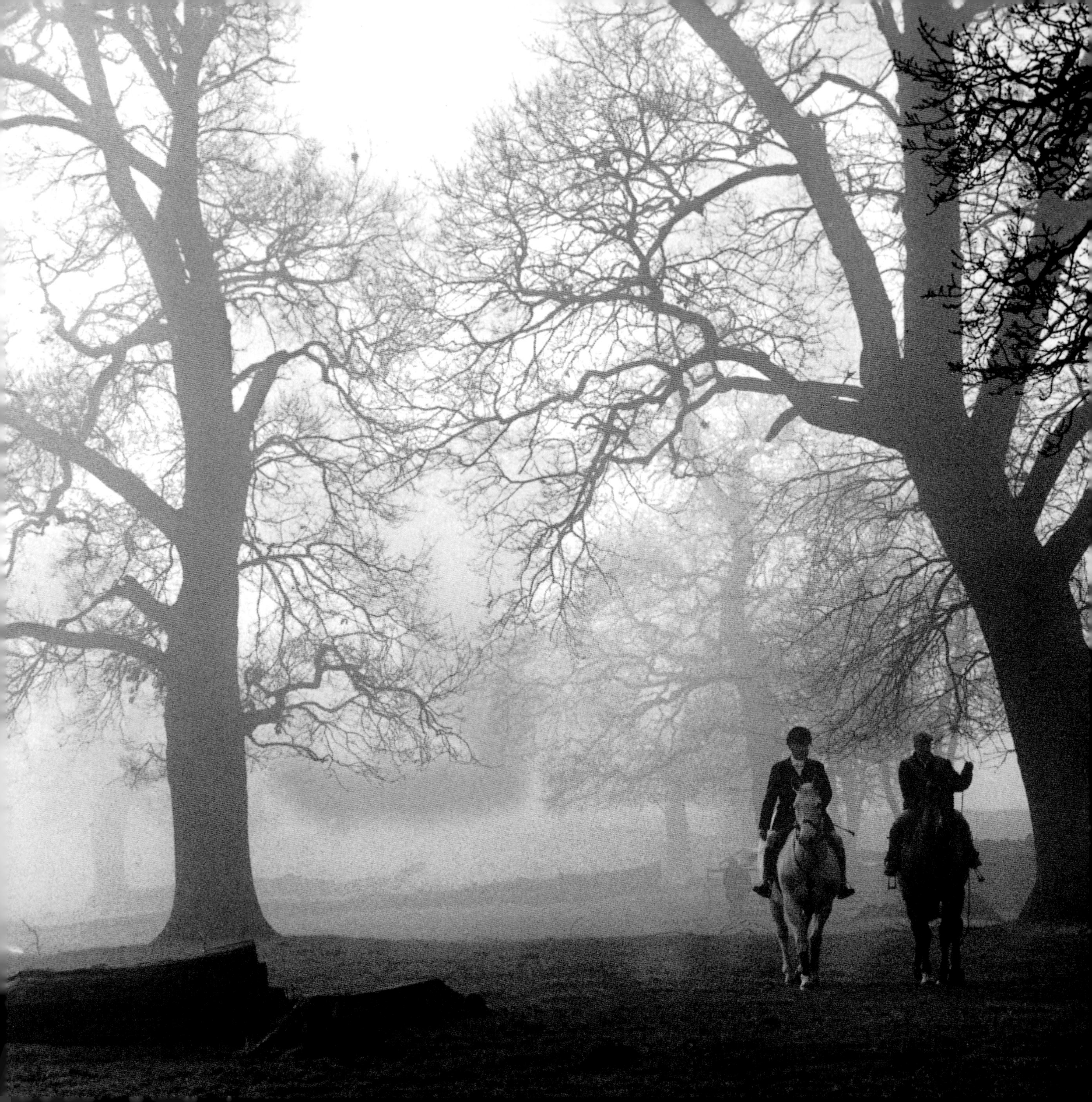

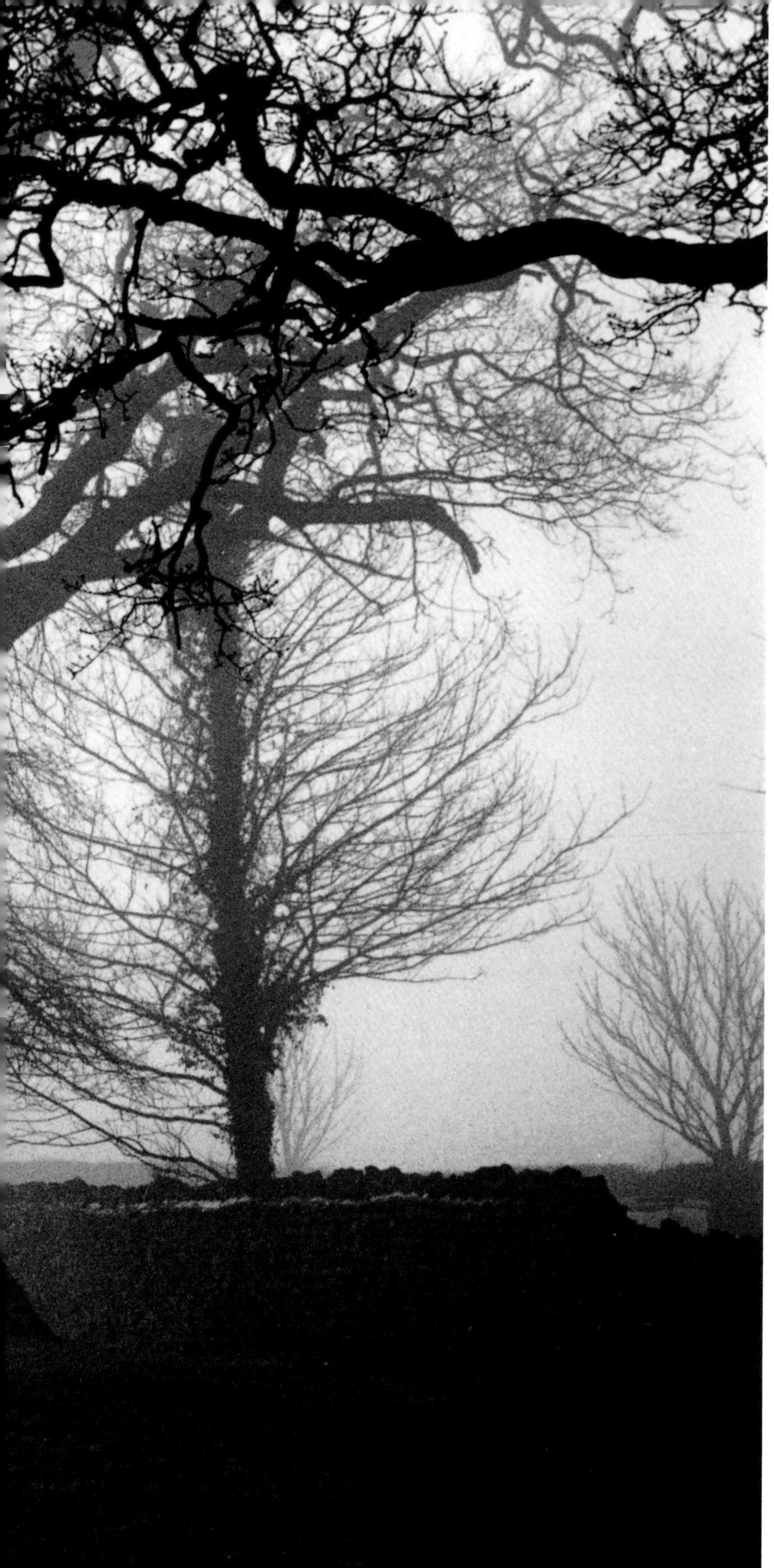

Two riders arriving at a meet of the Heythrop hunt

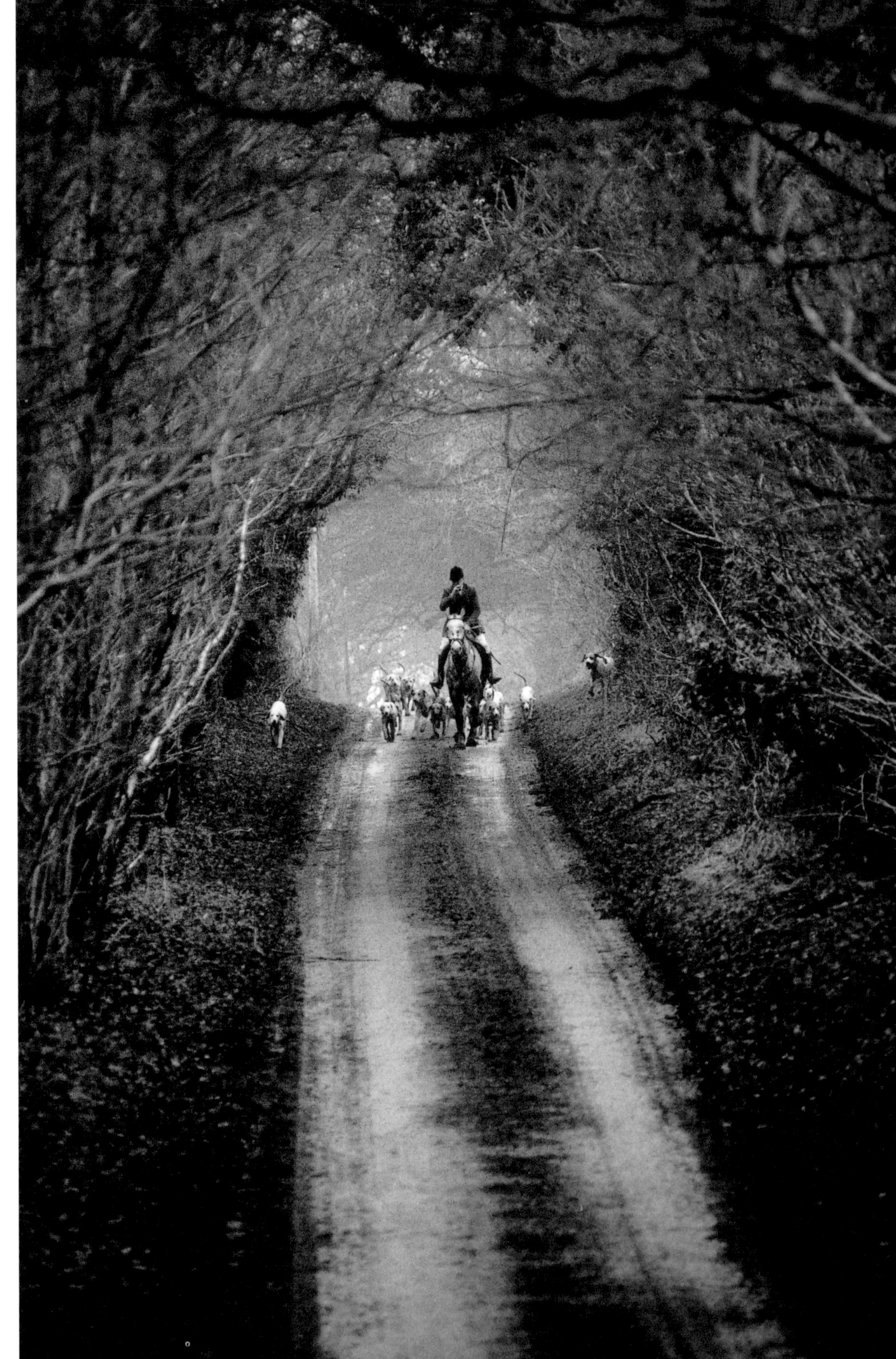

Julian Barnfield and the Cotswold hounds

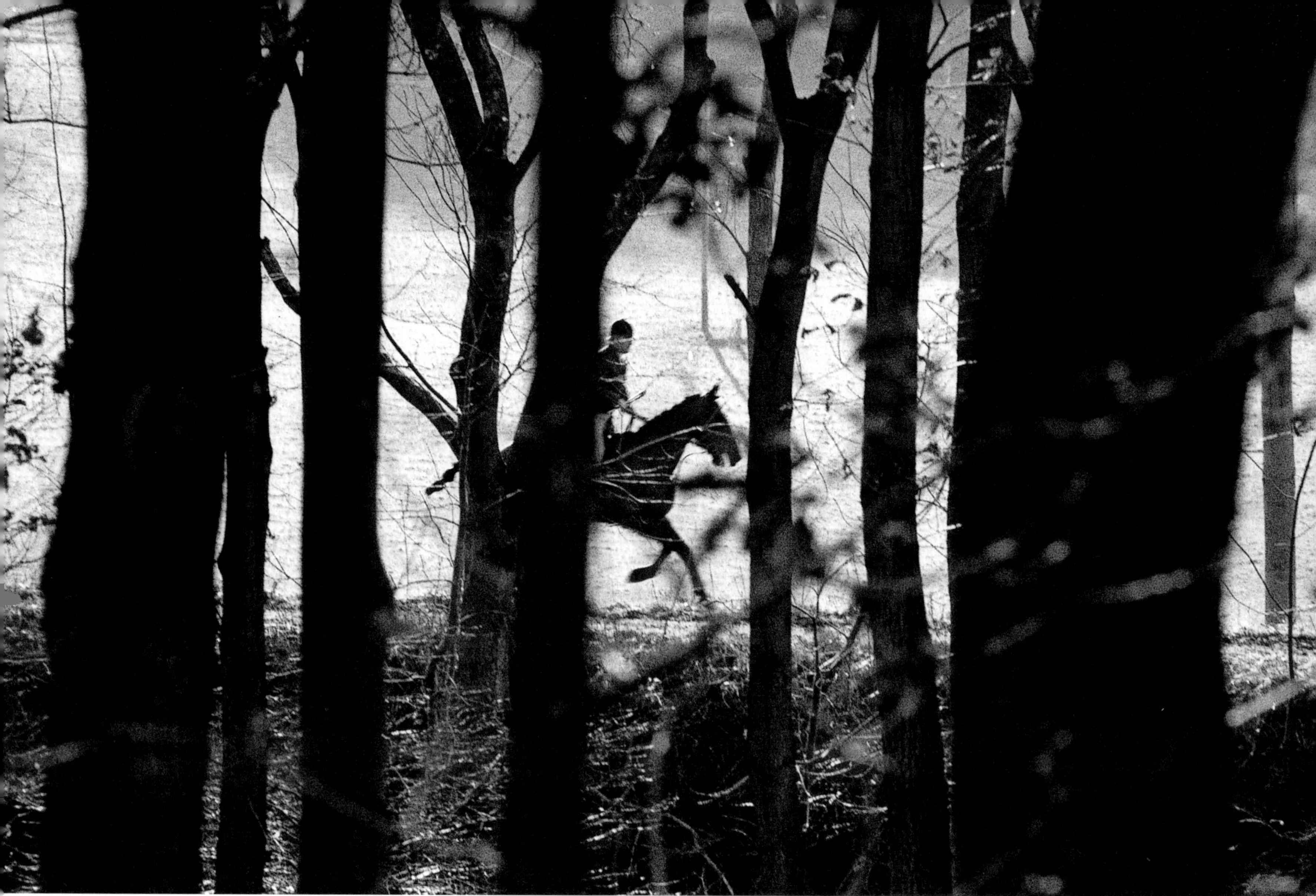

A follower of the Middleton hunt

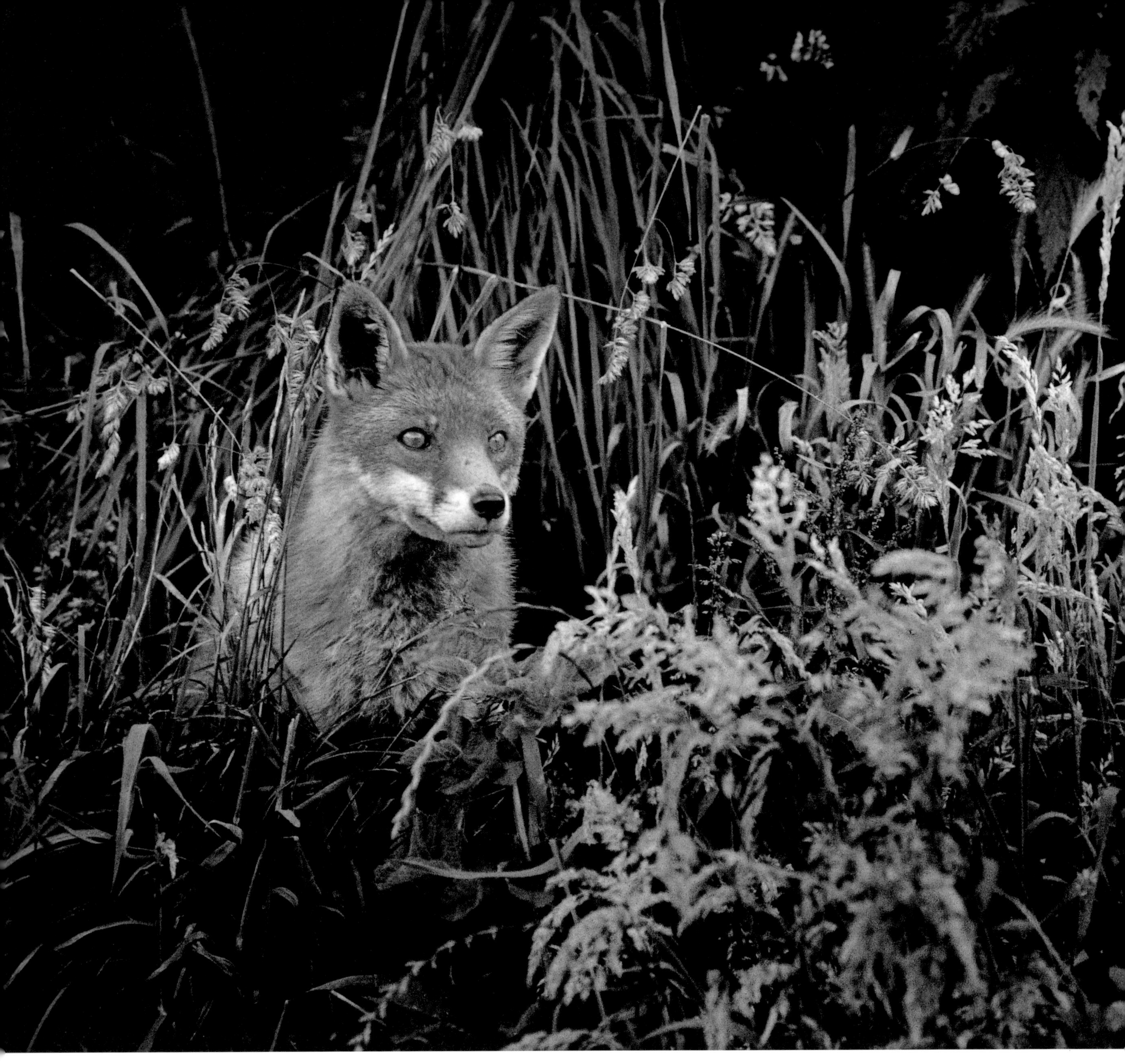

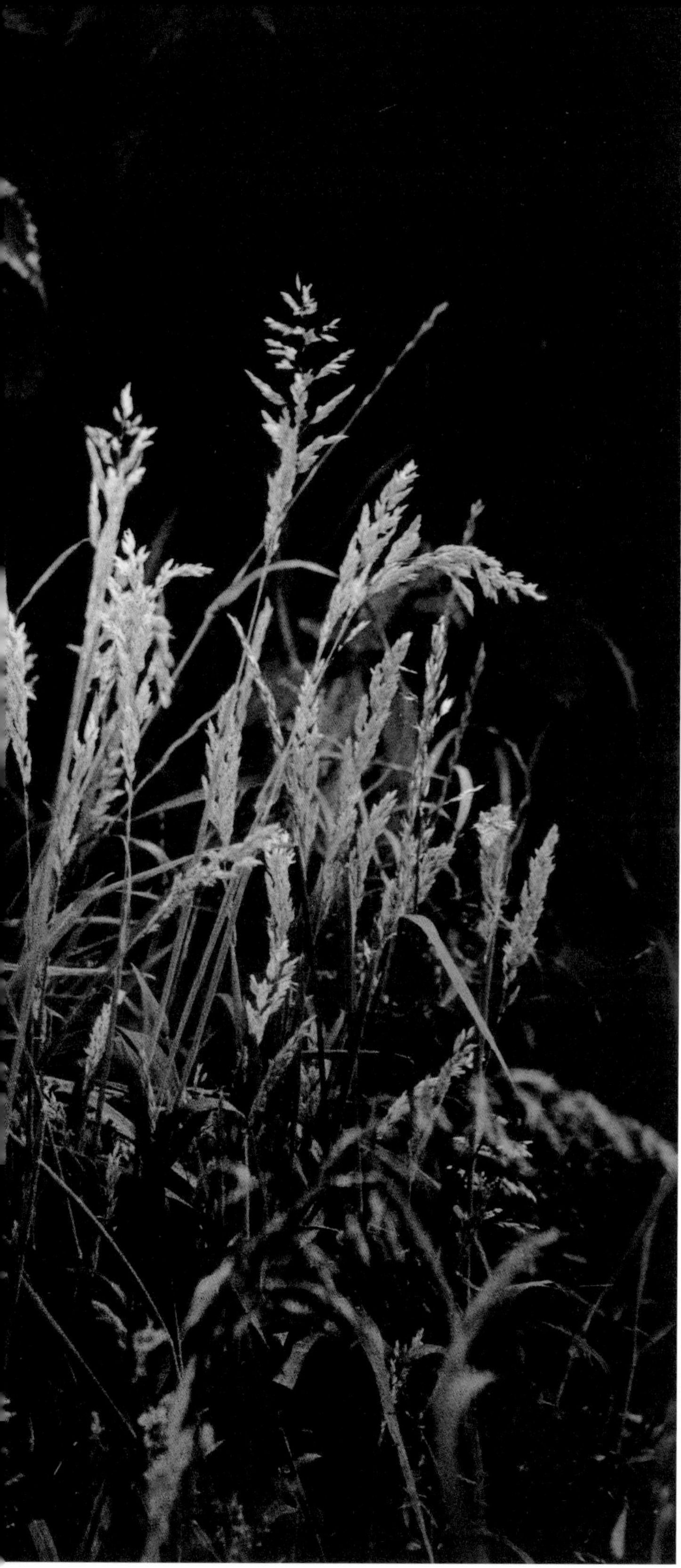

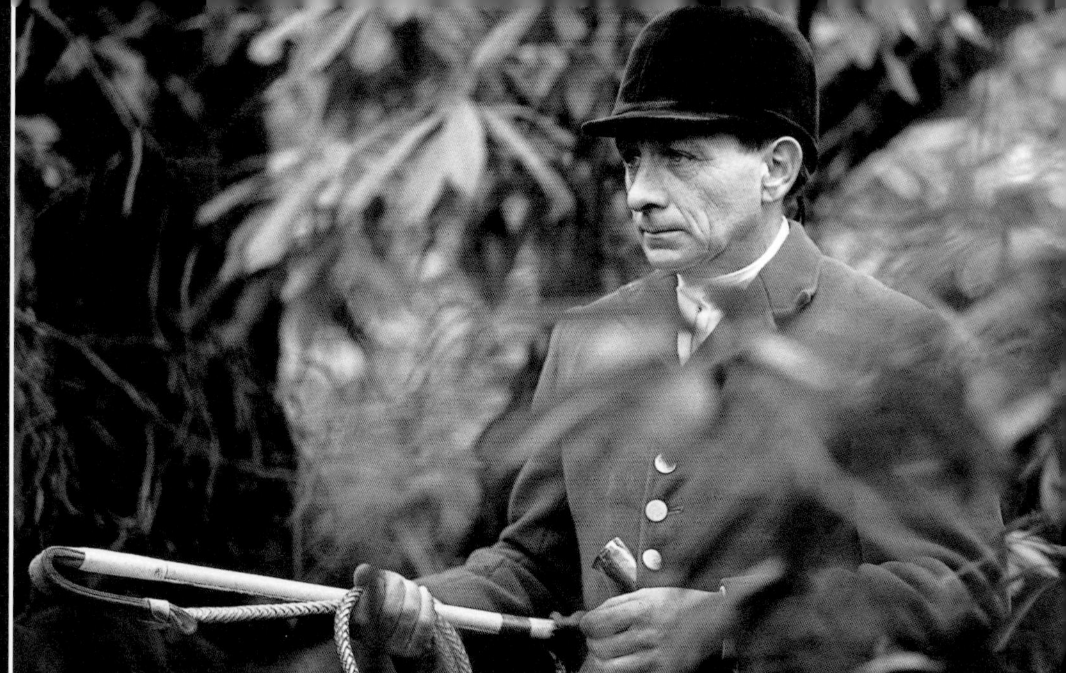

Barlow huntsman Lindsay Hall

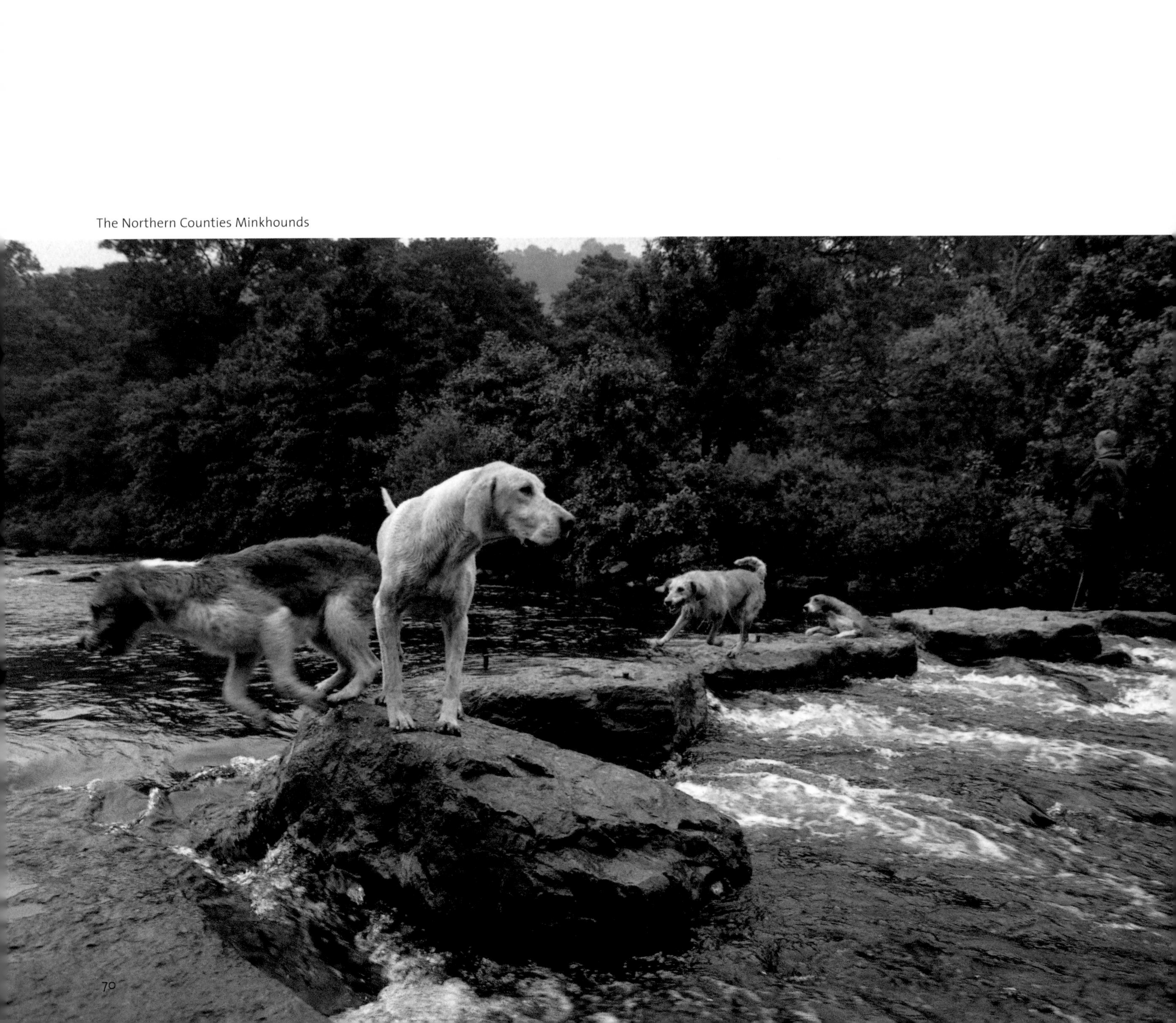

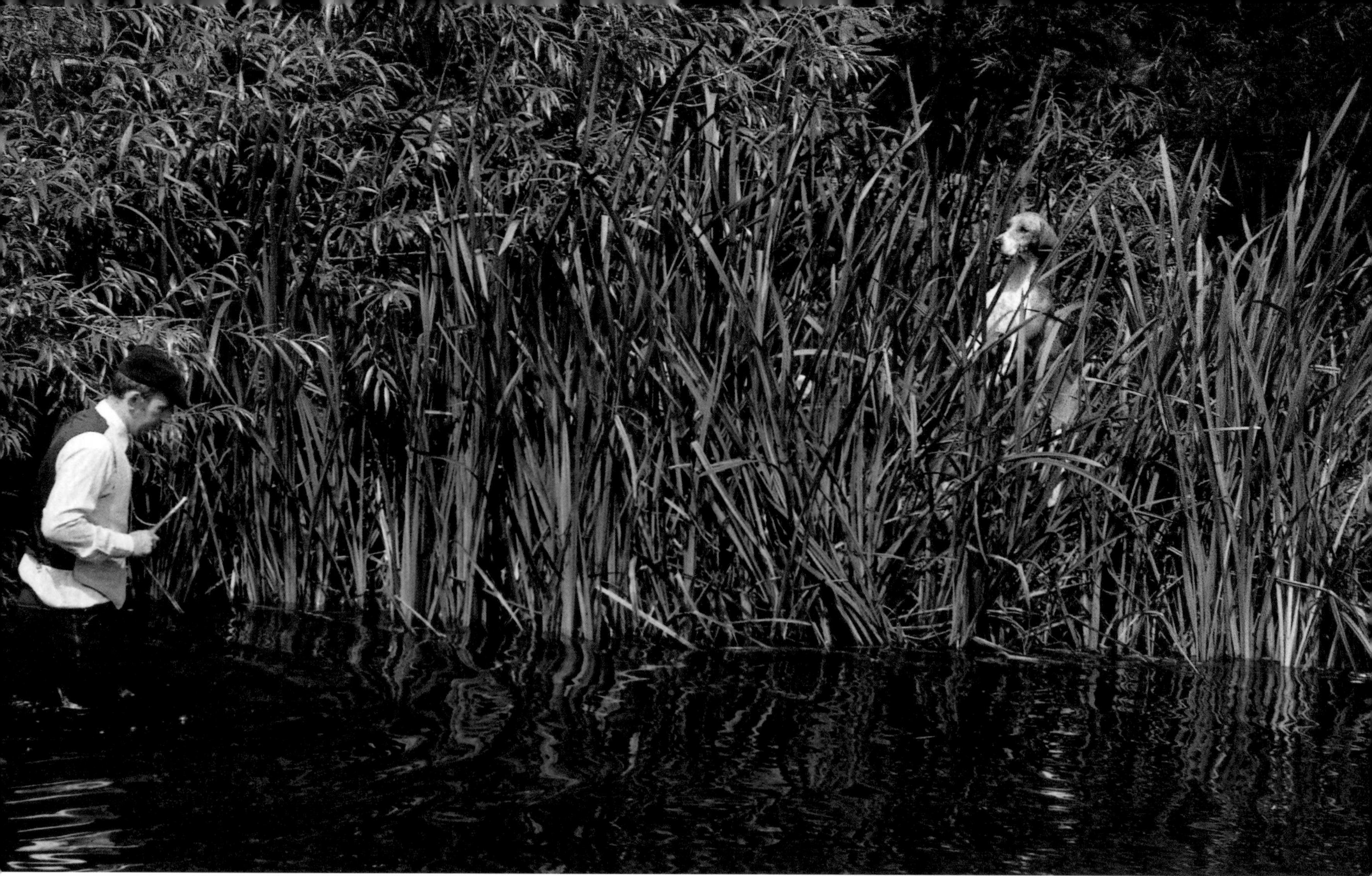

Martin Spilsbury, huntsman of the Northern Counties Minkhounds

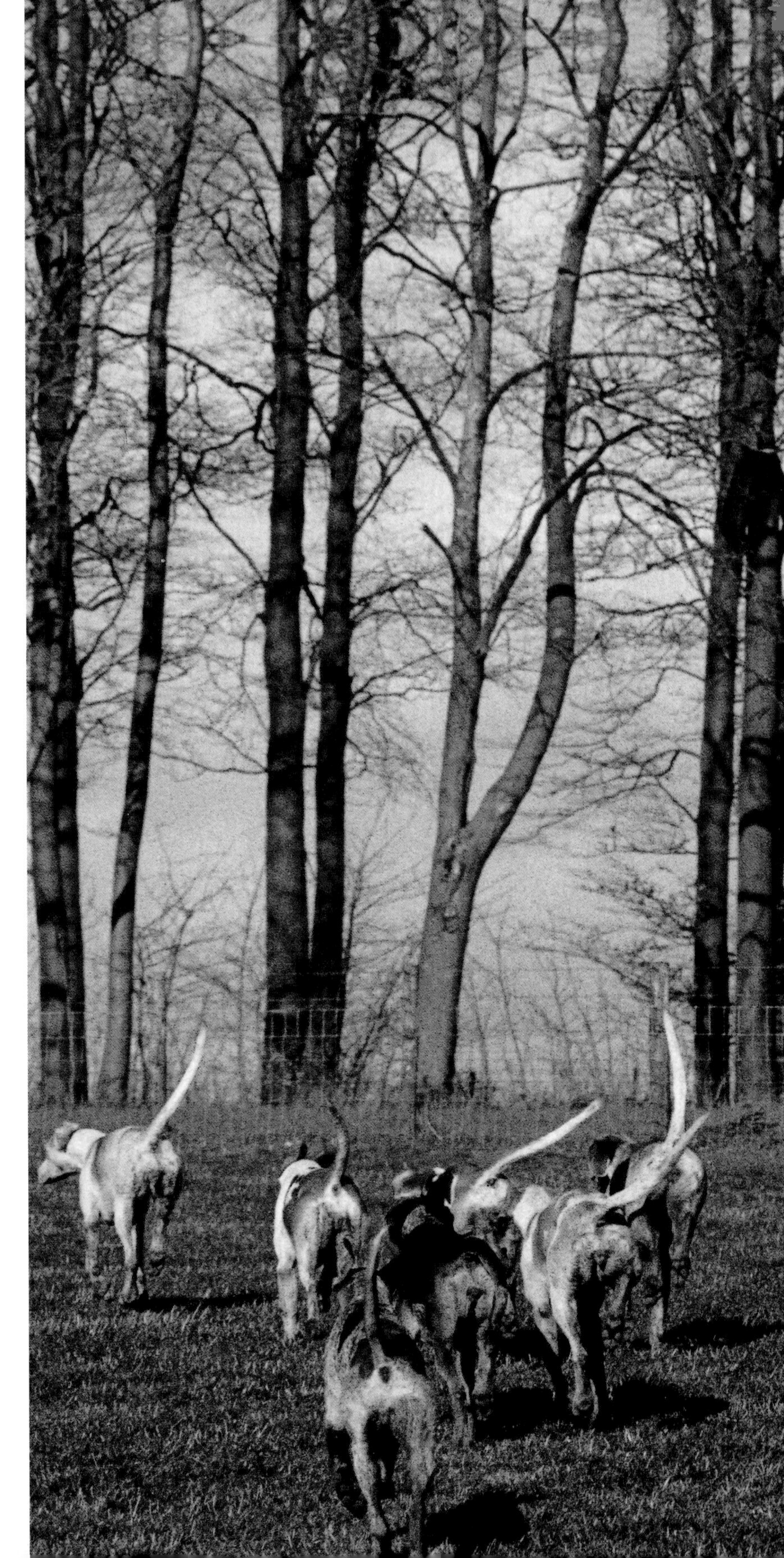

The Heythrop hounds

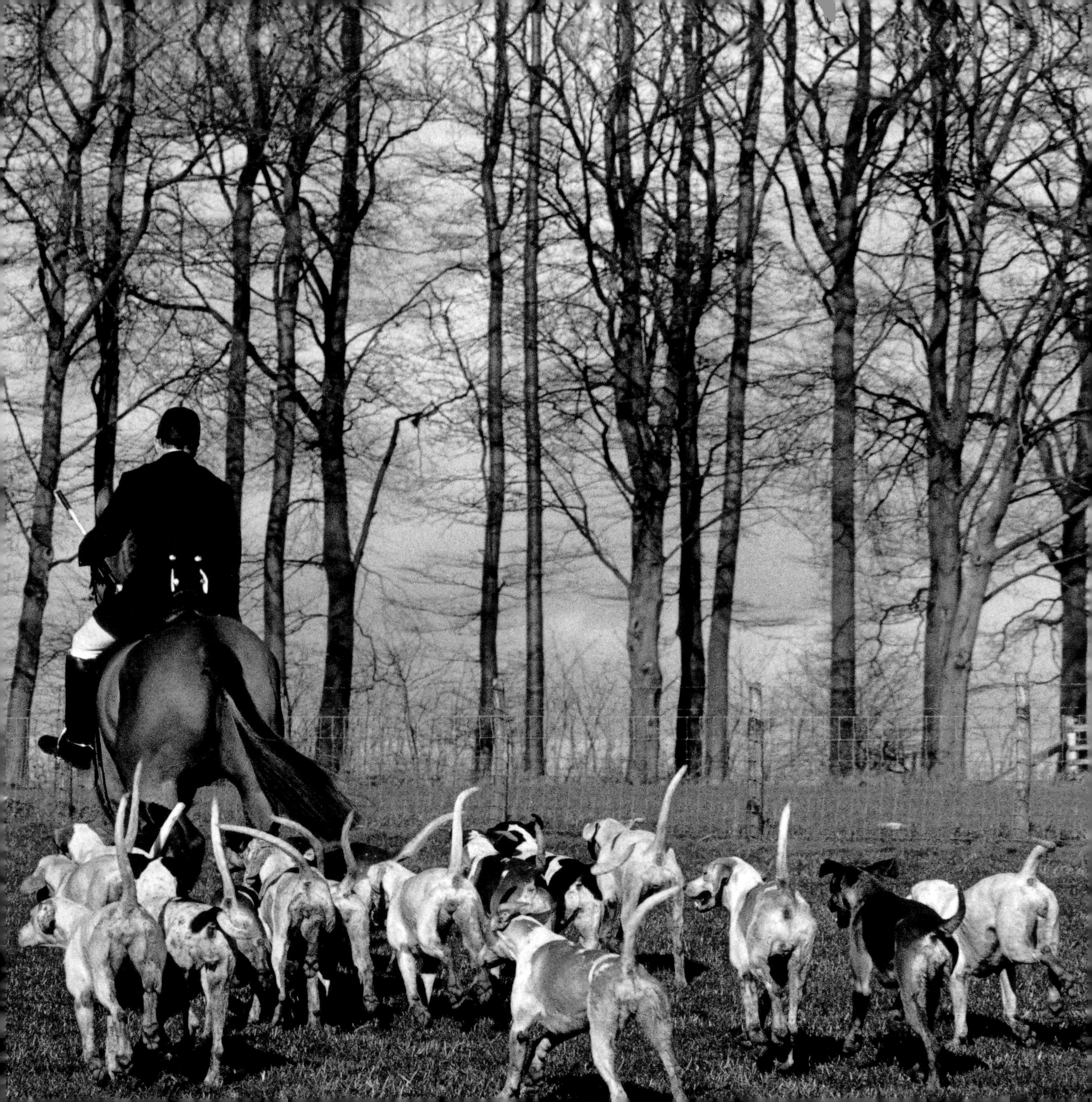

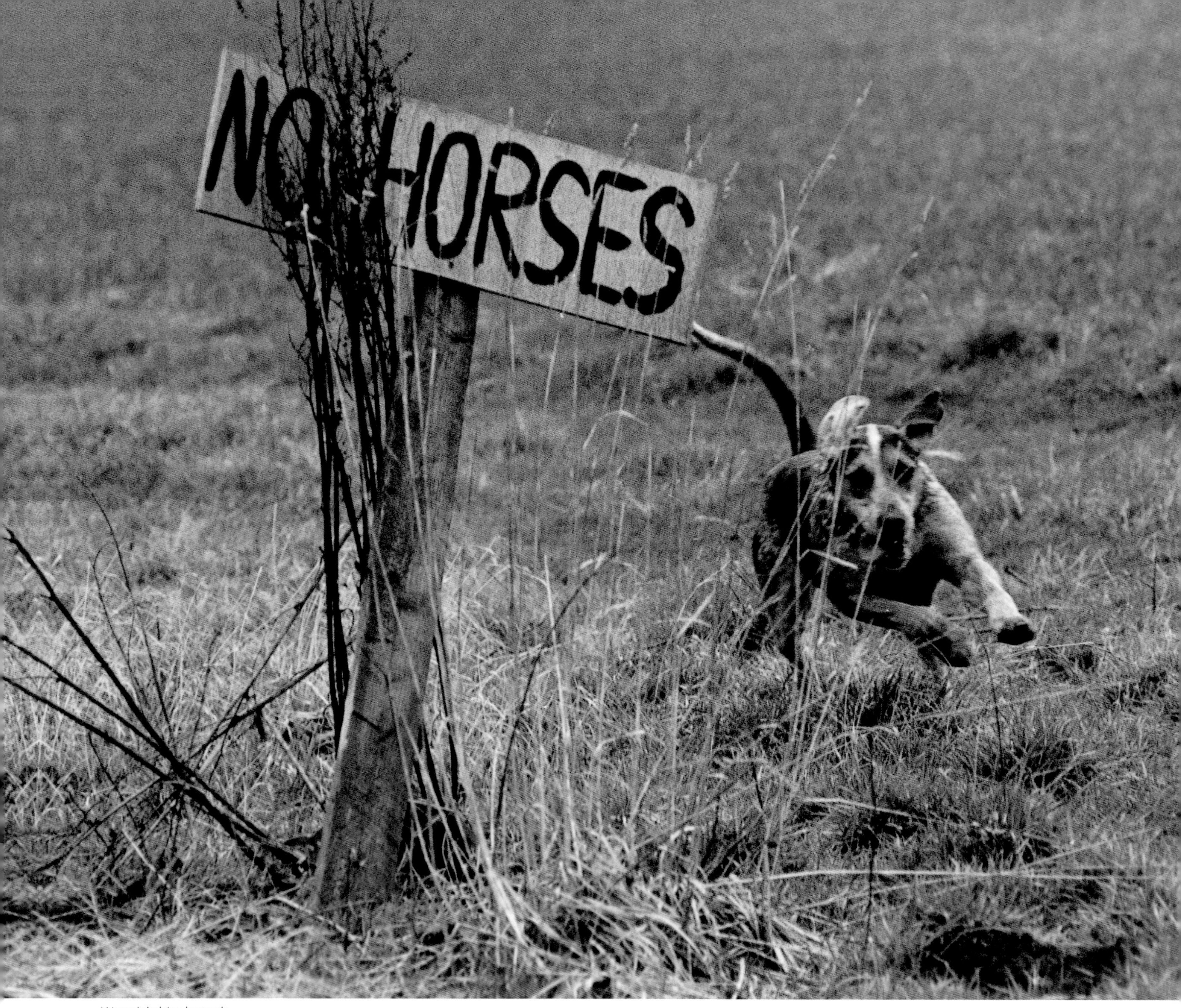

Warwickshire hounds

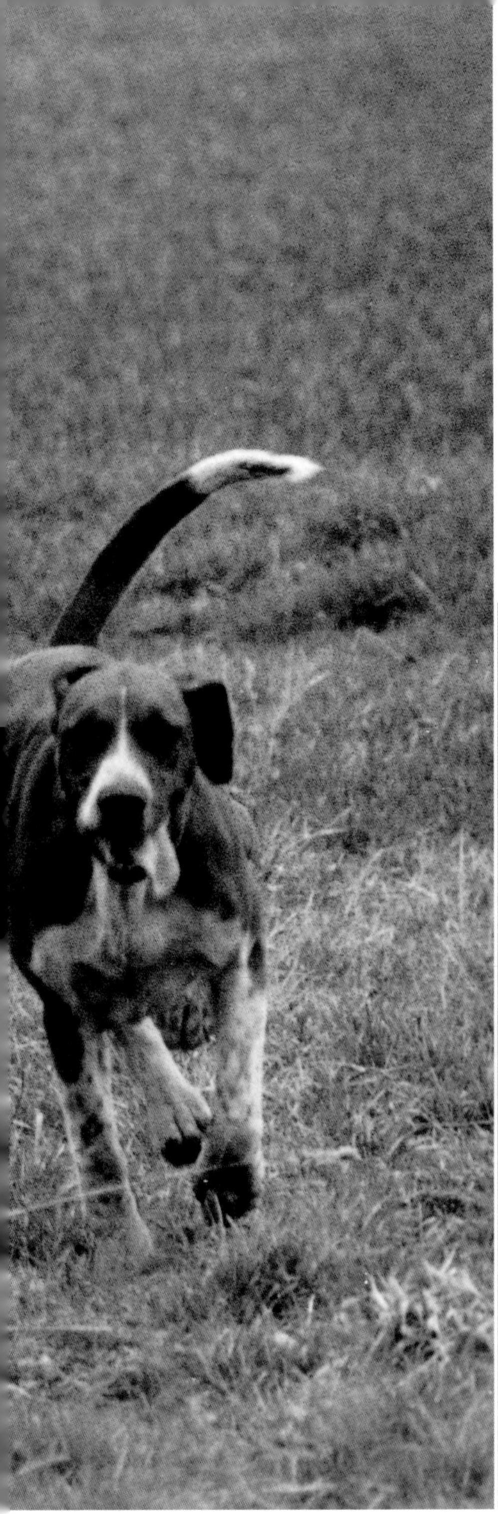

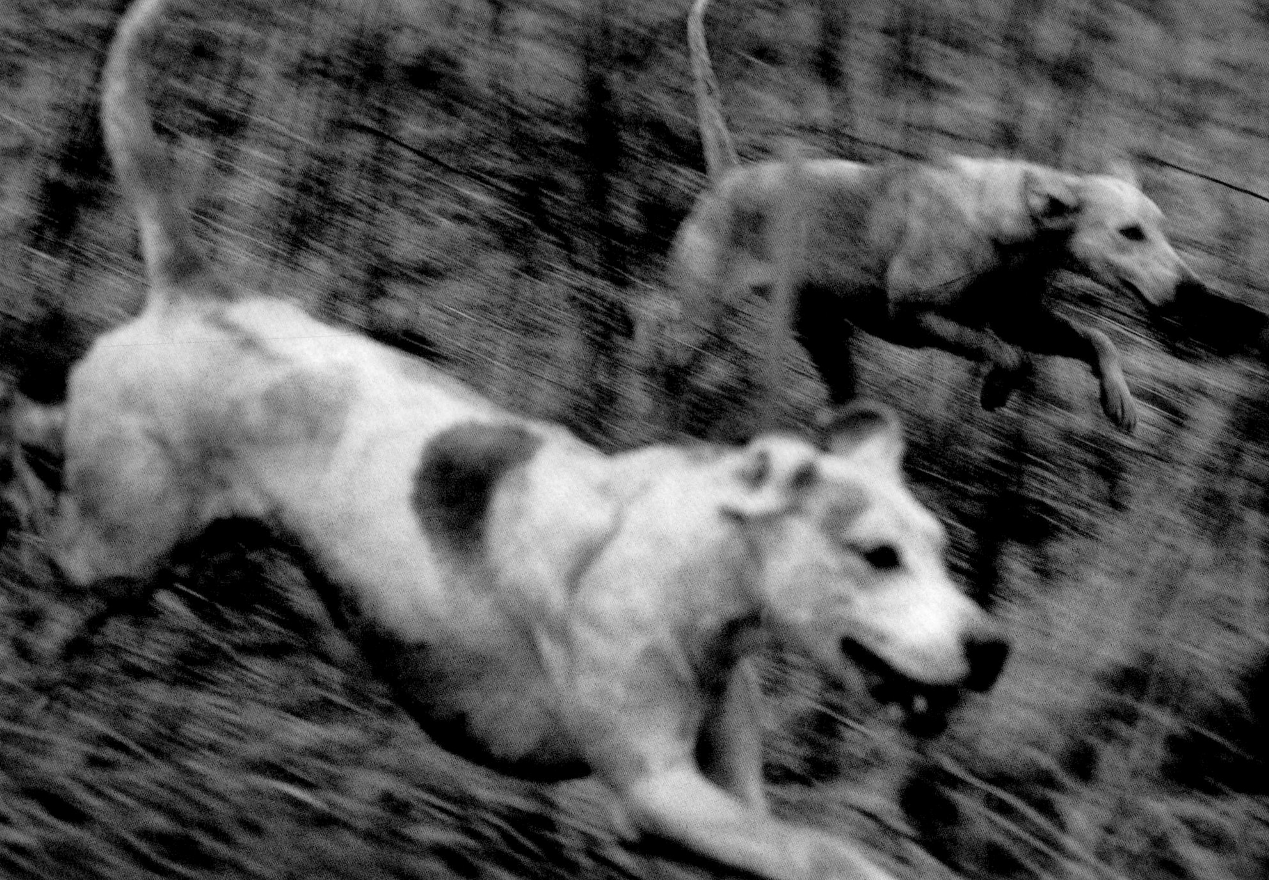

Bicester hounds running

Mounted followers of the Fife Hunt

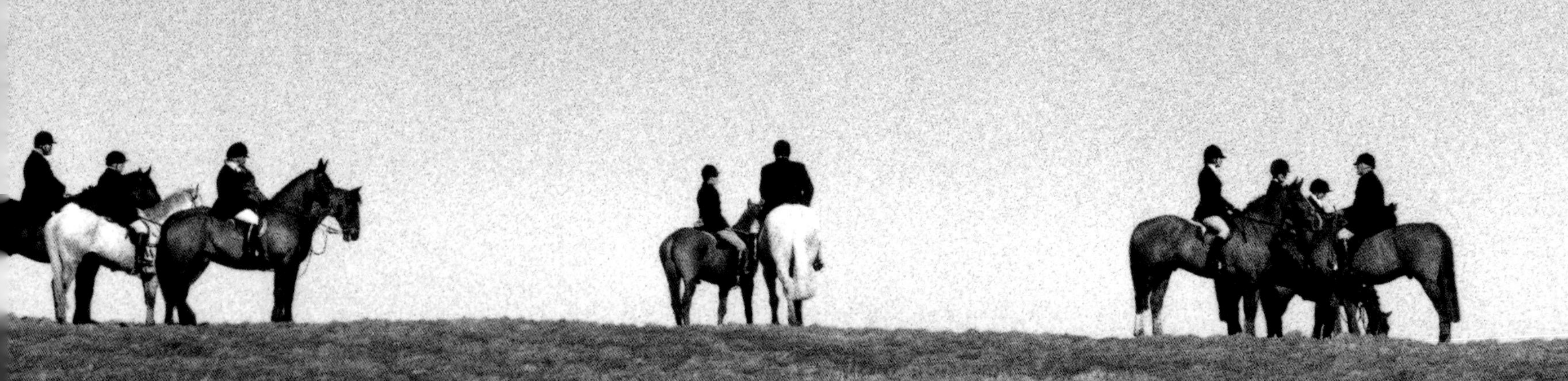

A morning's cubbing with the Bicester and Whaddon Chase

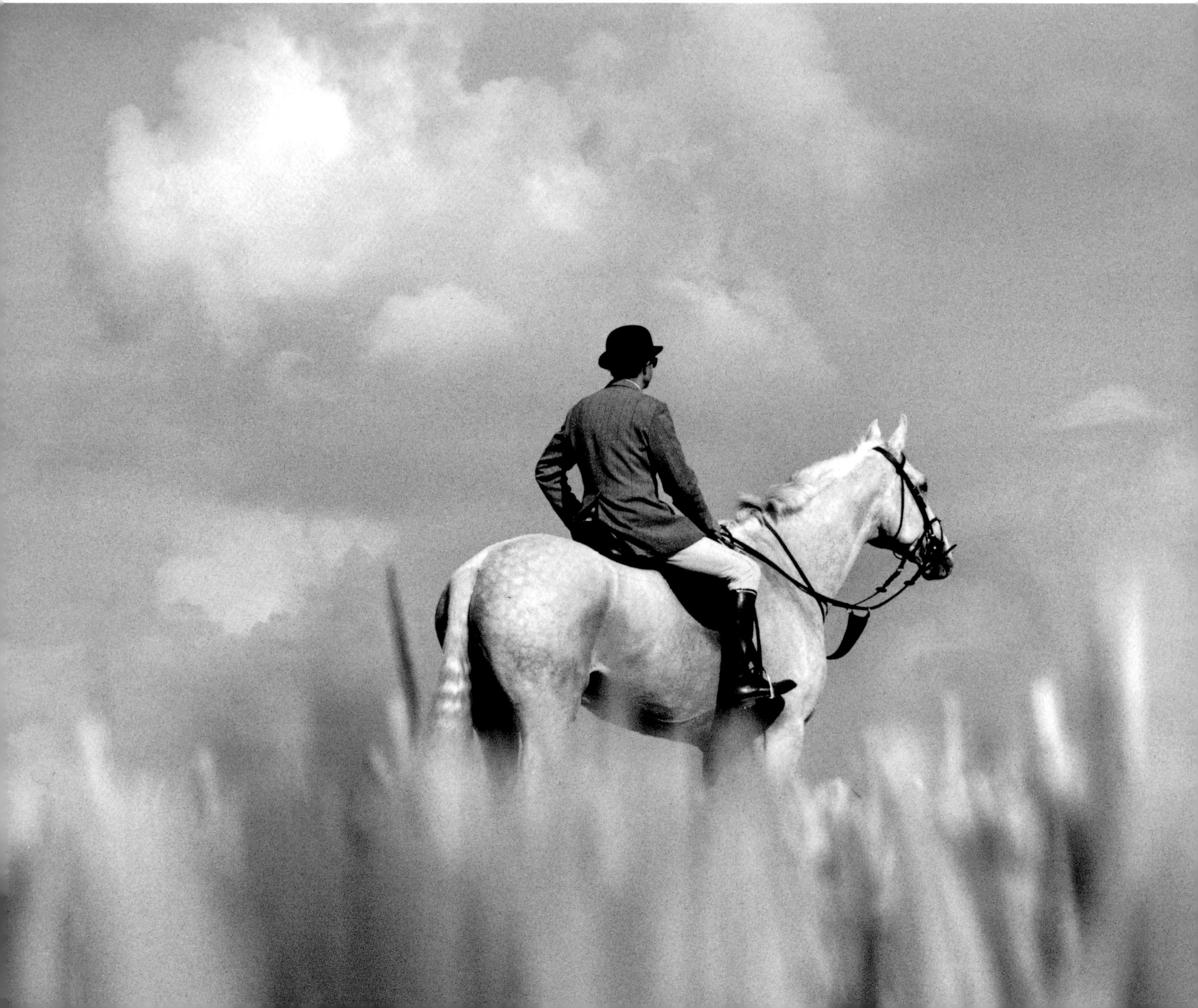

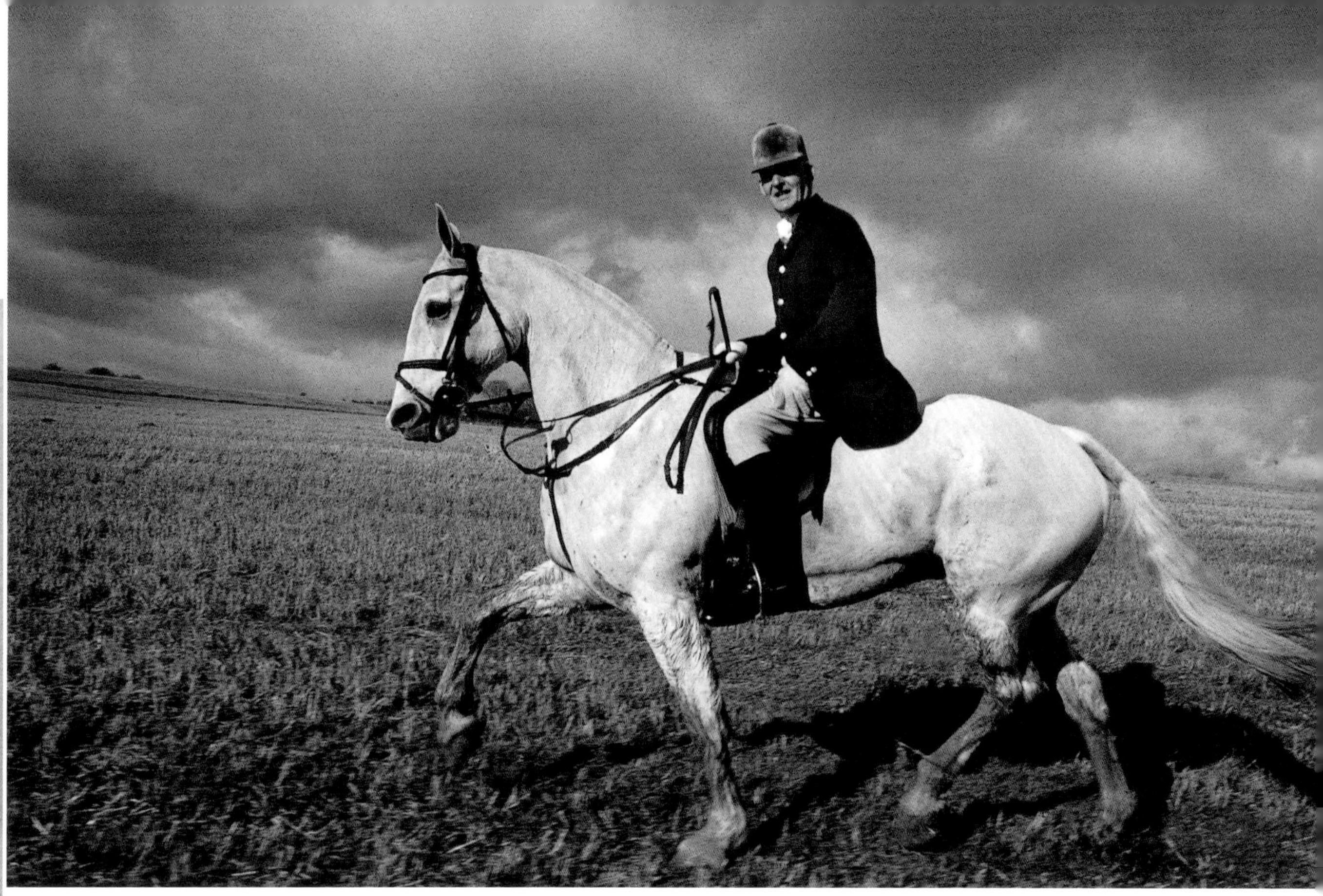

Roddy Fleming, member of the Heythrop hunt

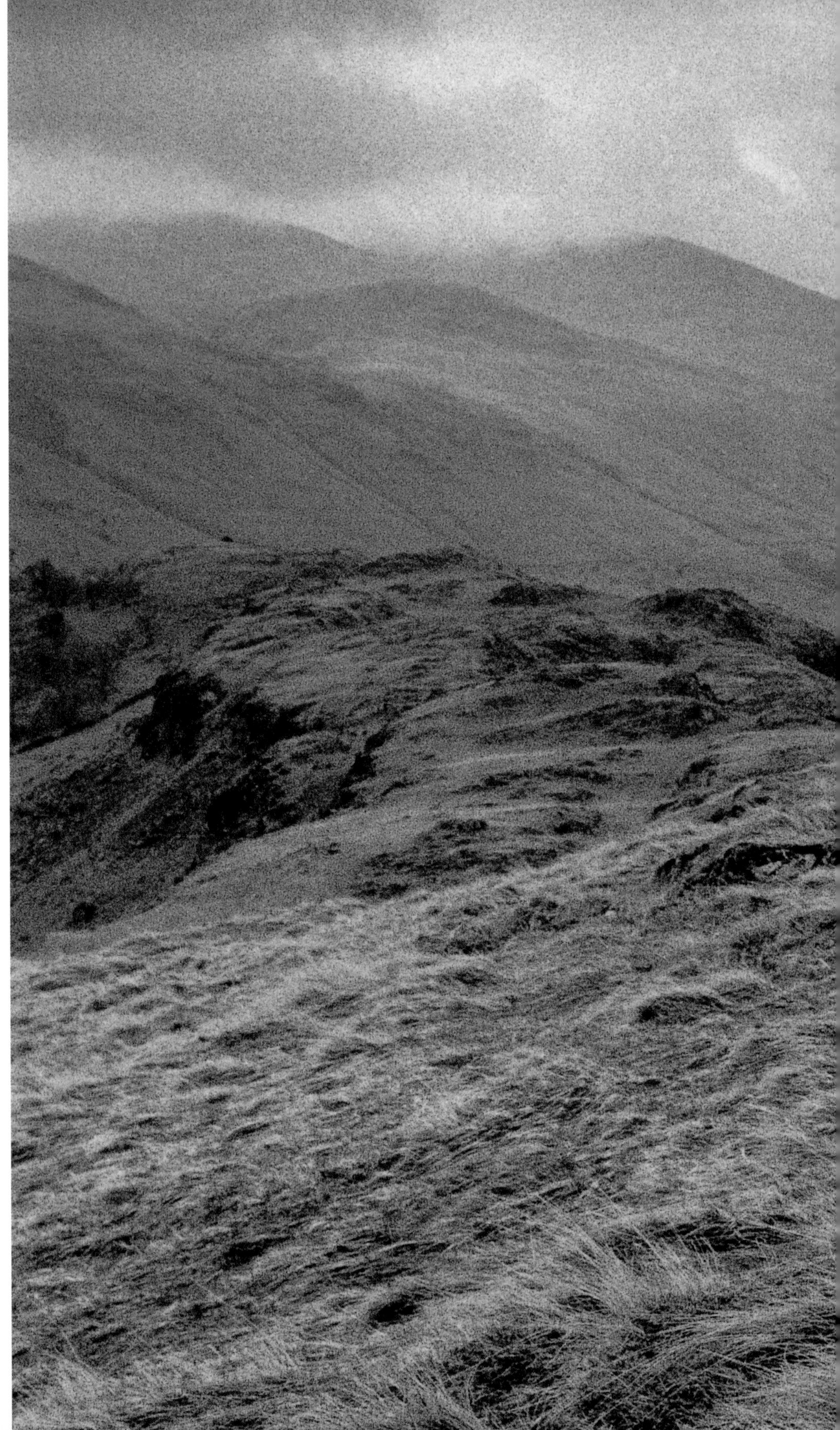

David Norris, fell follower

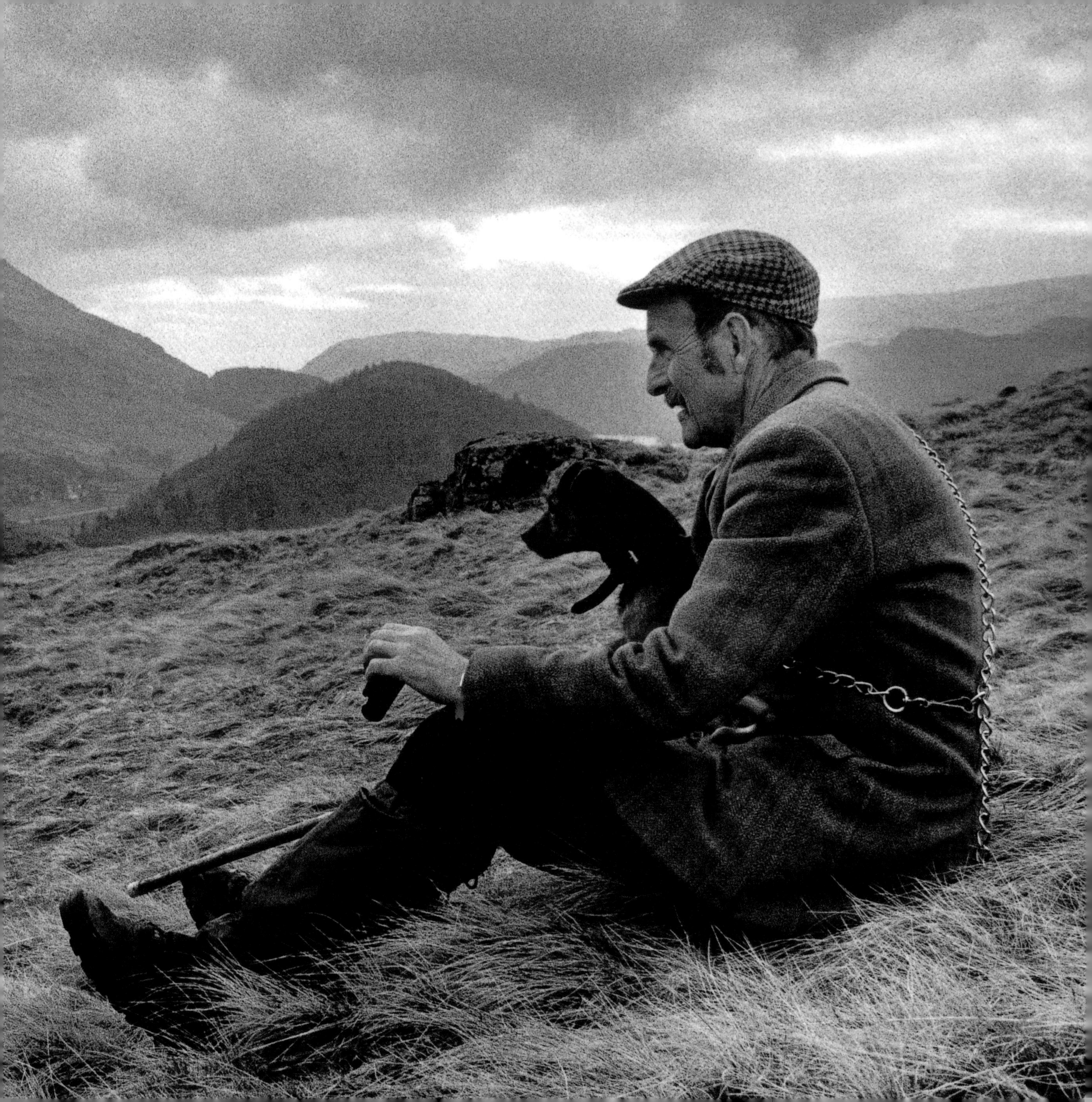

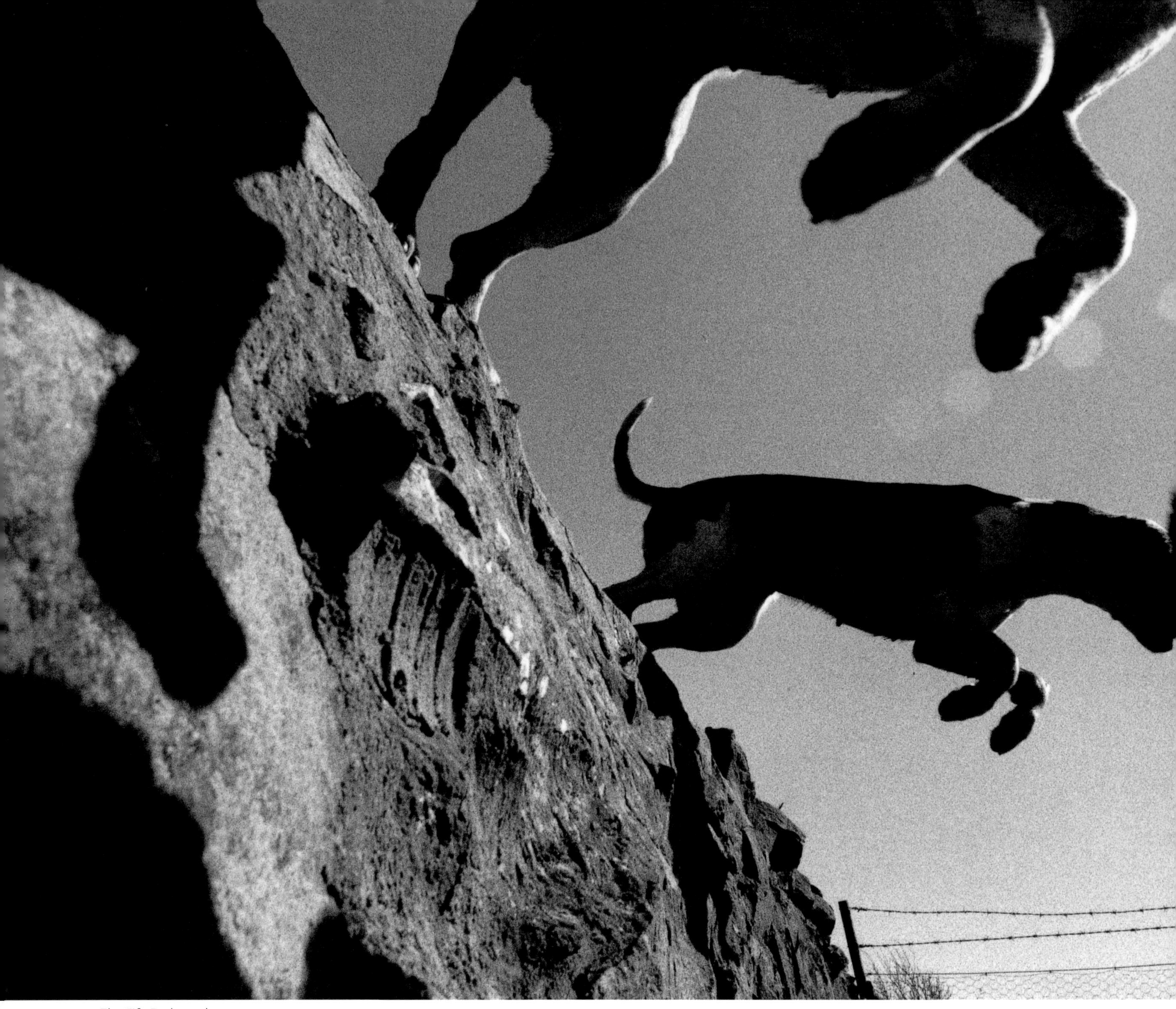

The Fife Foxhounds

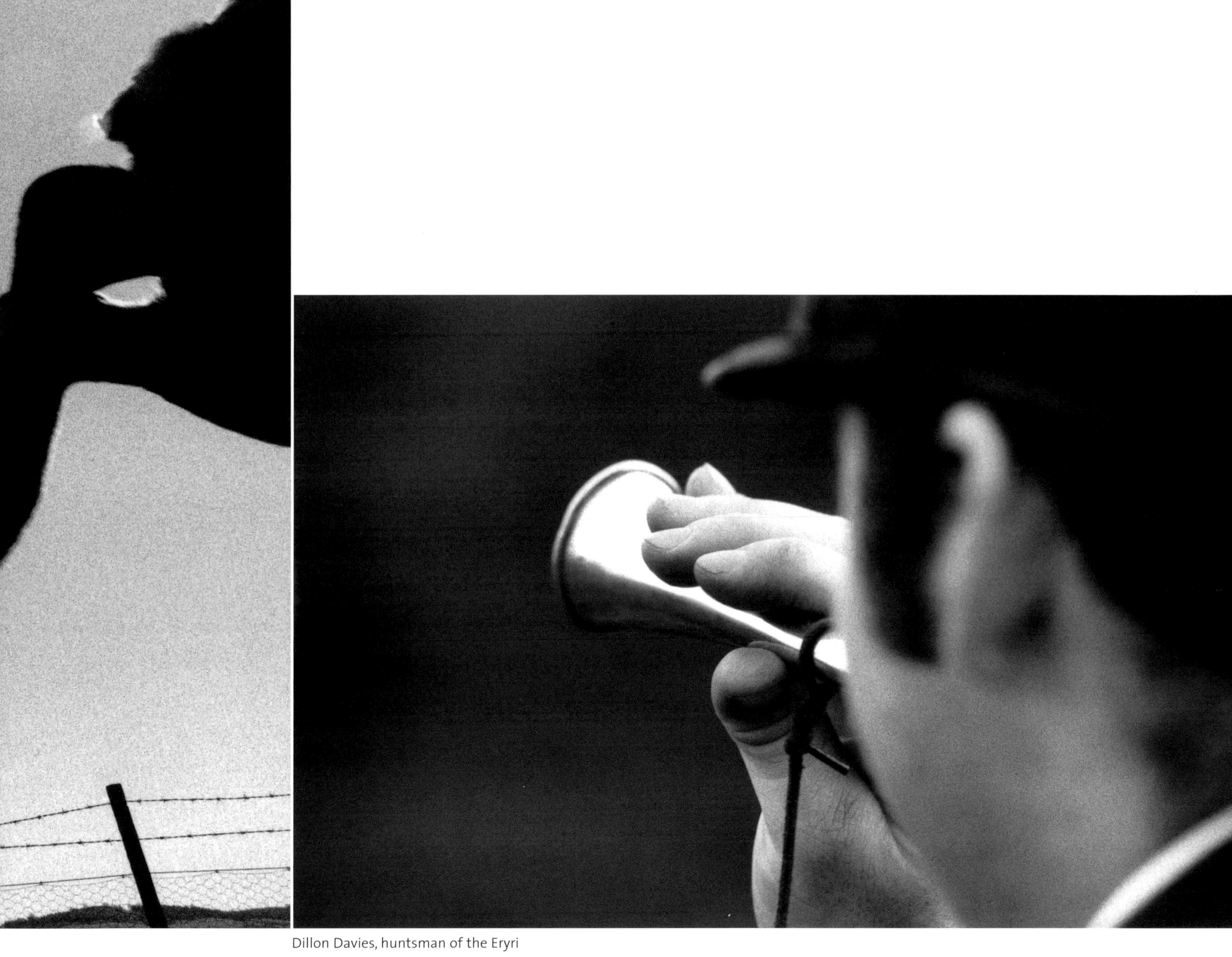

Dillon Davies, huntsman of the Eryri

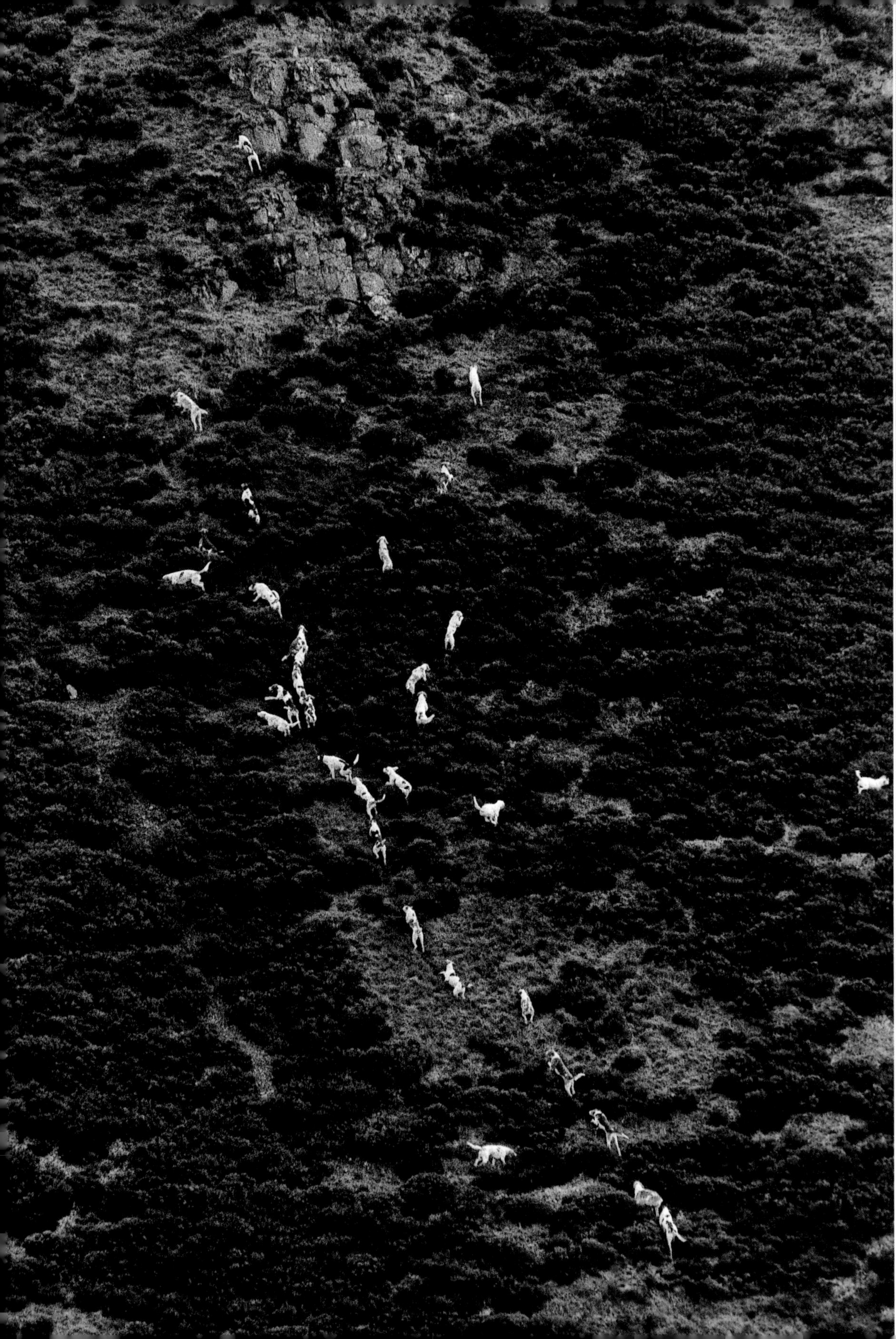

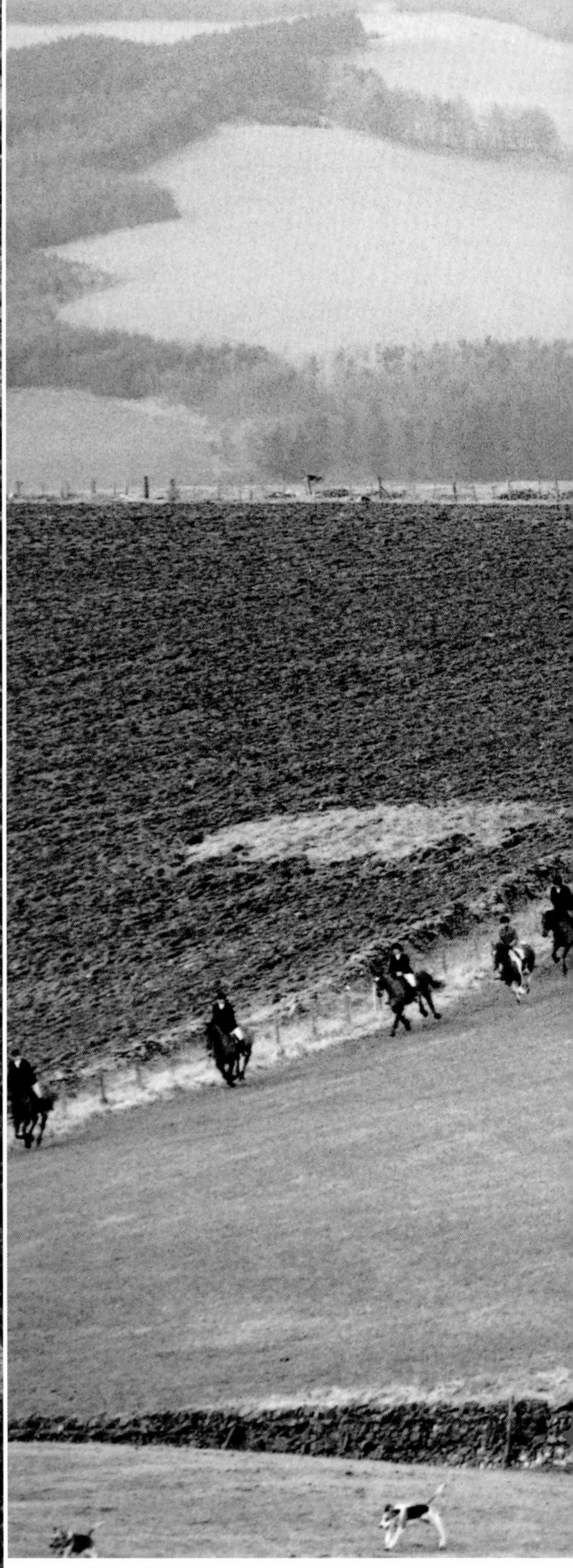

The Border Foxhounds

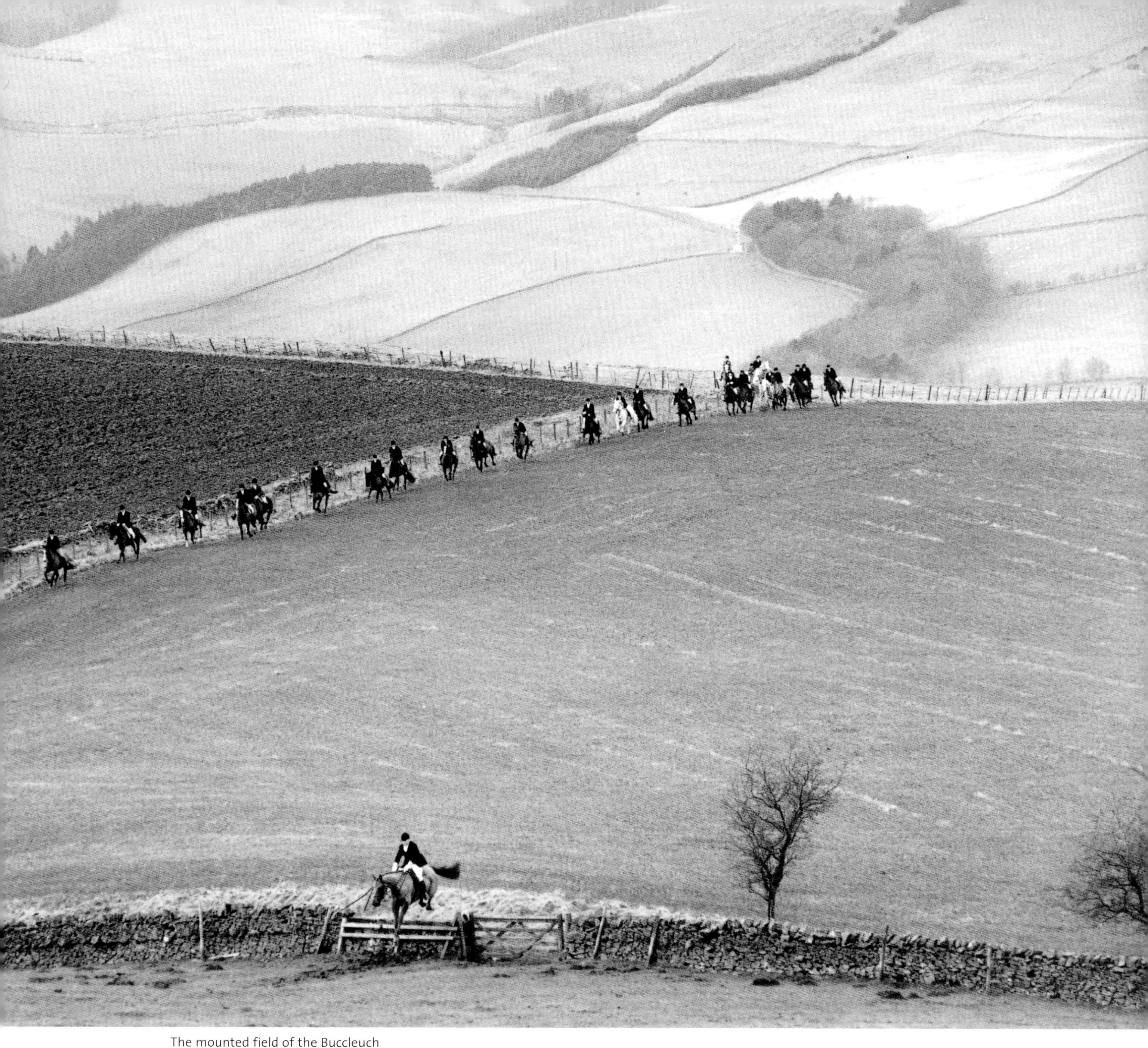

The mounted field of the Buccleuch

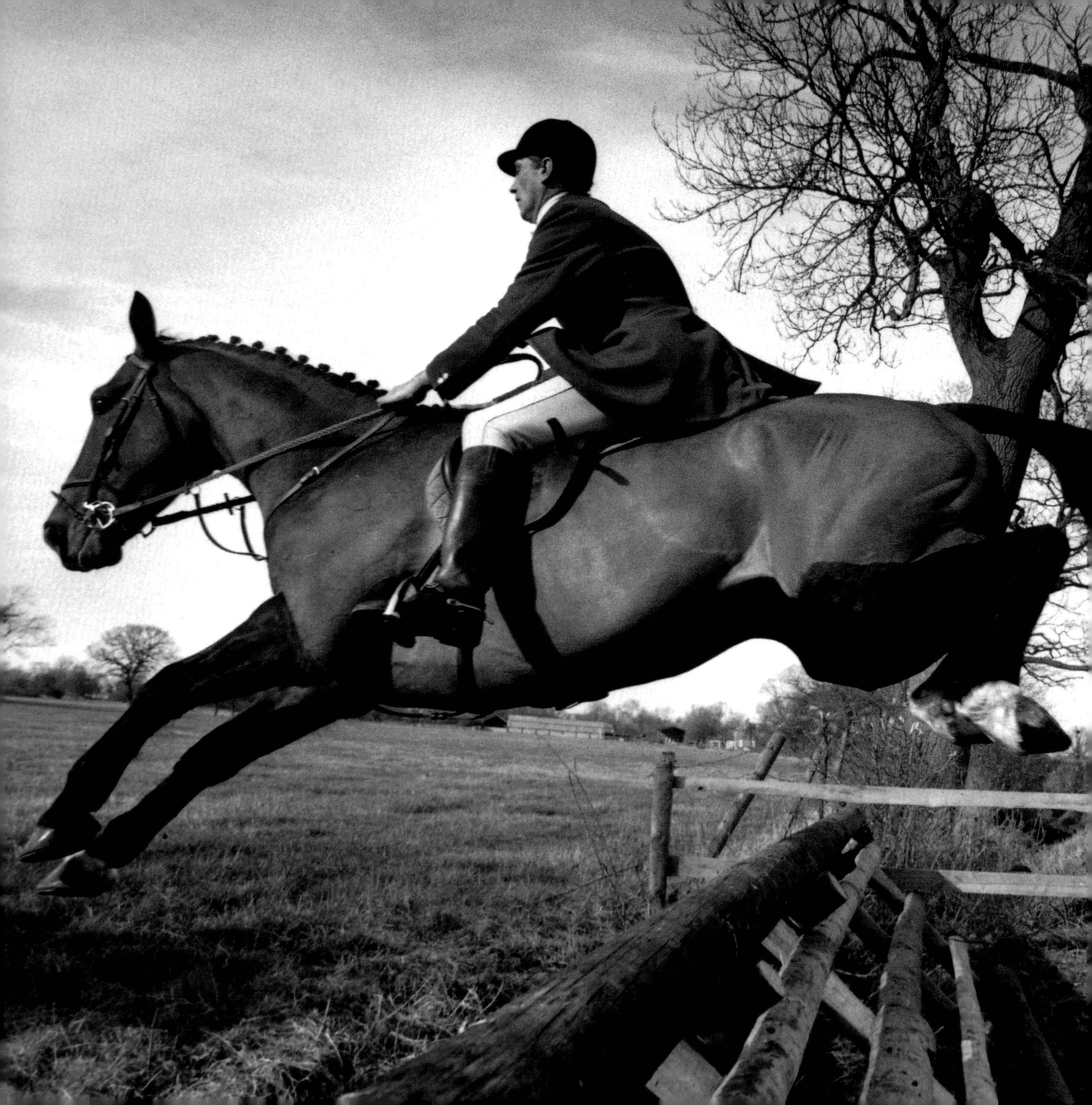

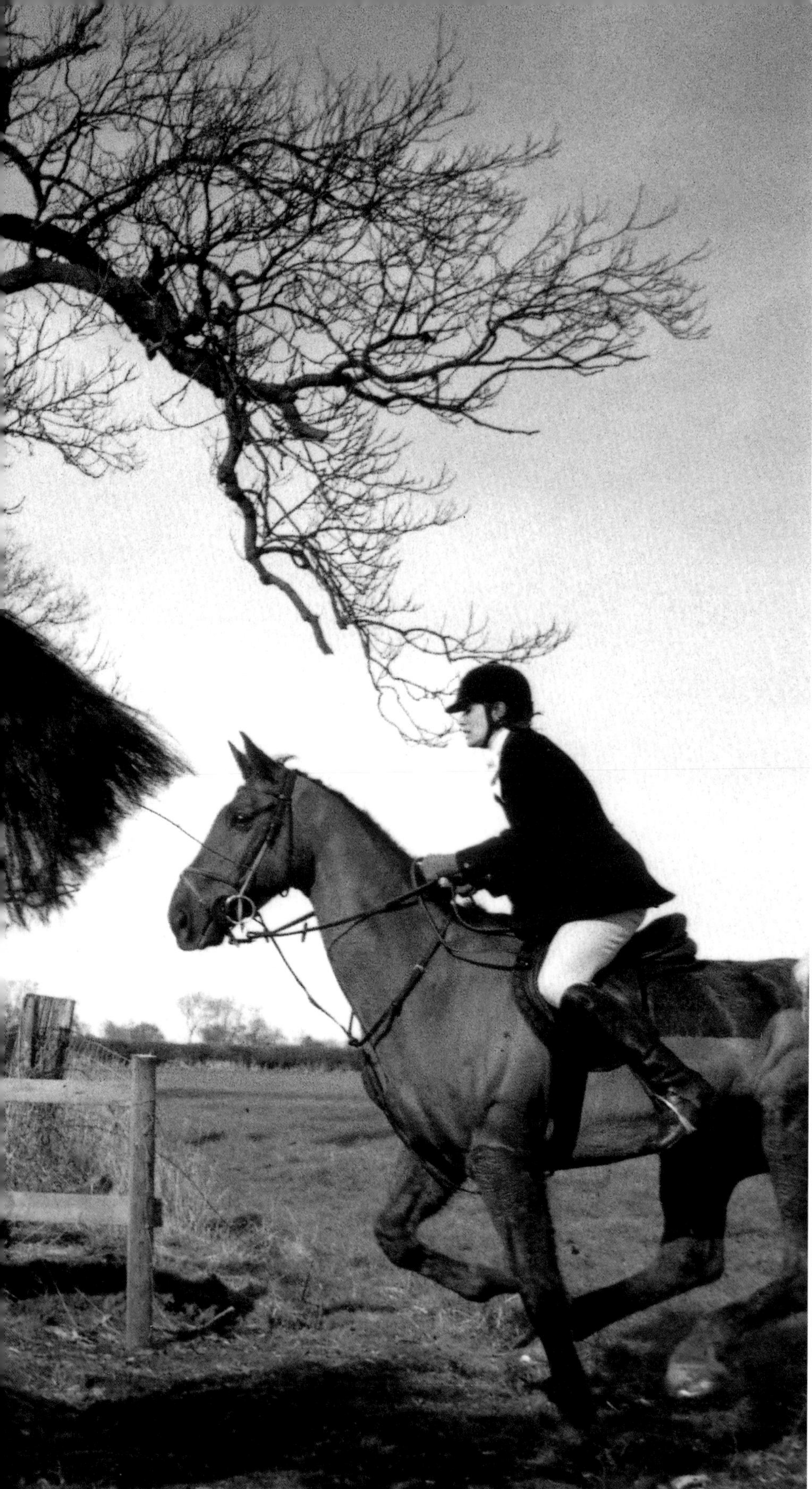

Mounted followers of the Atherstone

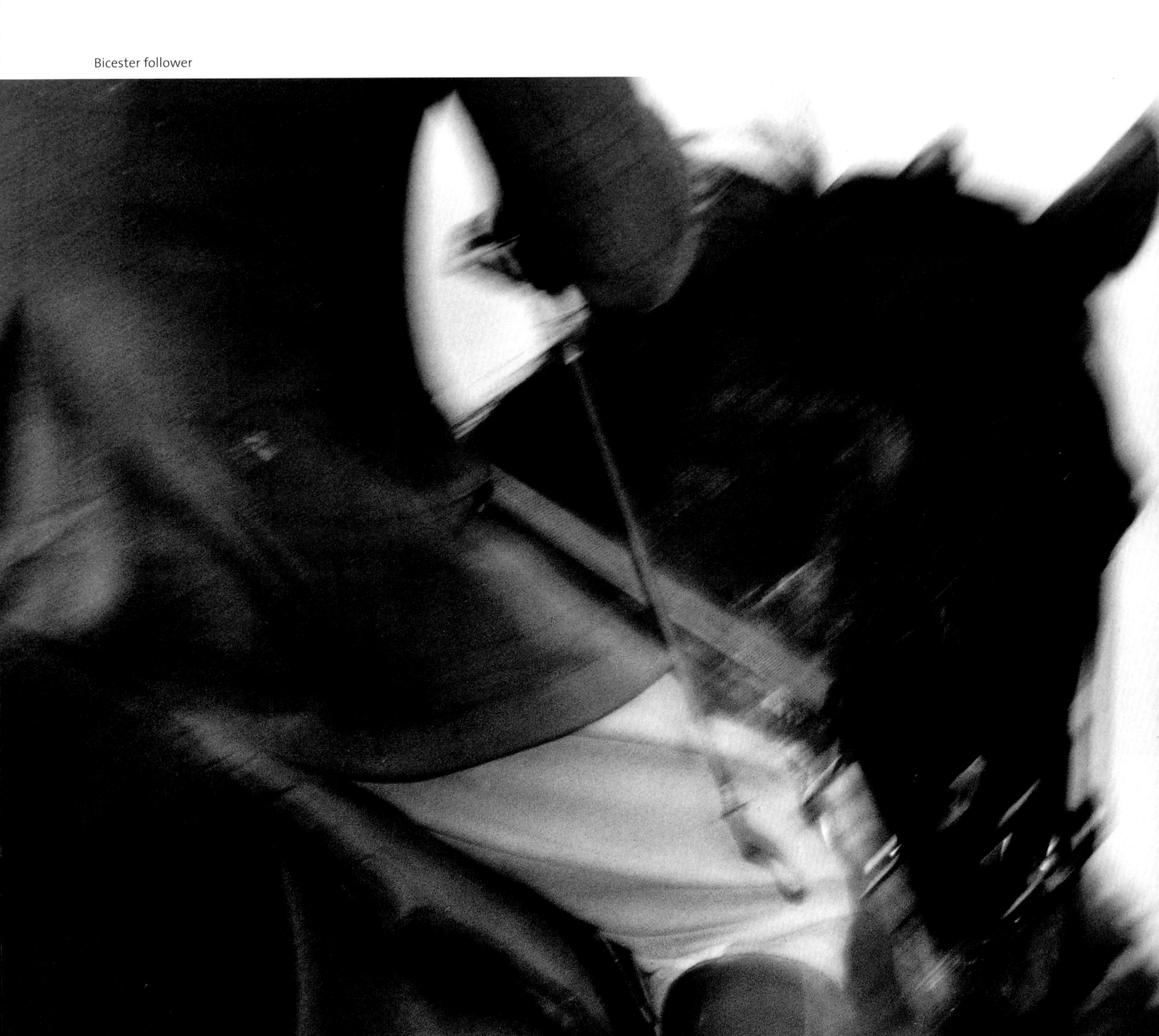

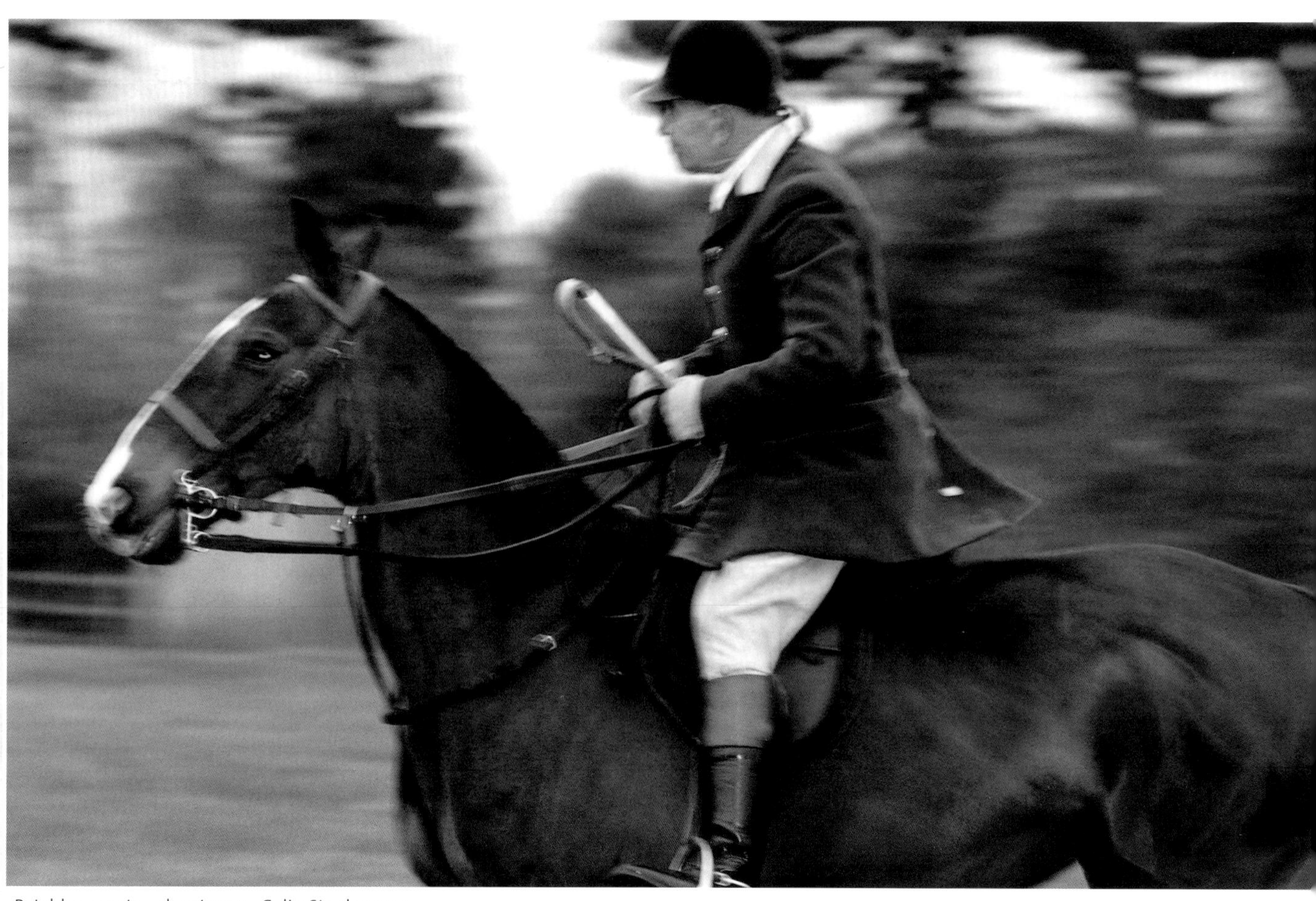

Pytchley amateur huntsman, Colin Stephenson

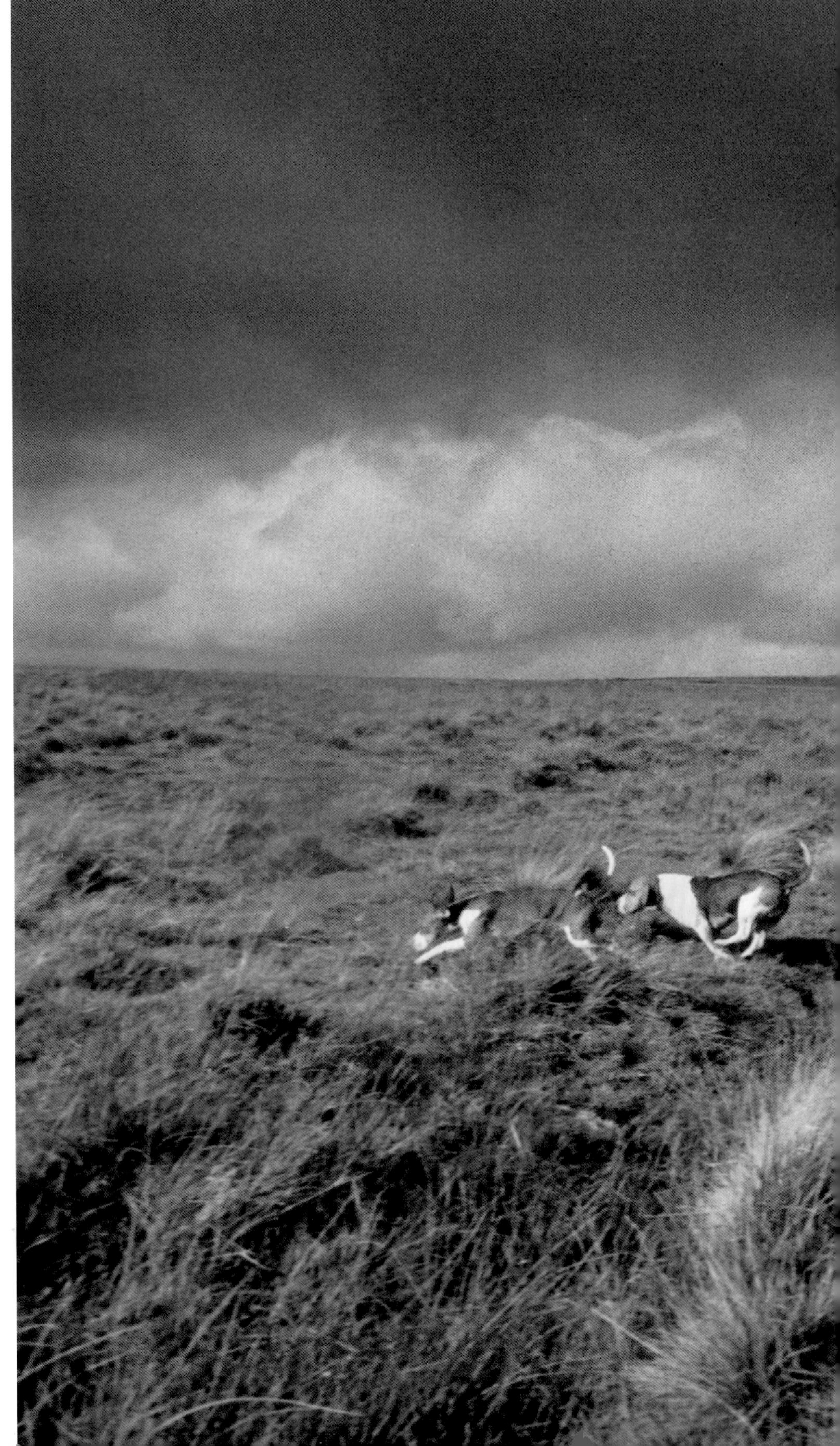

Matthew Higgs and the South Herts Beagles

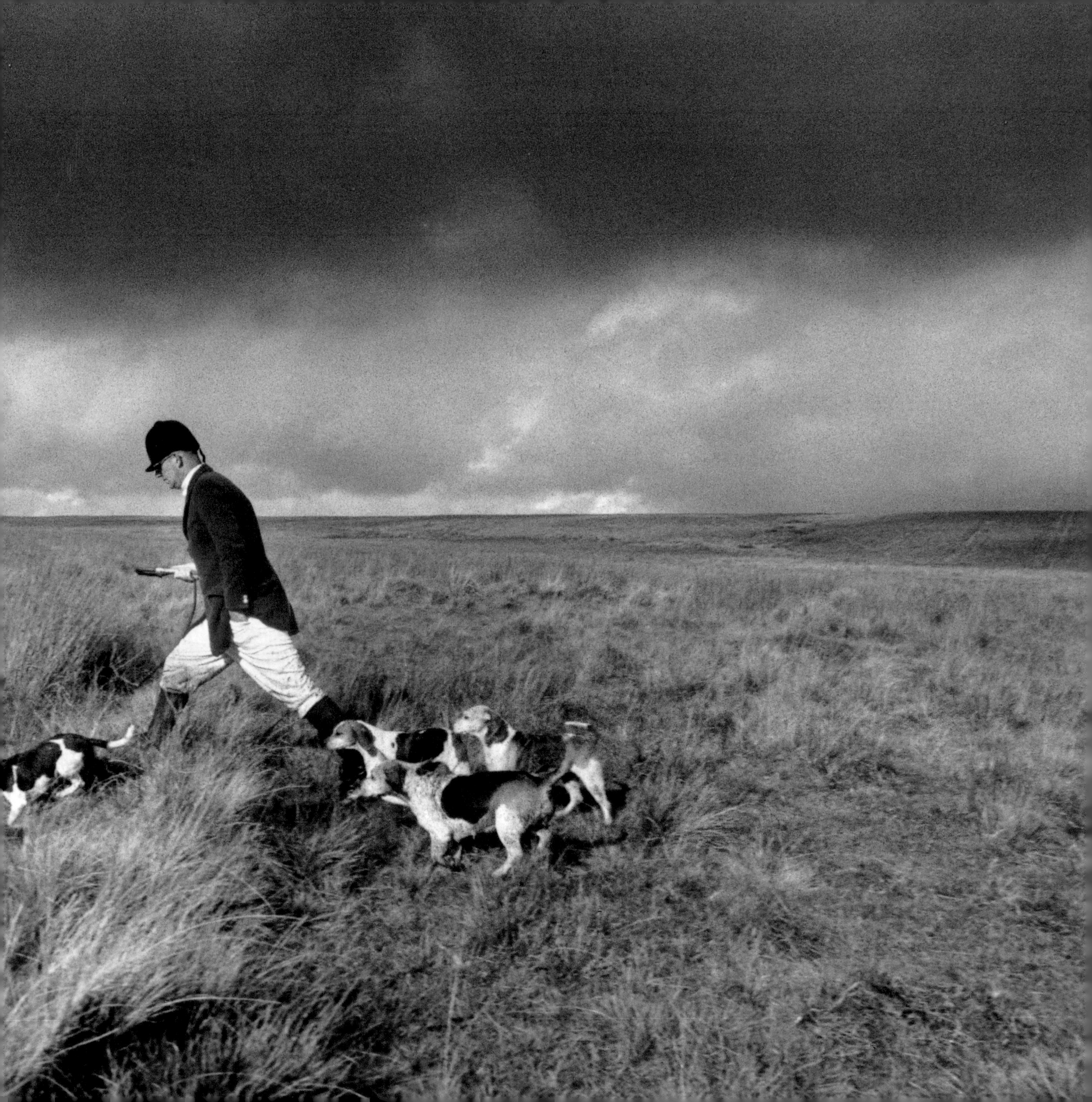

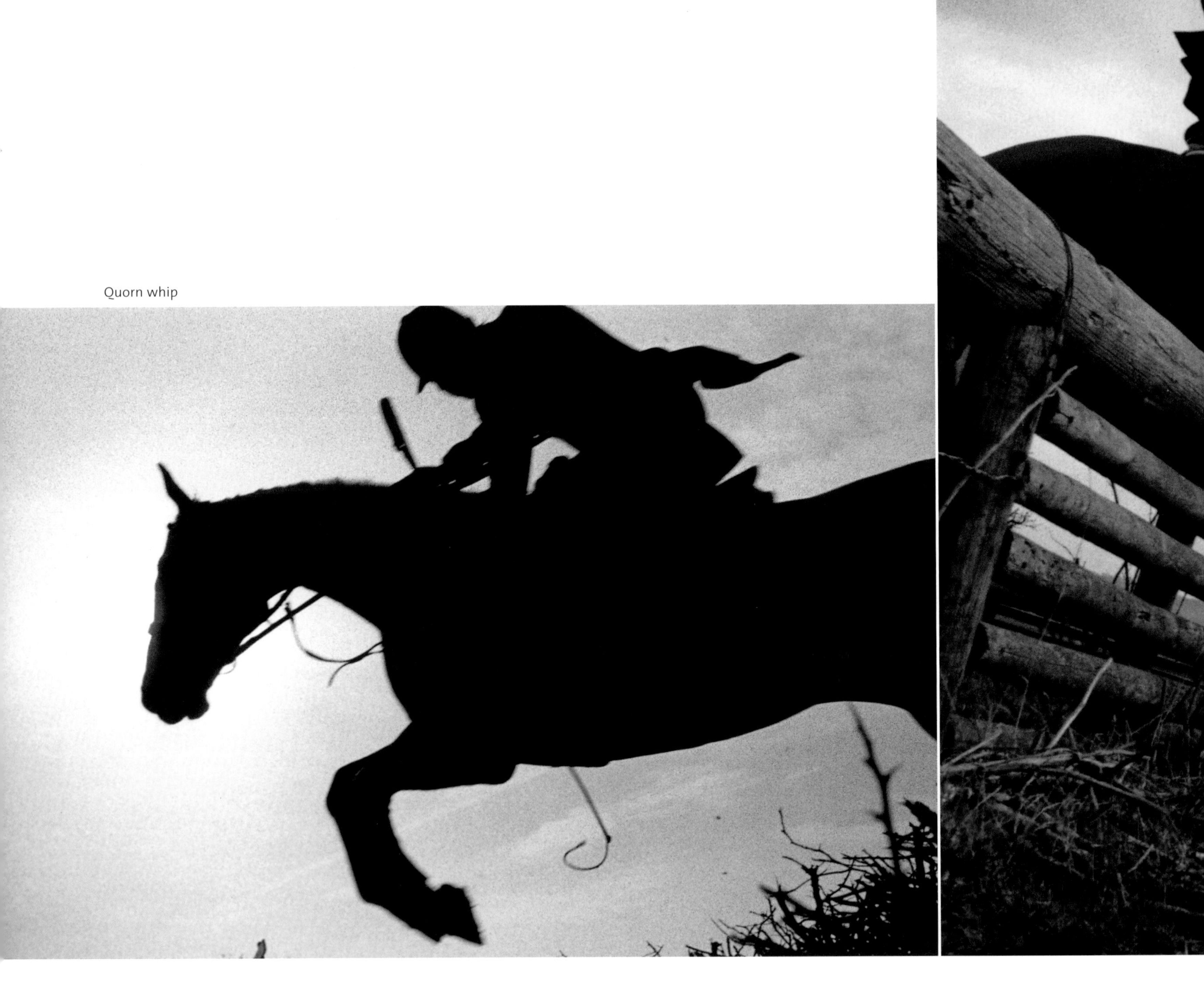

Quorn whip

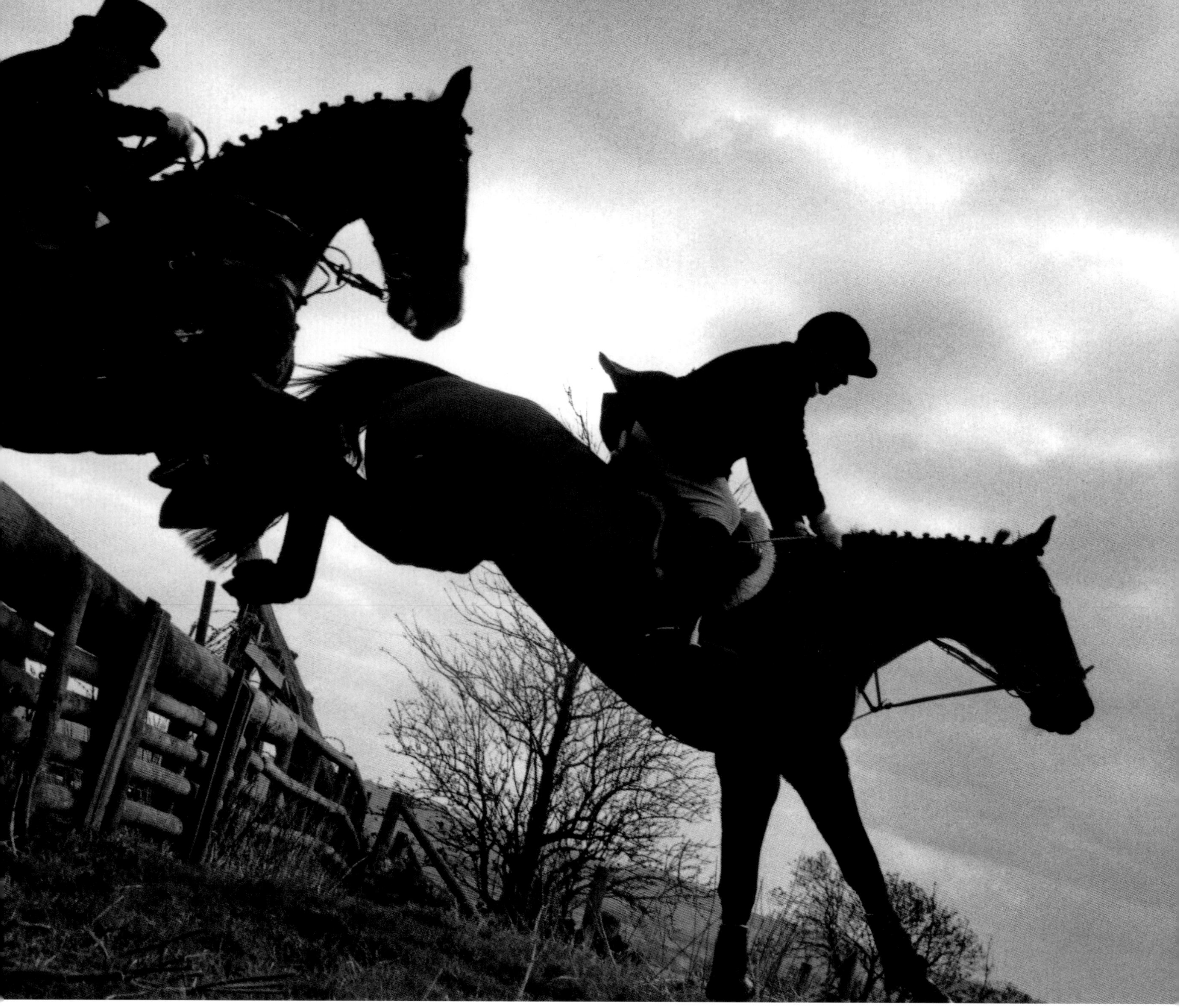

Quorn followers

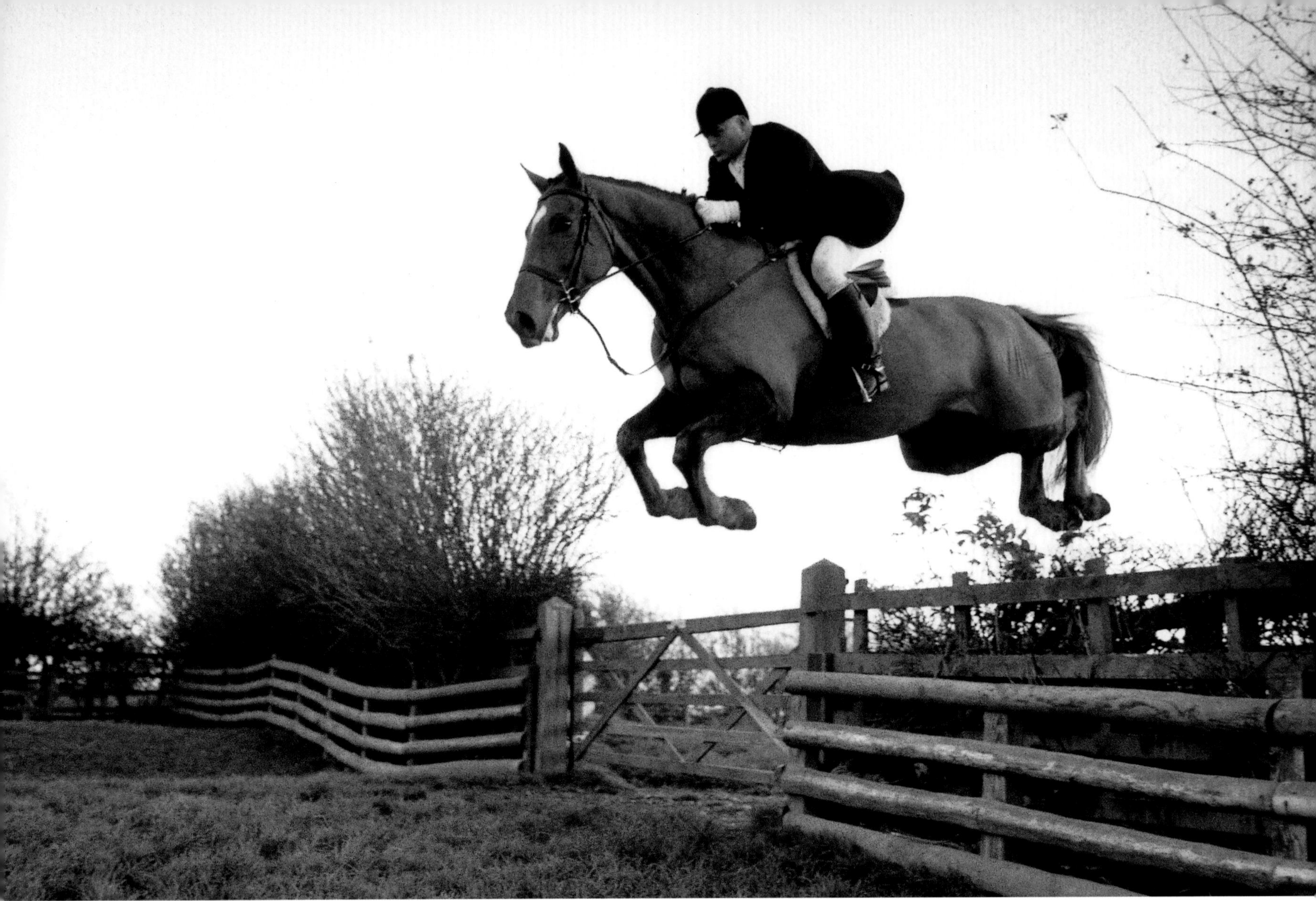

David Mee, Quorn

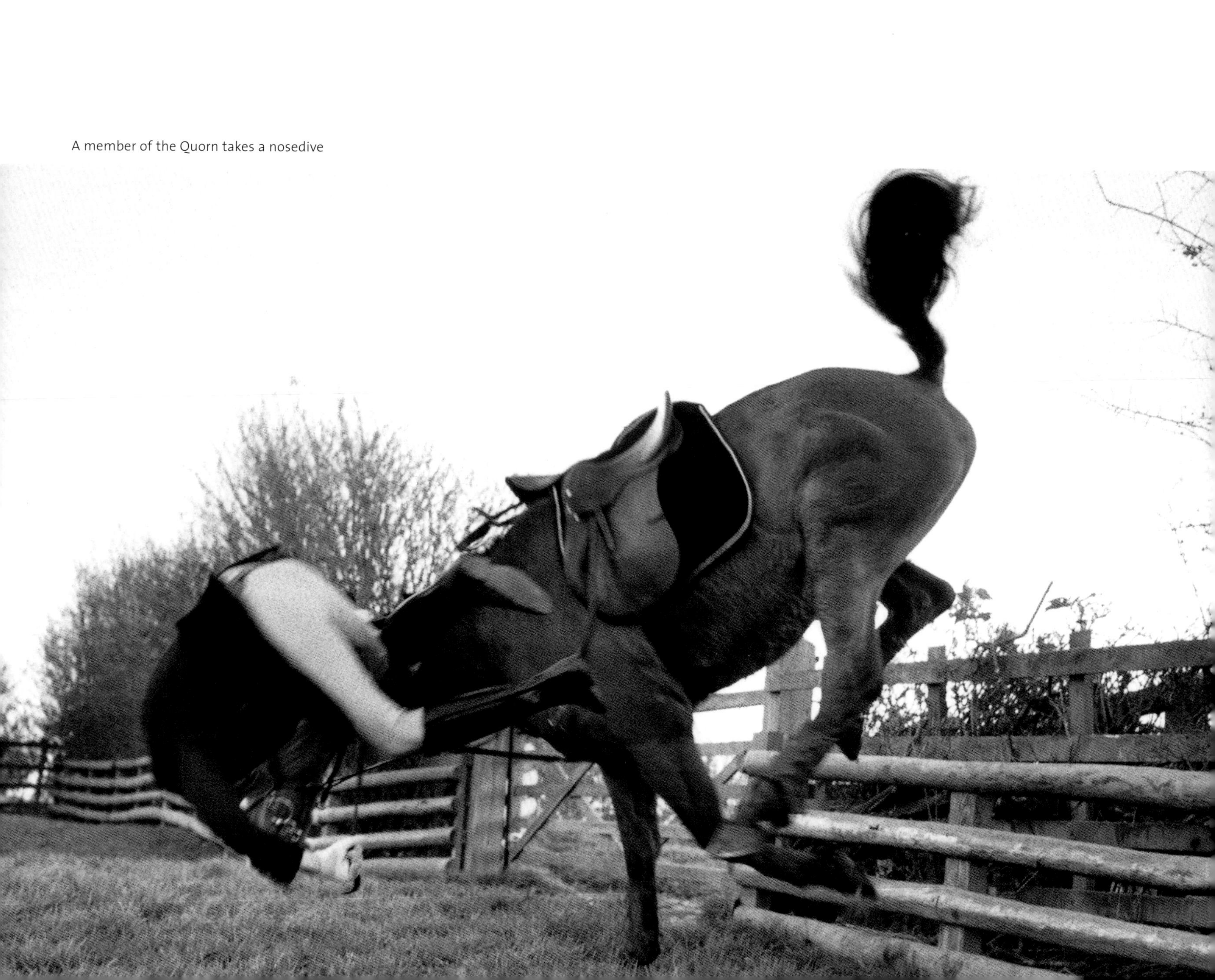

A member of the Quorn takes a nosedive

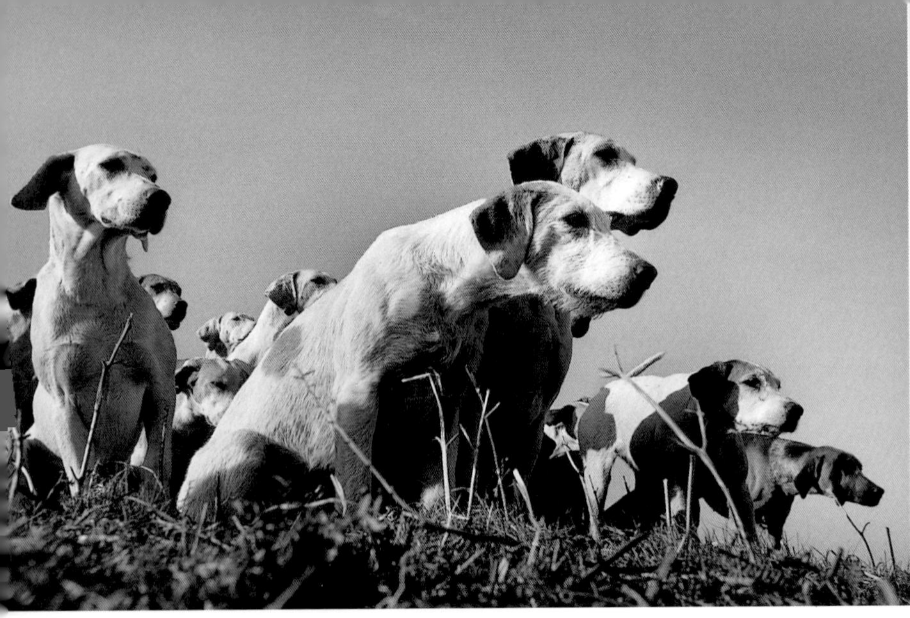

Hounds of the Mid Devon hunt

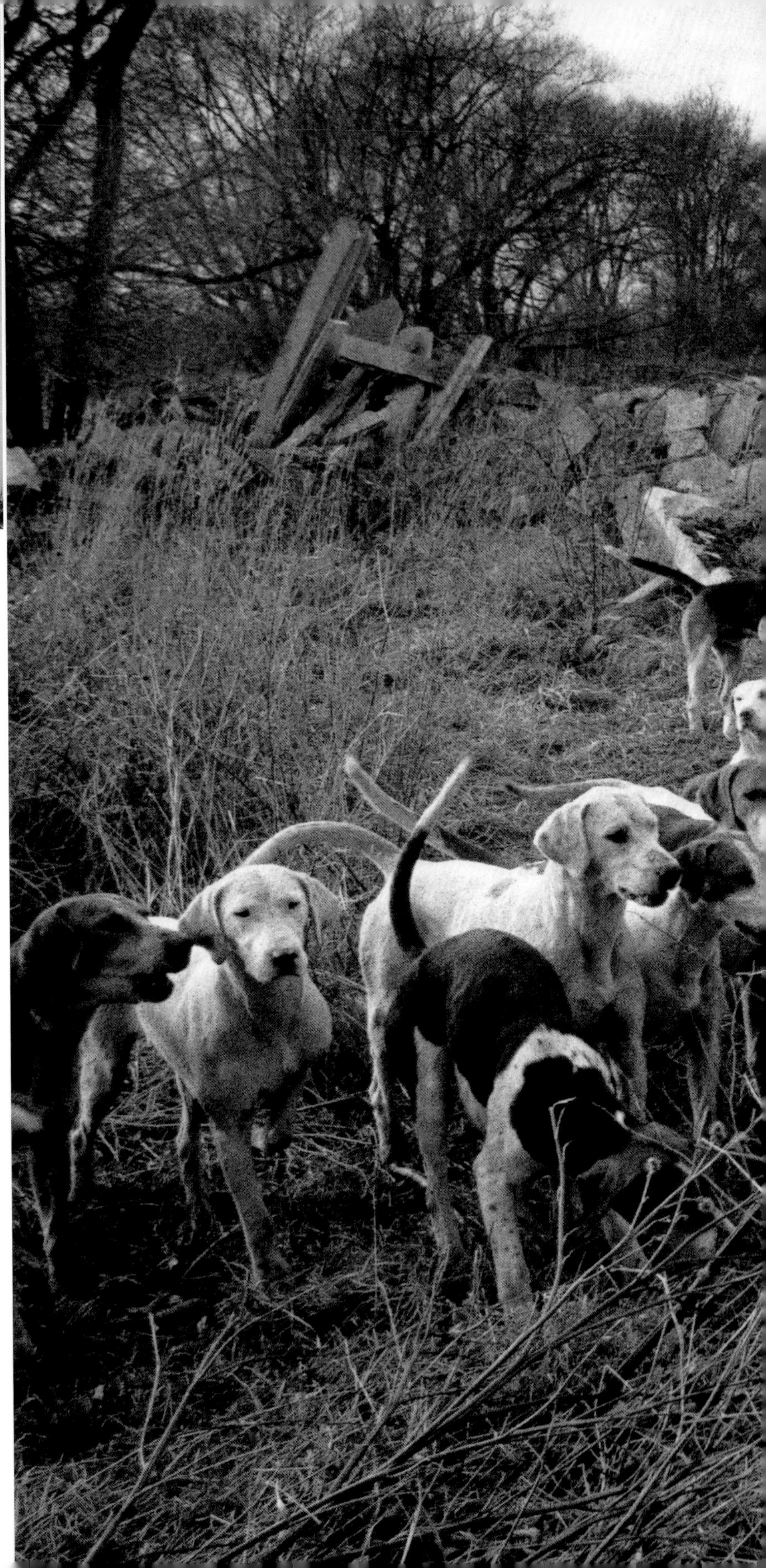

Charlie Frampton, Bedale huntsman, and former kennel huntsman, Joe Townsend

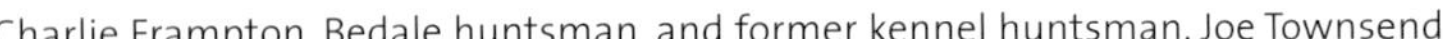

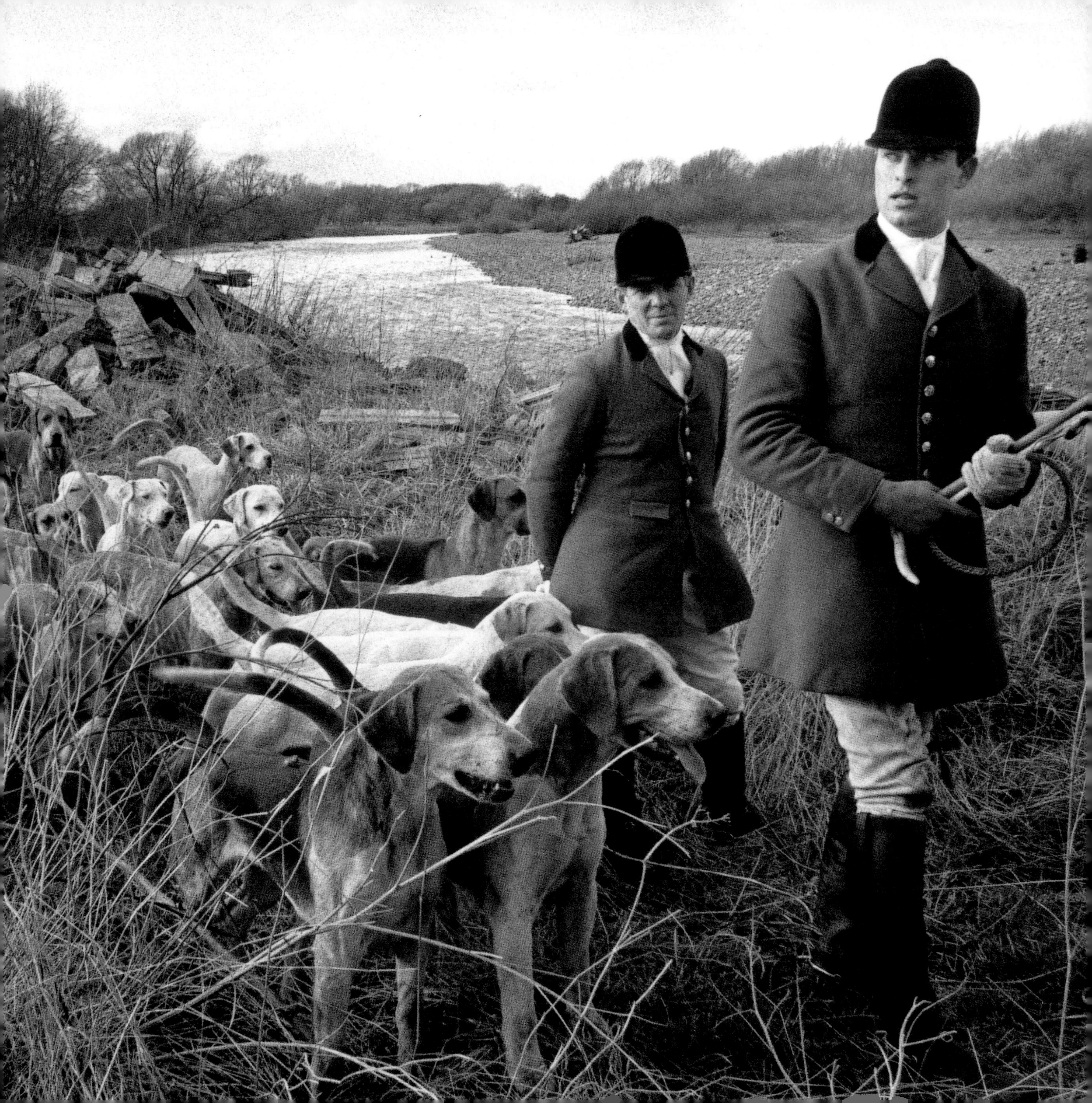

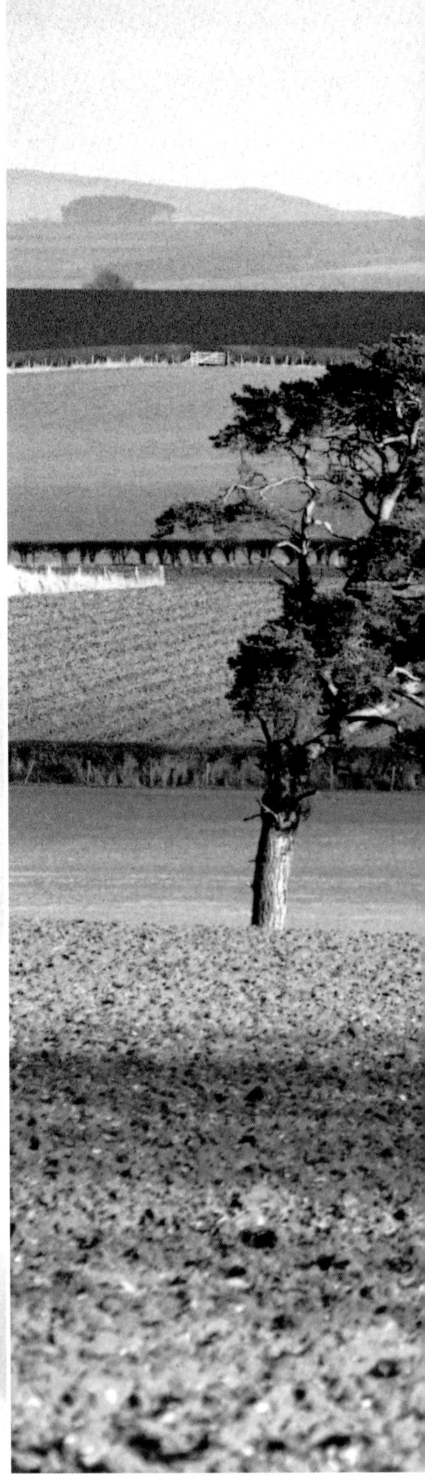

Warwickshire holloa

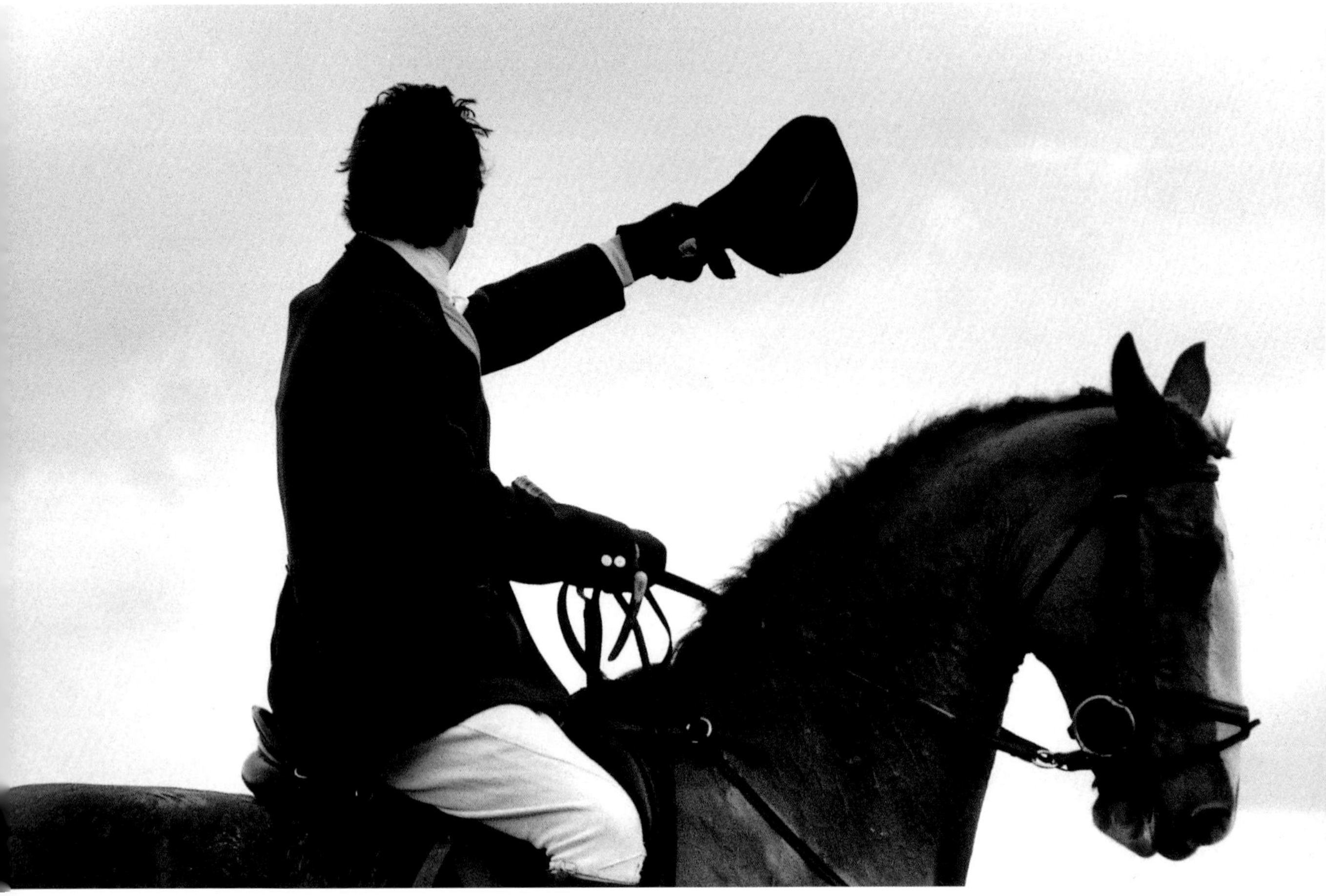

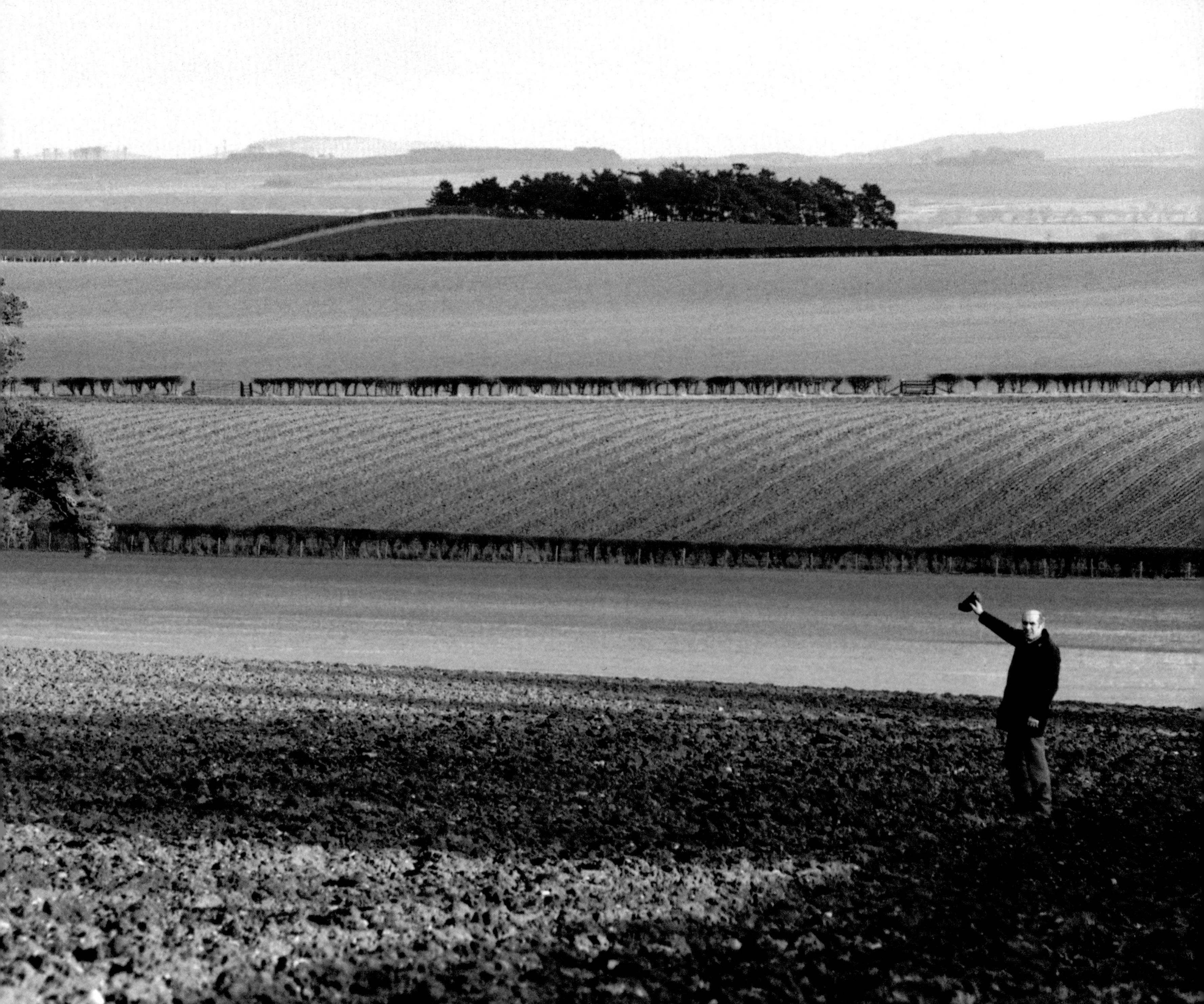

Buccleuch holloa

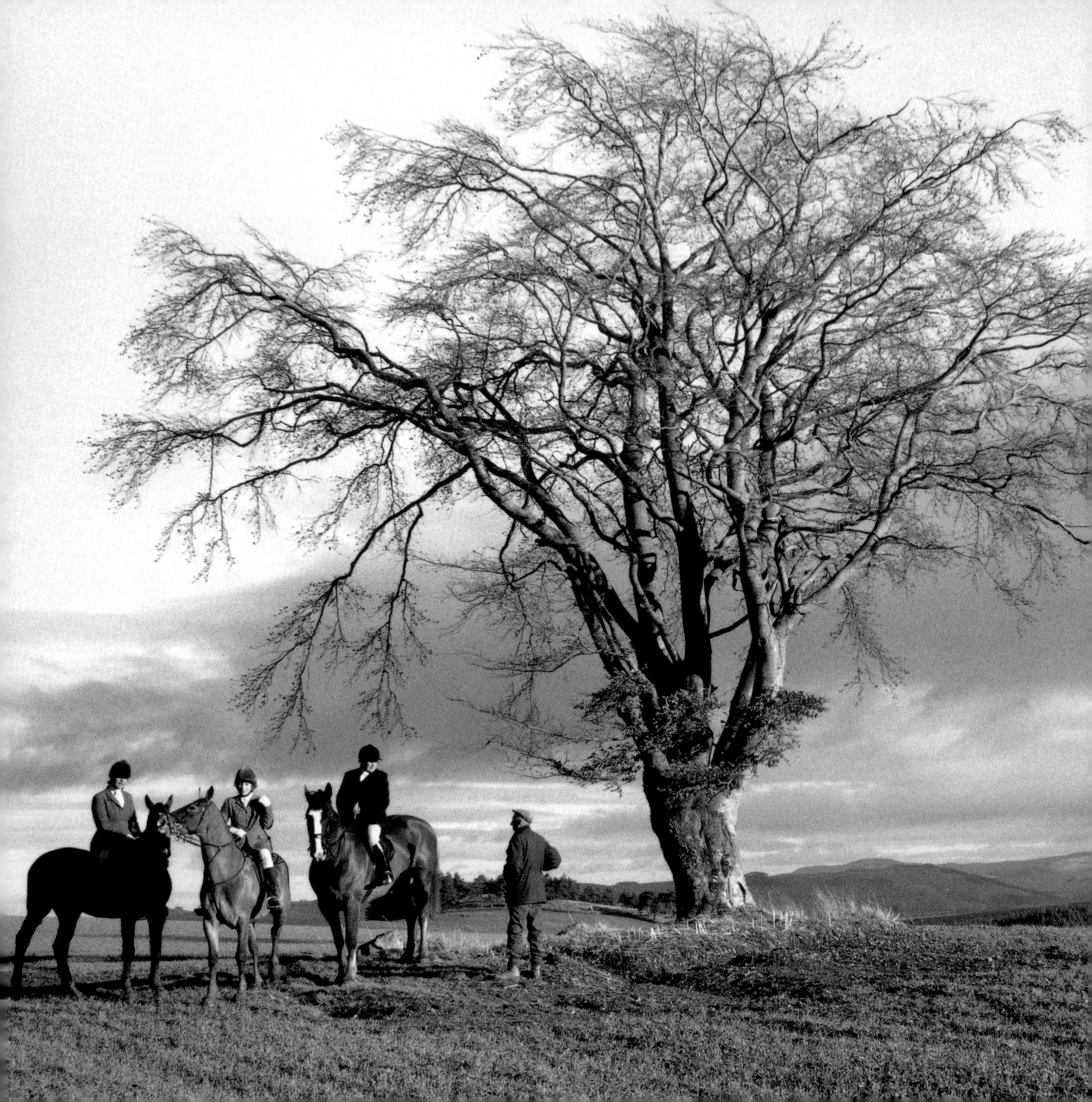

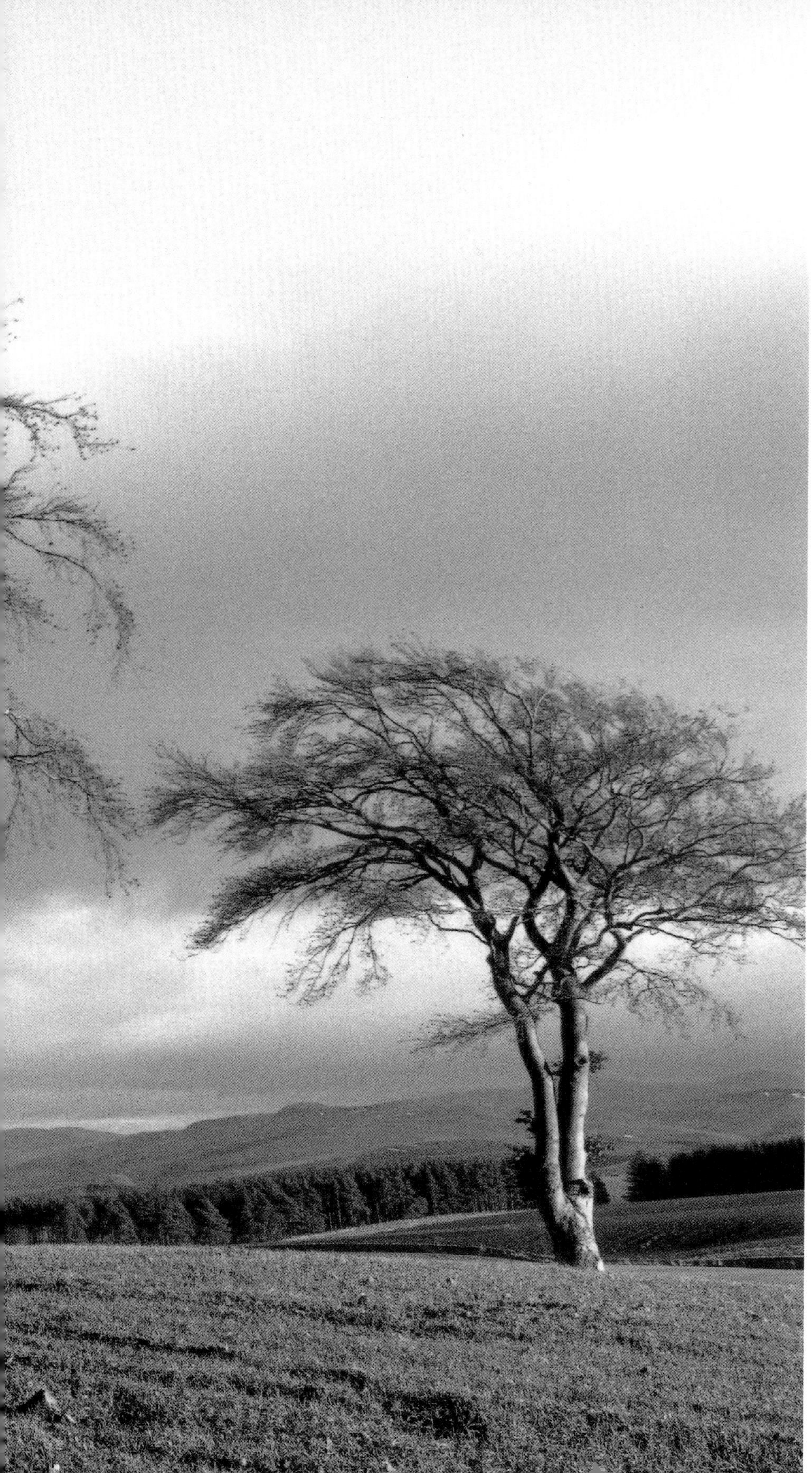

Members of the Buccleuch hunt

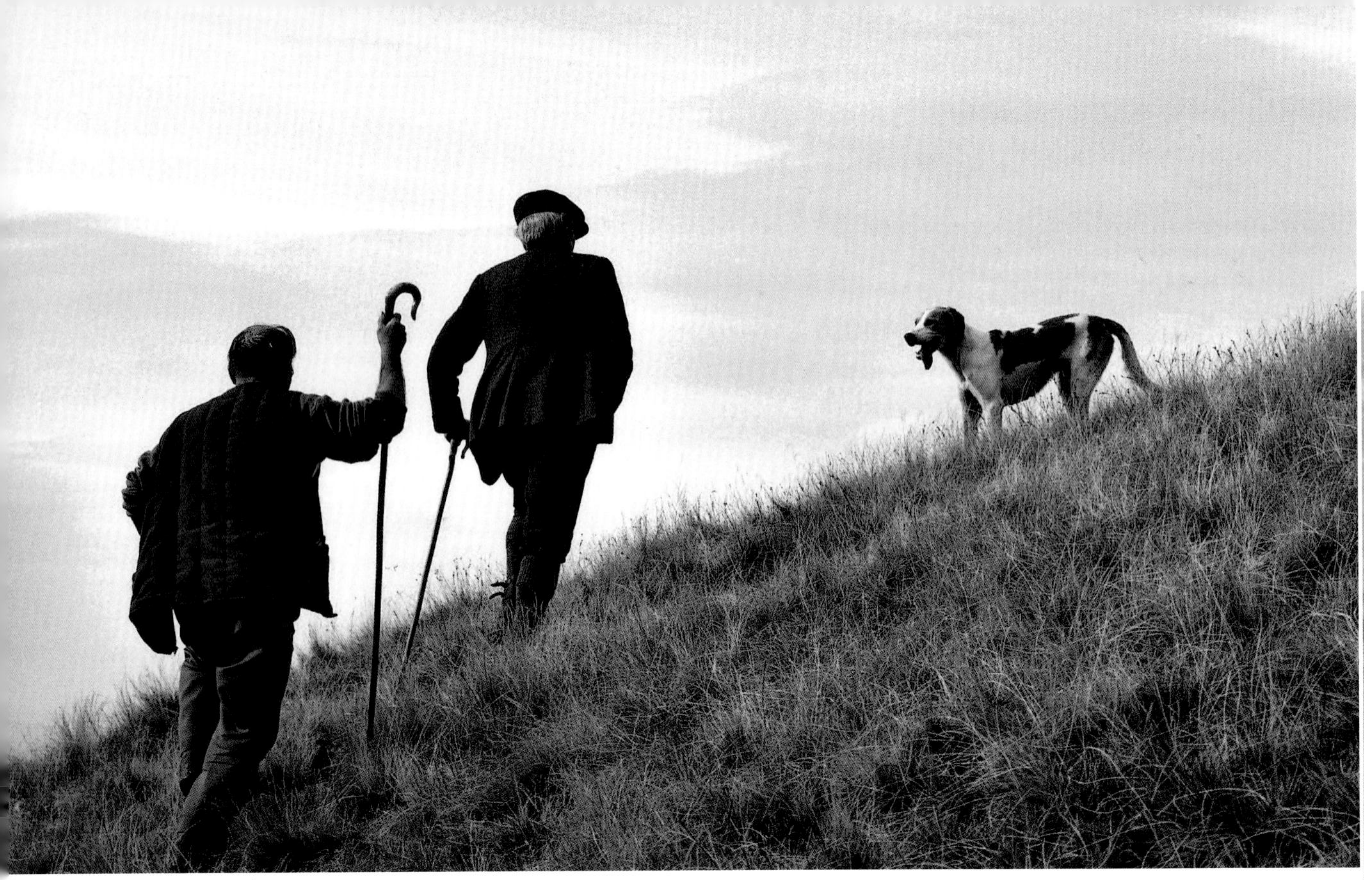

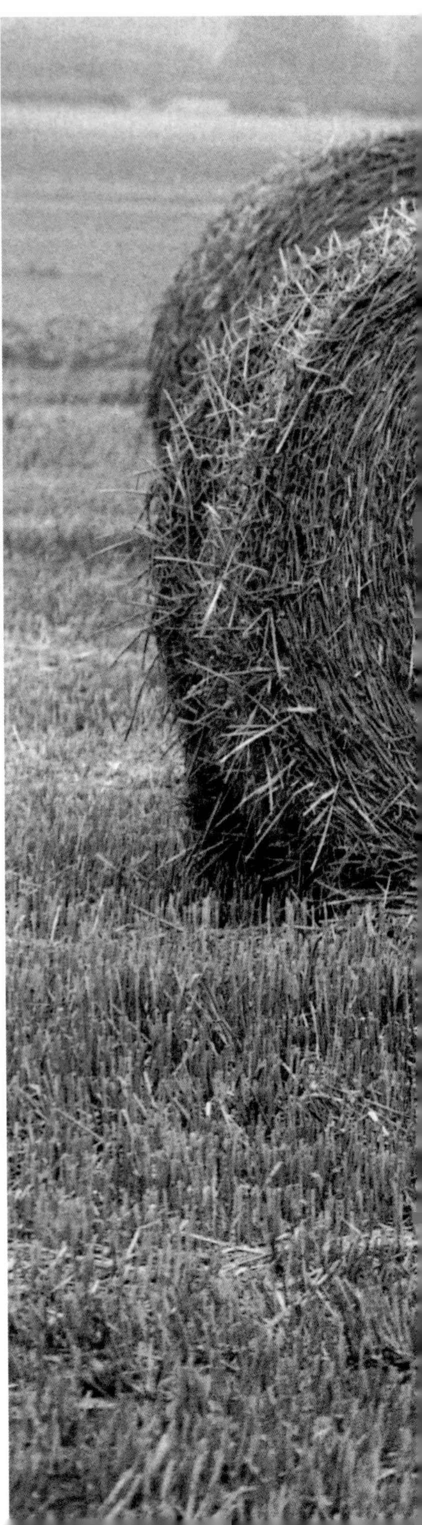

Ullswater master, John Lothian leads the way uphill

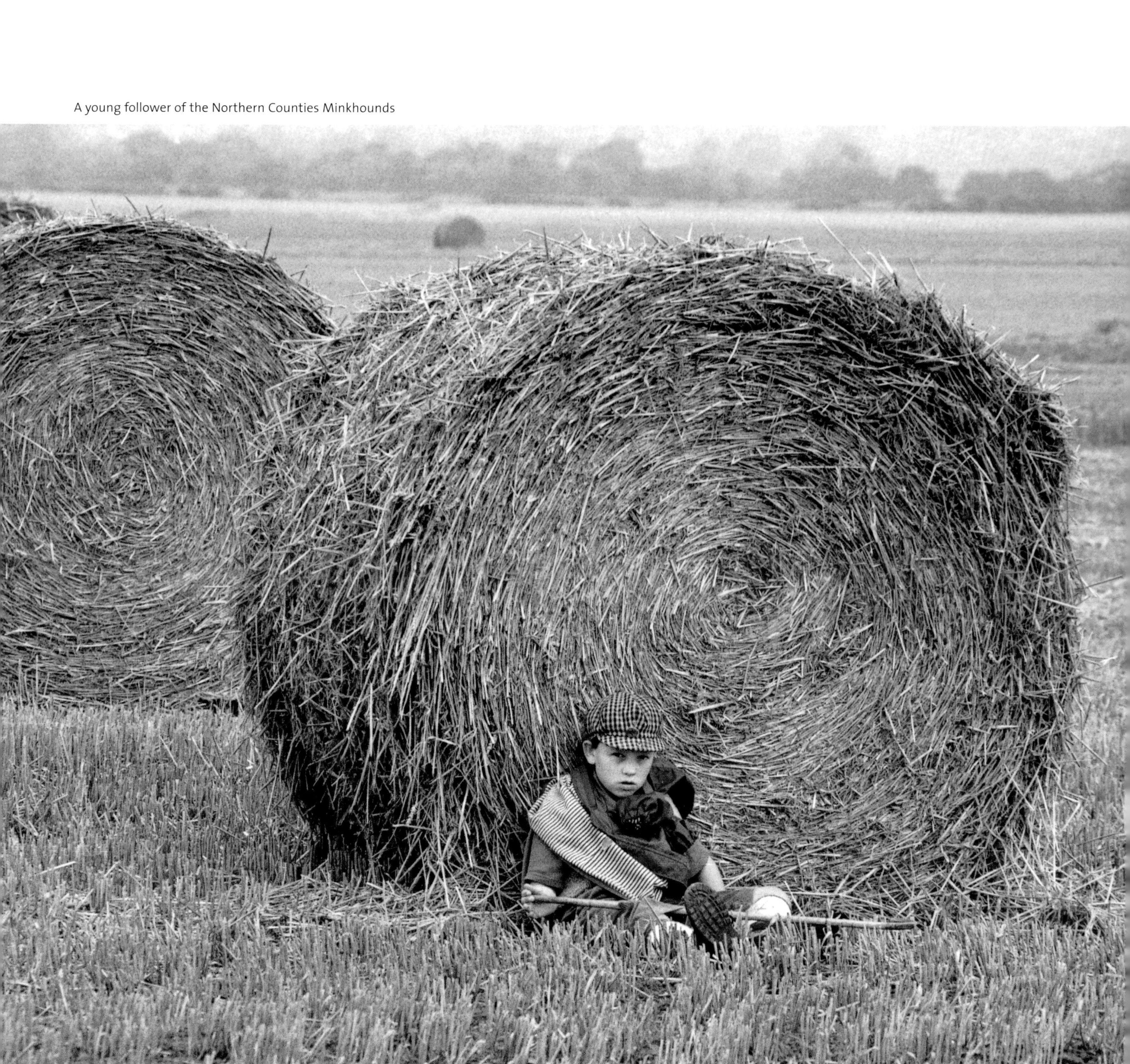

A young follower of the Northern Counties Minkhounds

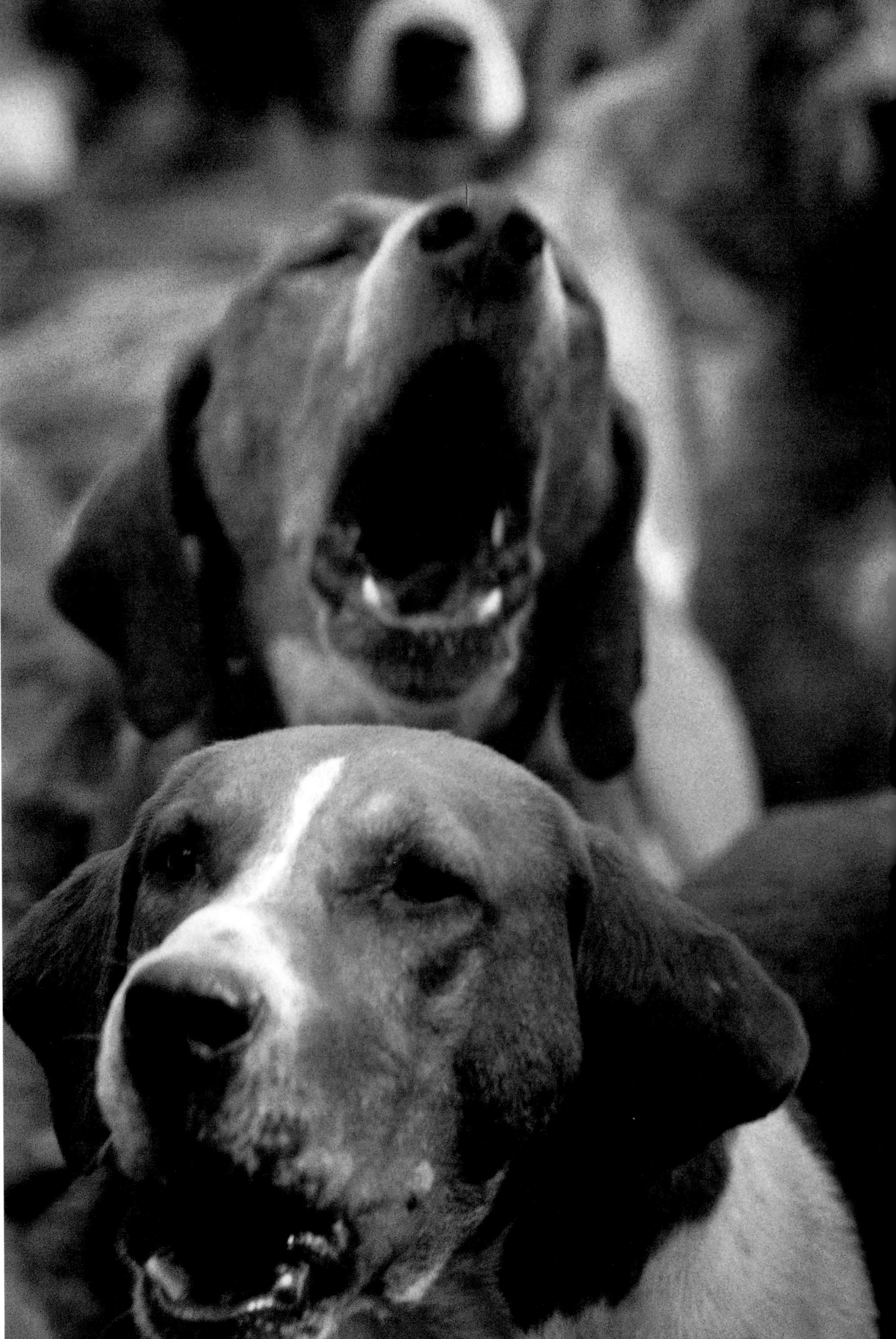

Northern Counties Minkhounds

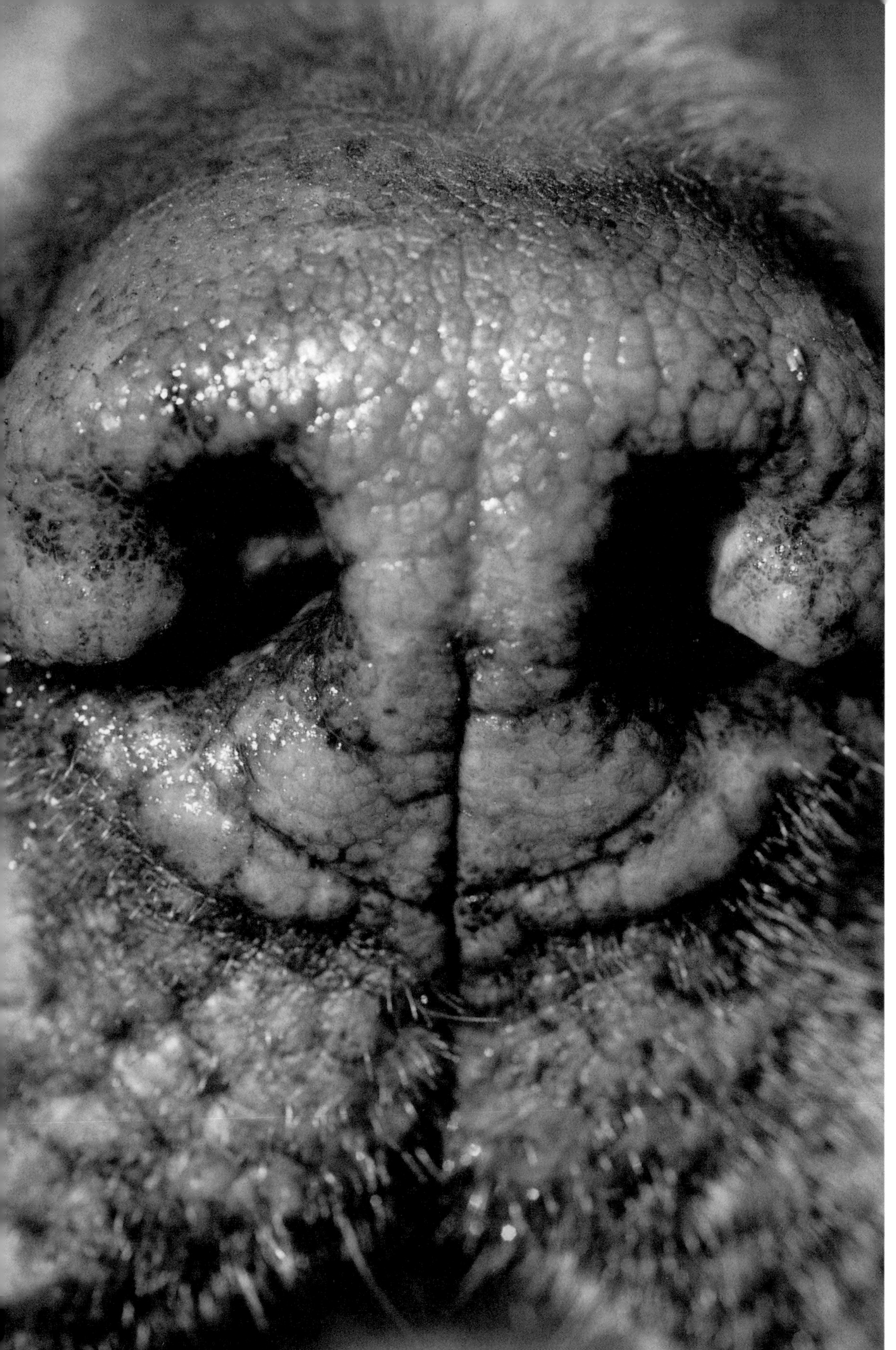

Morpeth hound nose

Bedale hound running

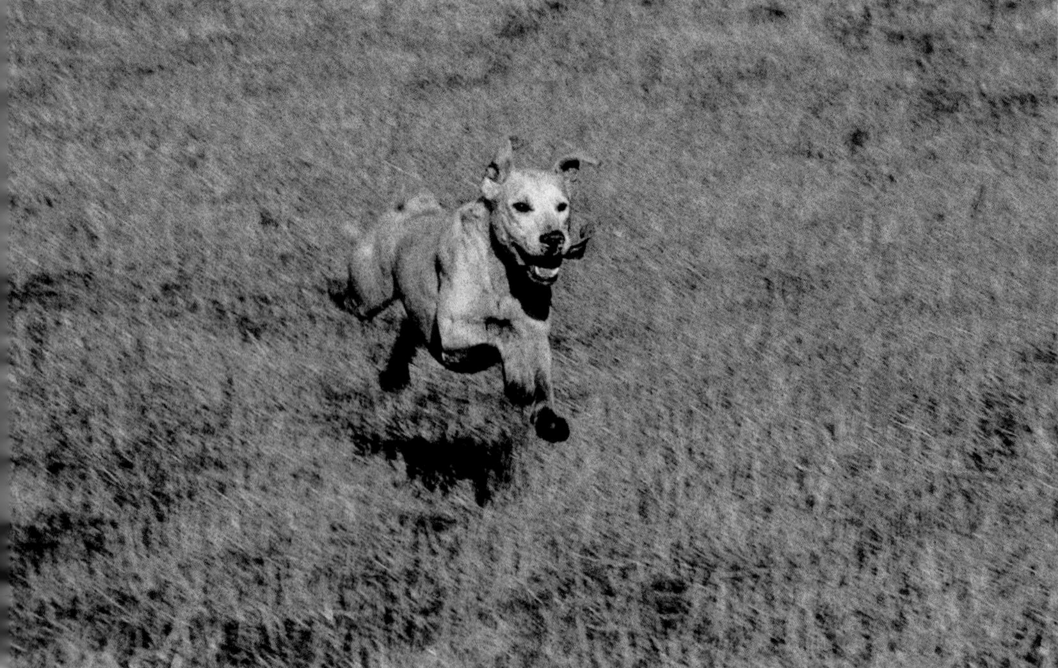

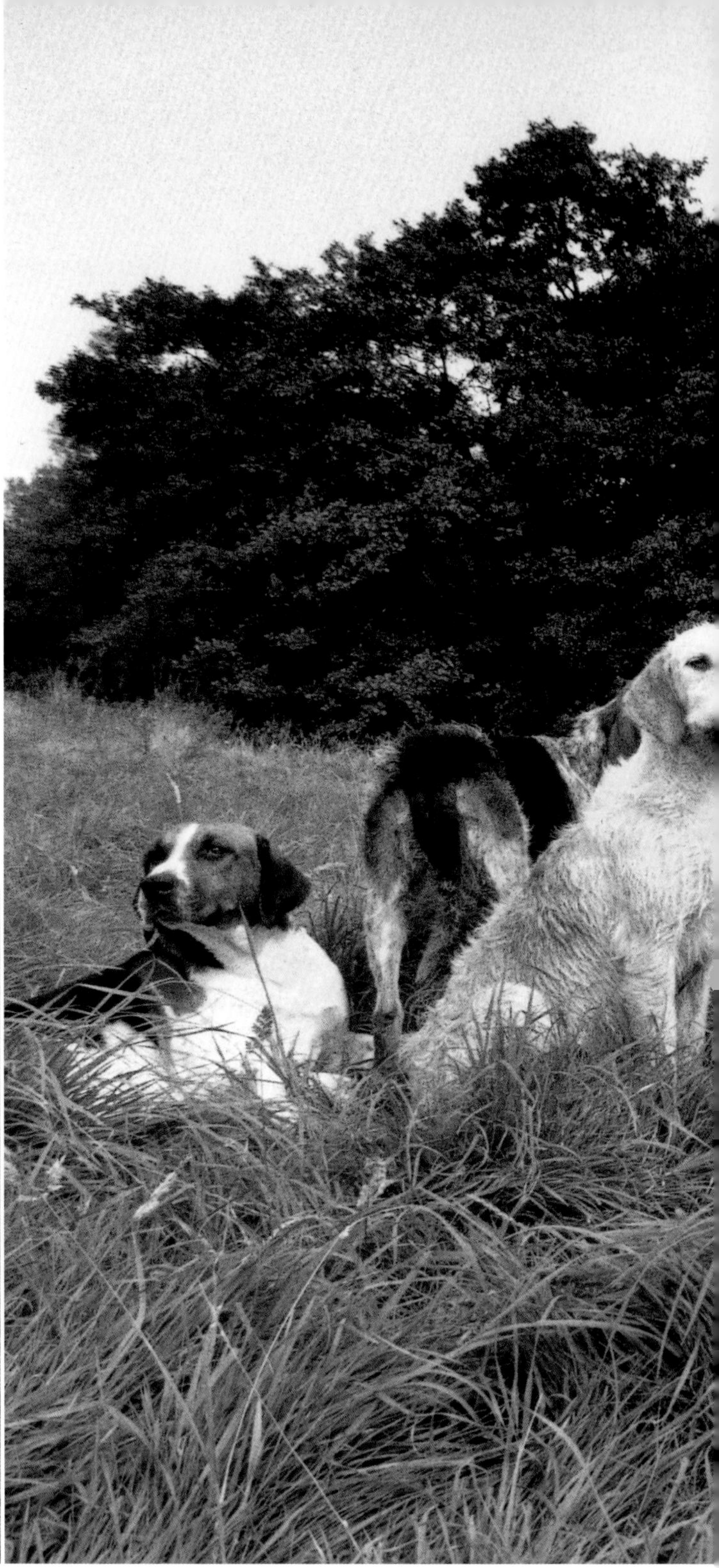

Martin Spilsbury and the Northern Counties Minkhounds

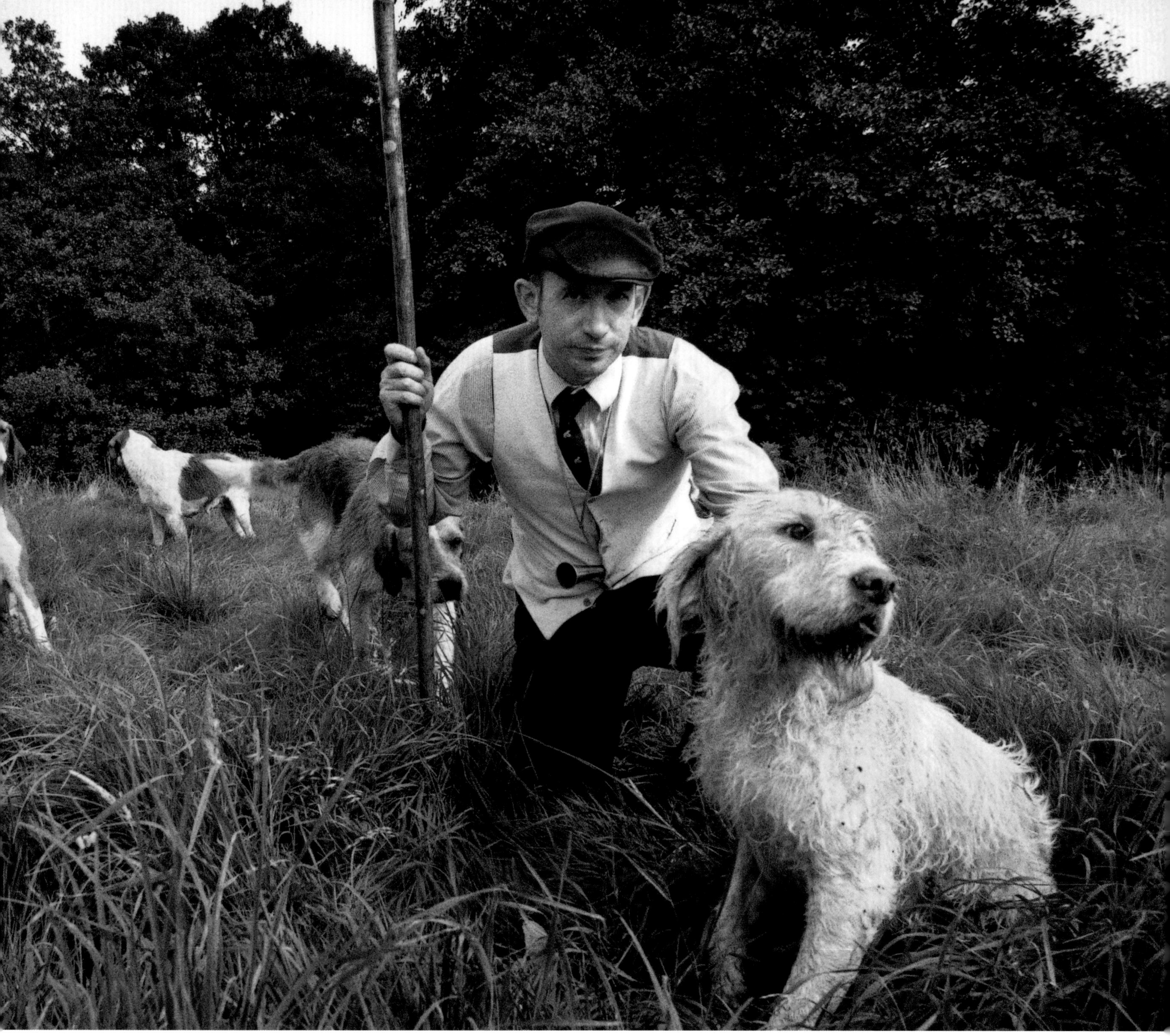

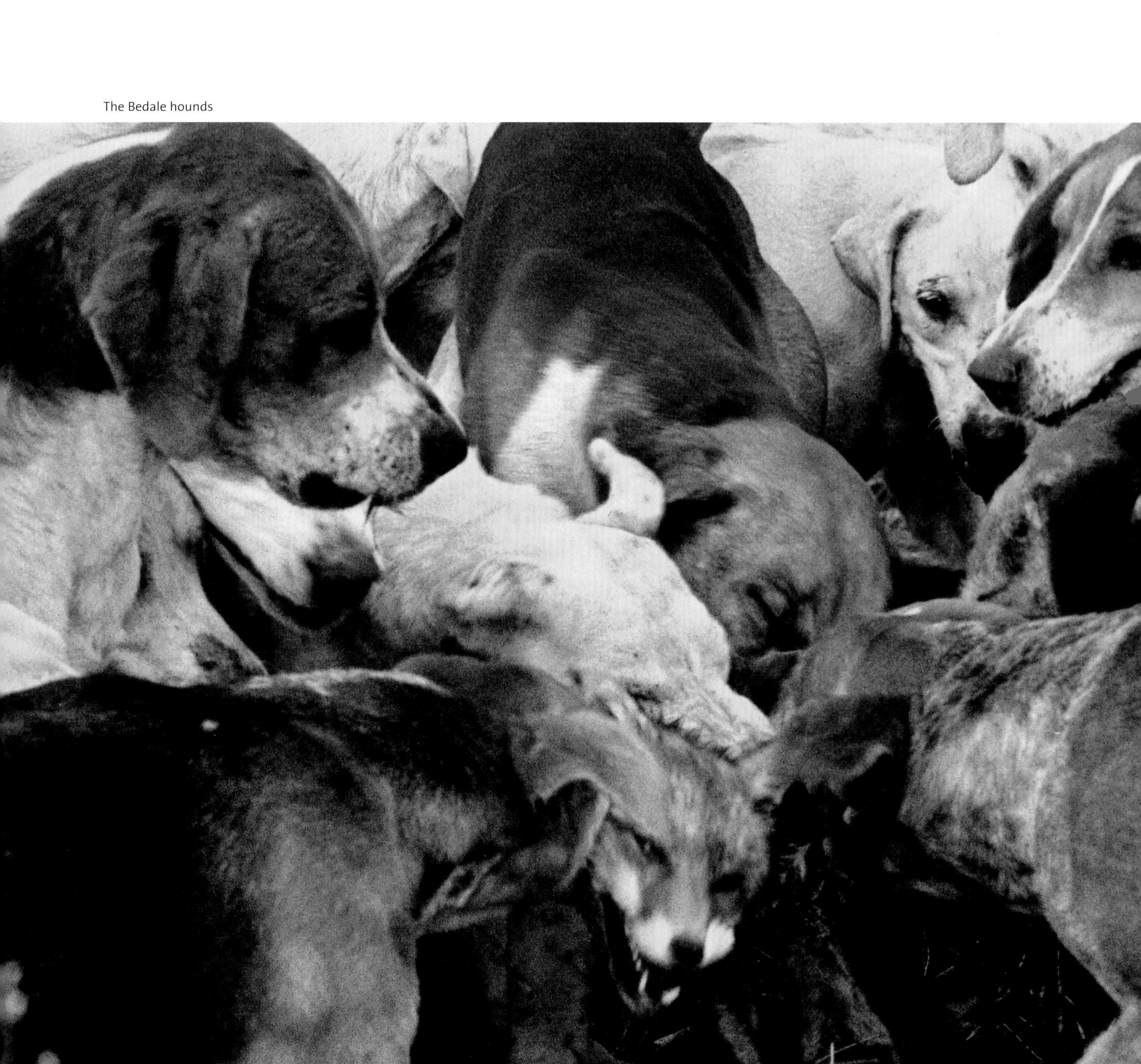

The Bedale hounds

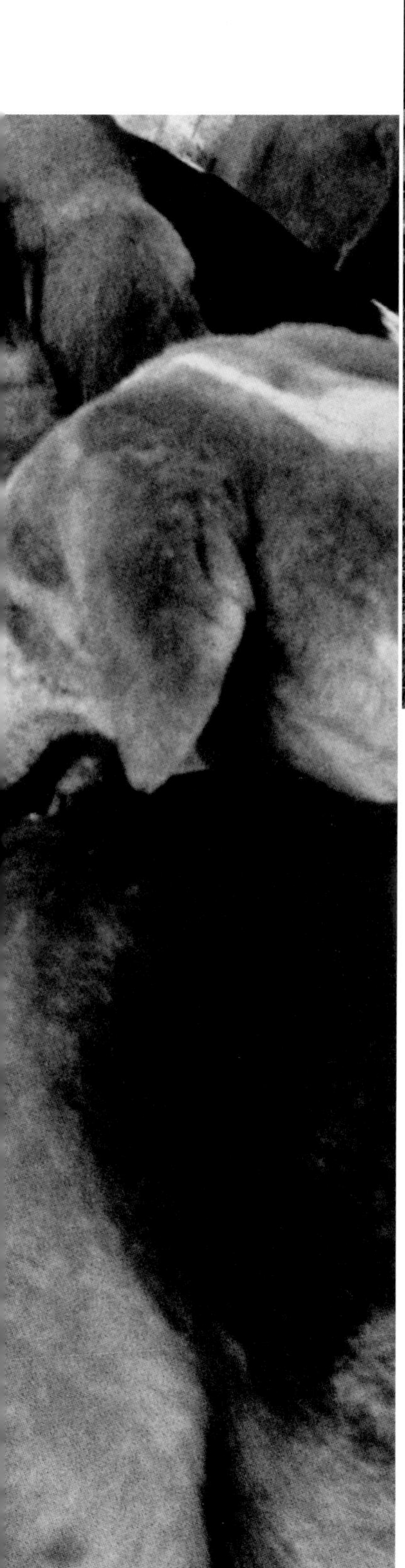

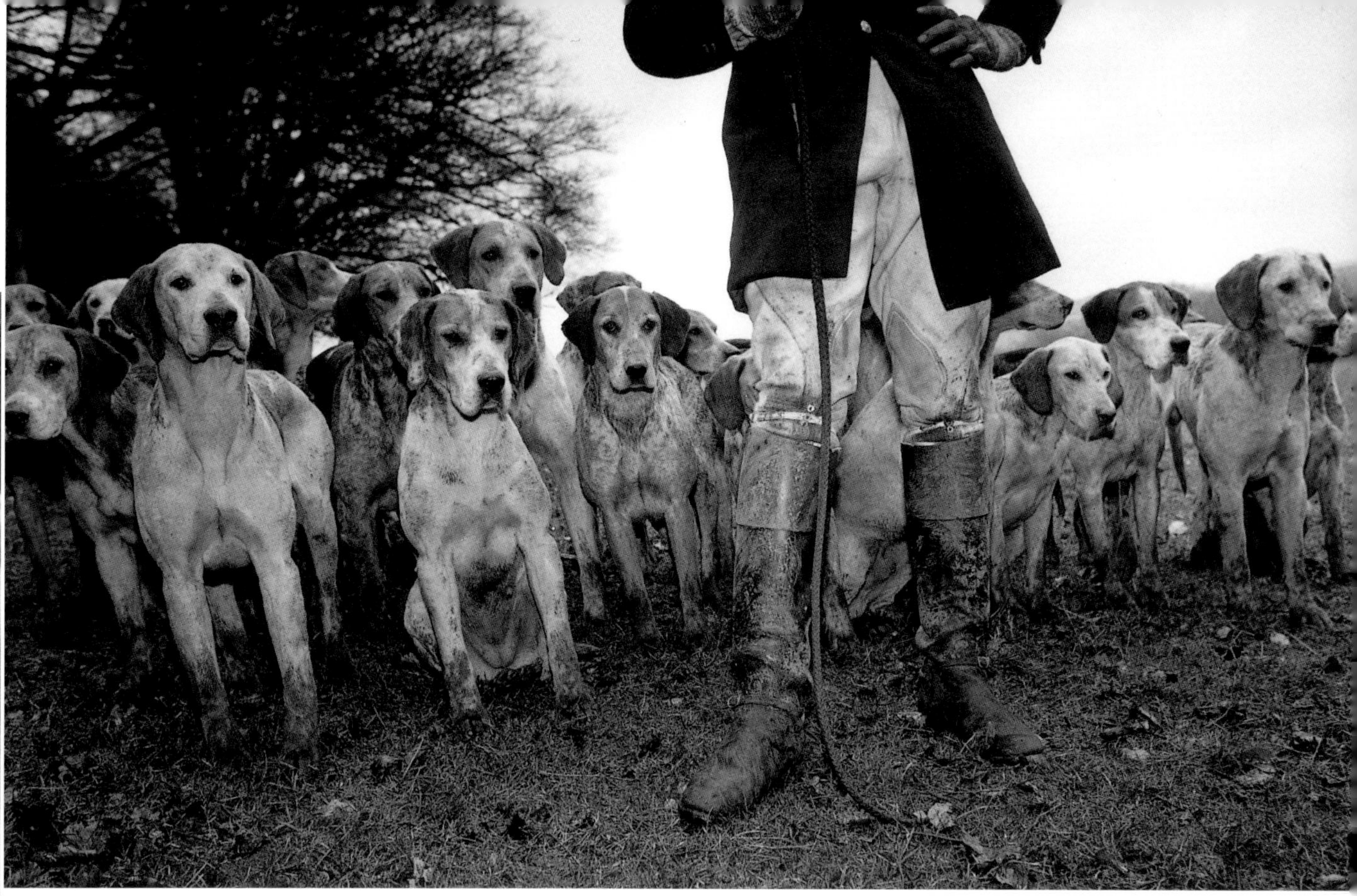

The Eglinton hounds

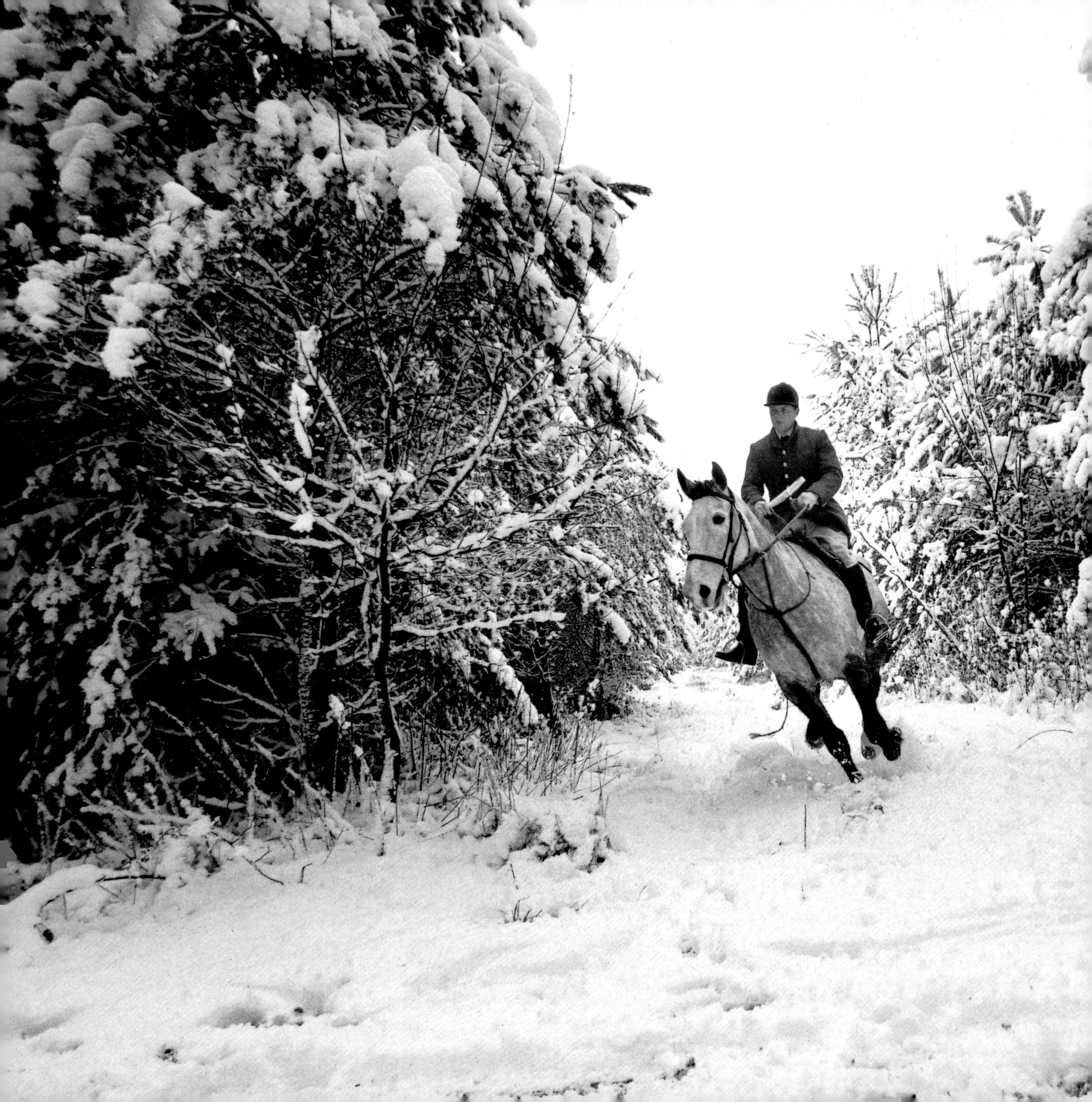

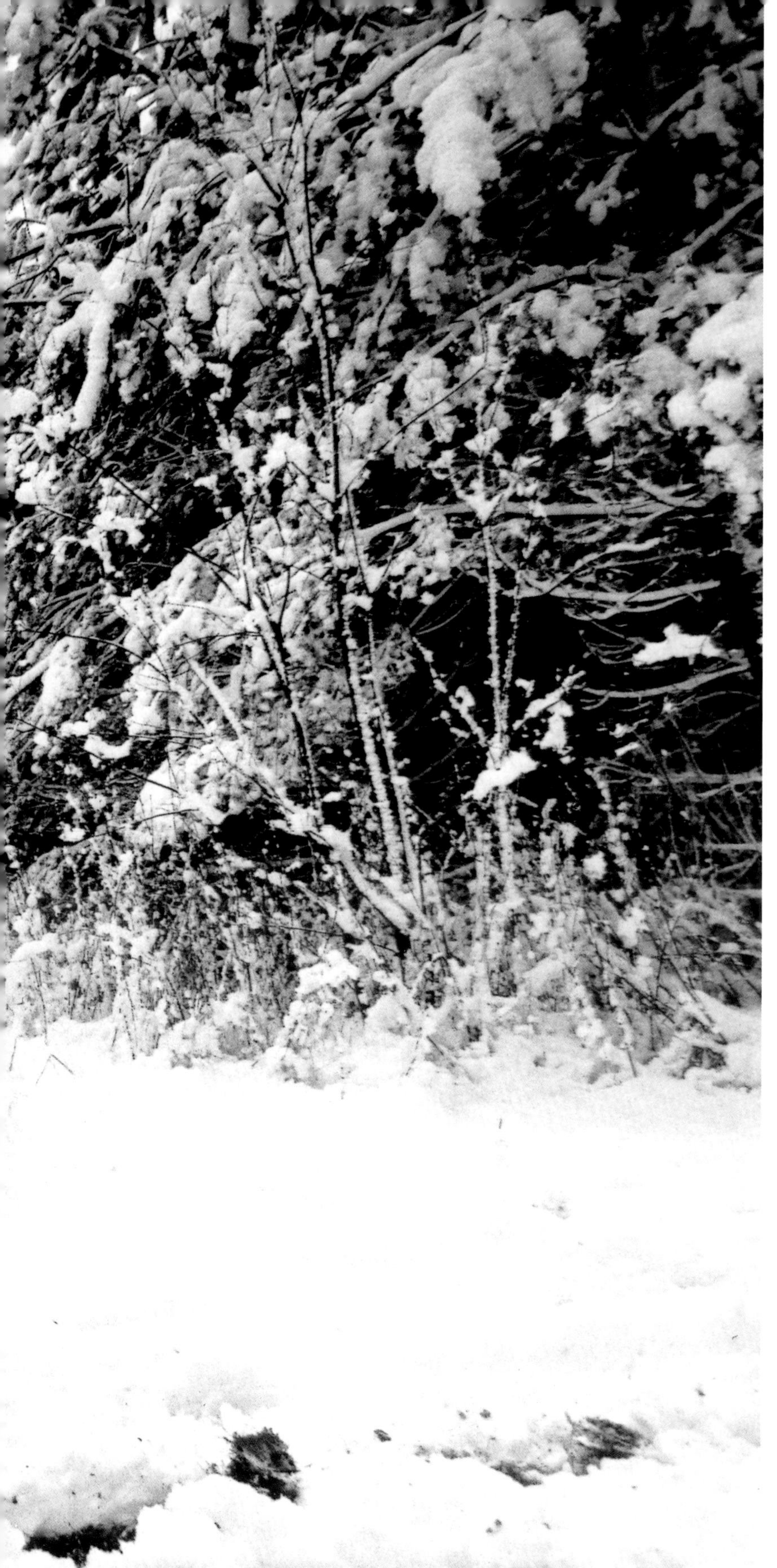

Rory Innes, former huntsman of the Jedforest

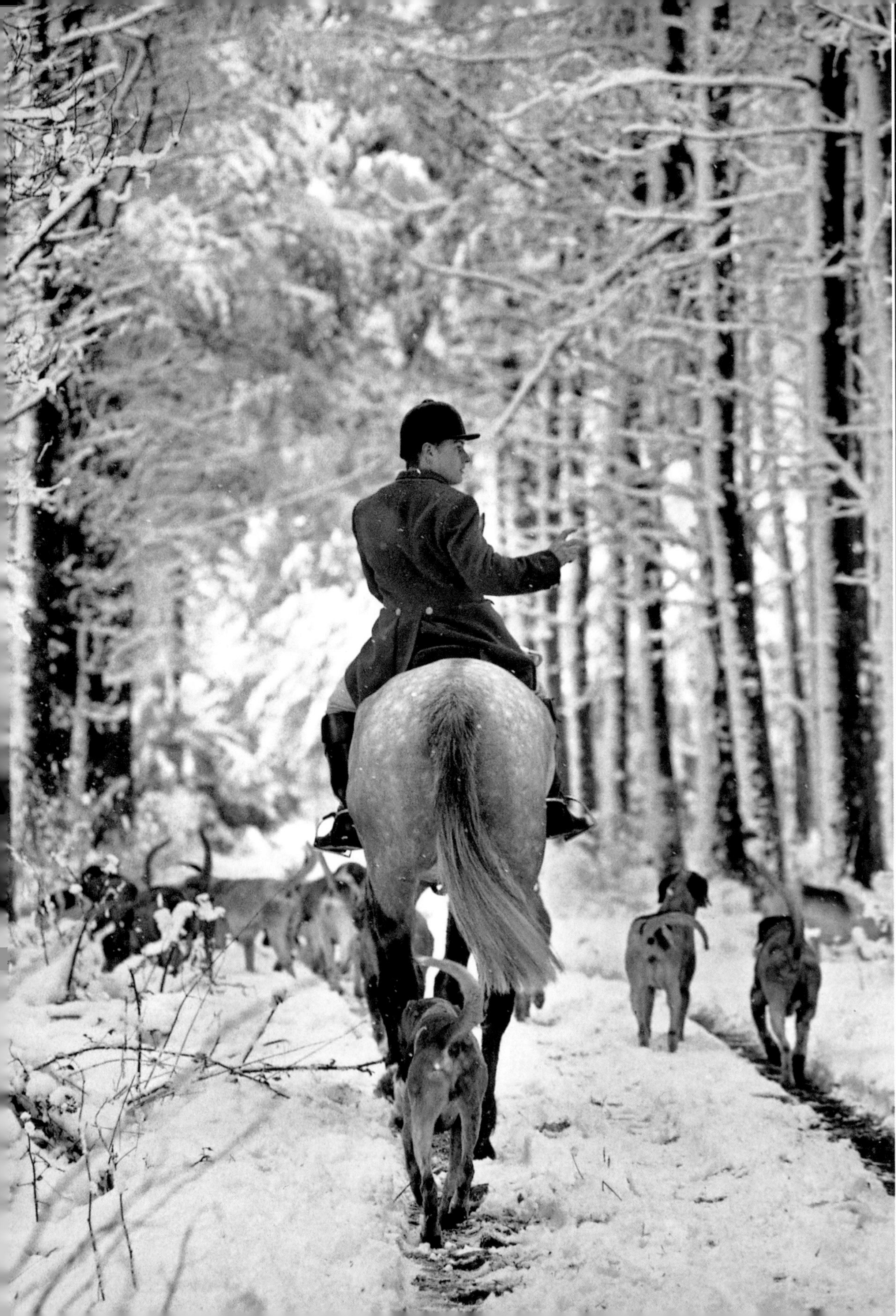

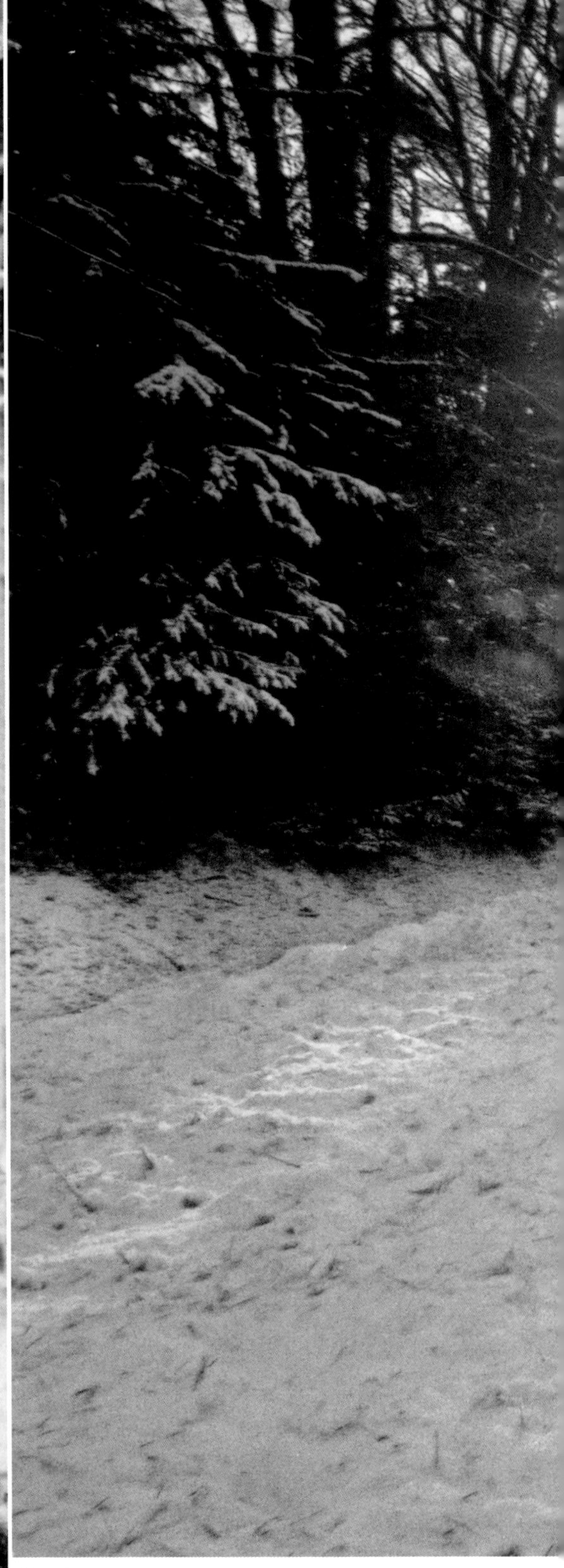

Rory Innes

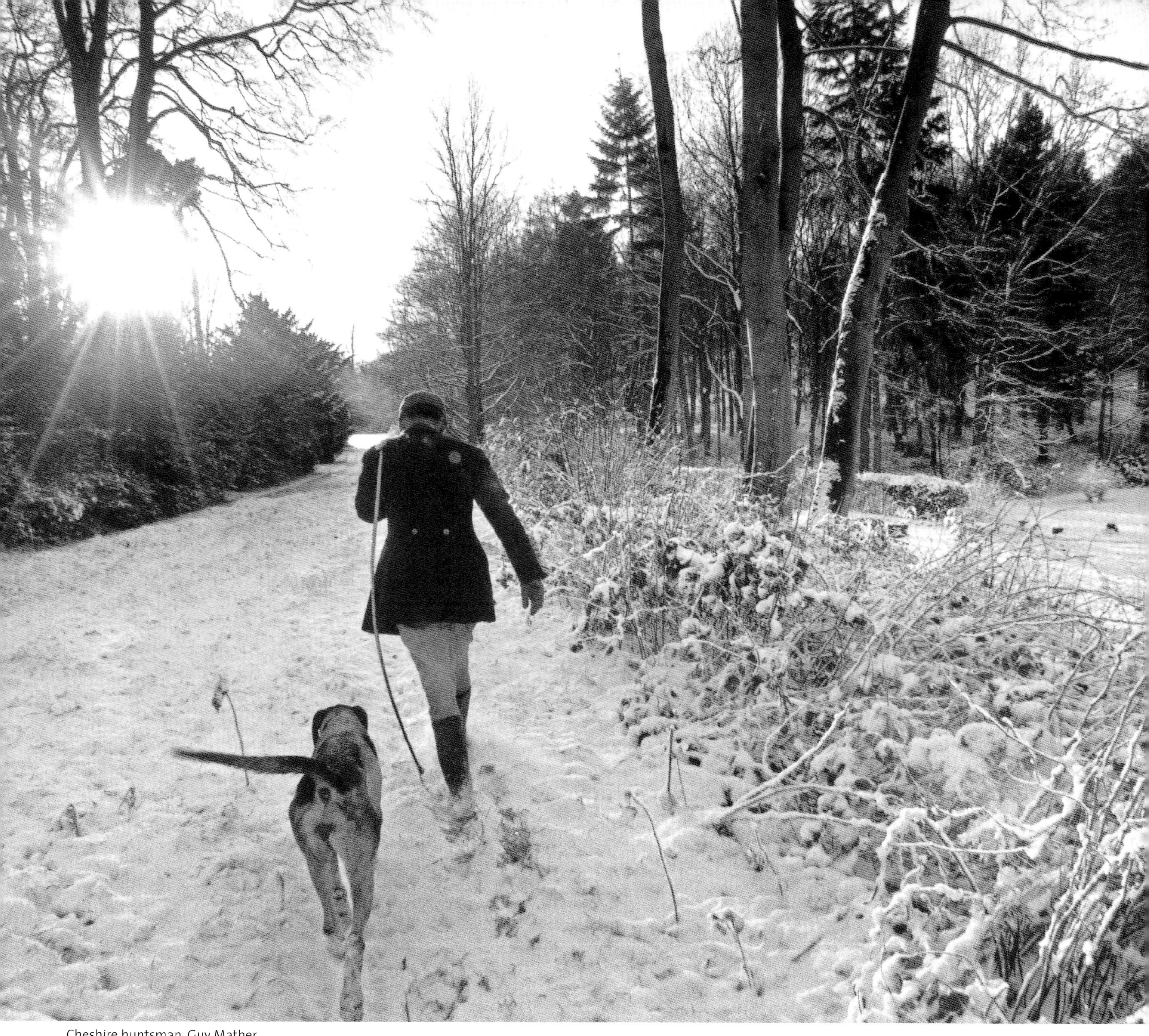

Cheshire huntsman, Guy Mather

Members of The Vale of White Horse Hunt (VWH) at the end of a run

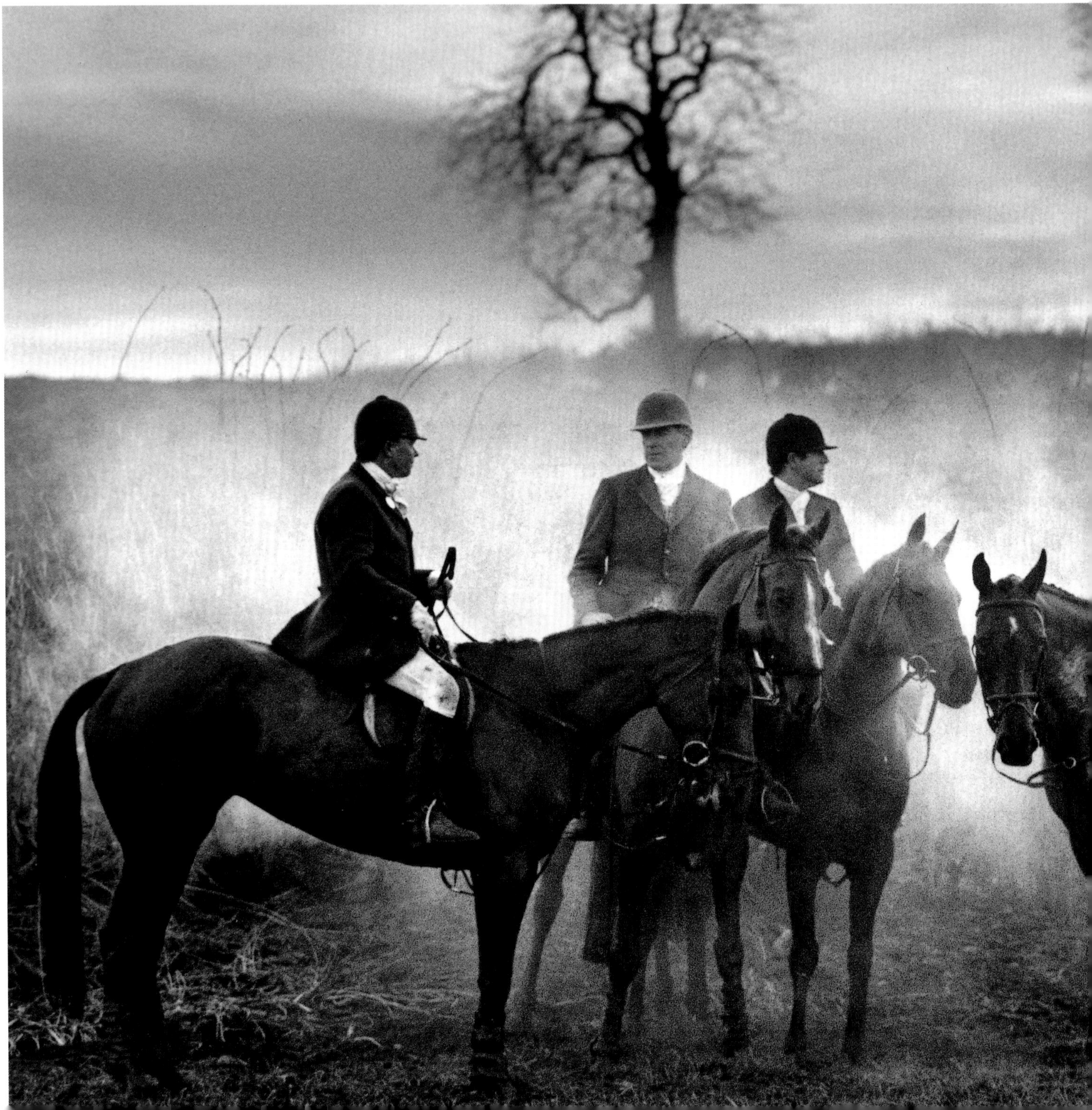

Members of the Berkeley

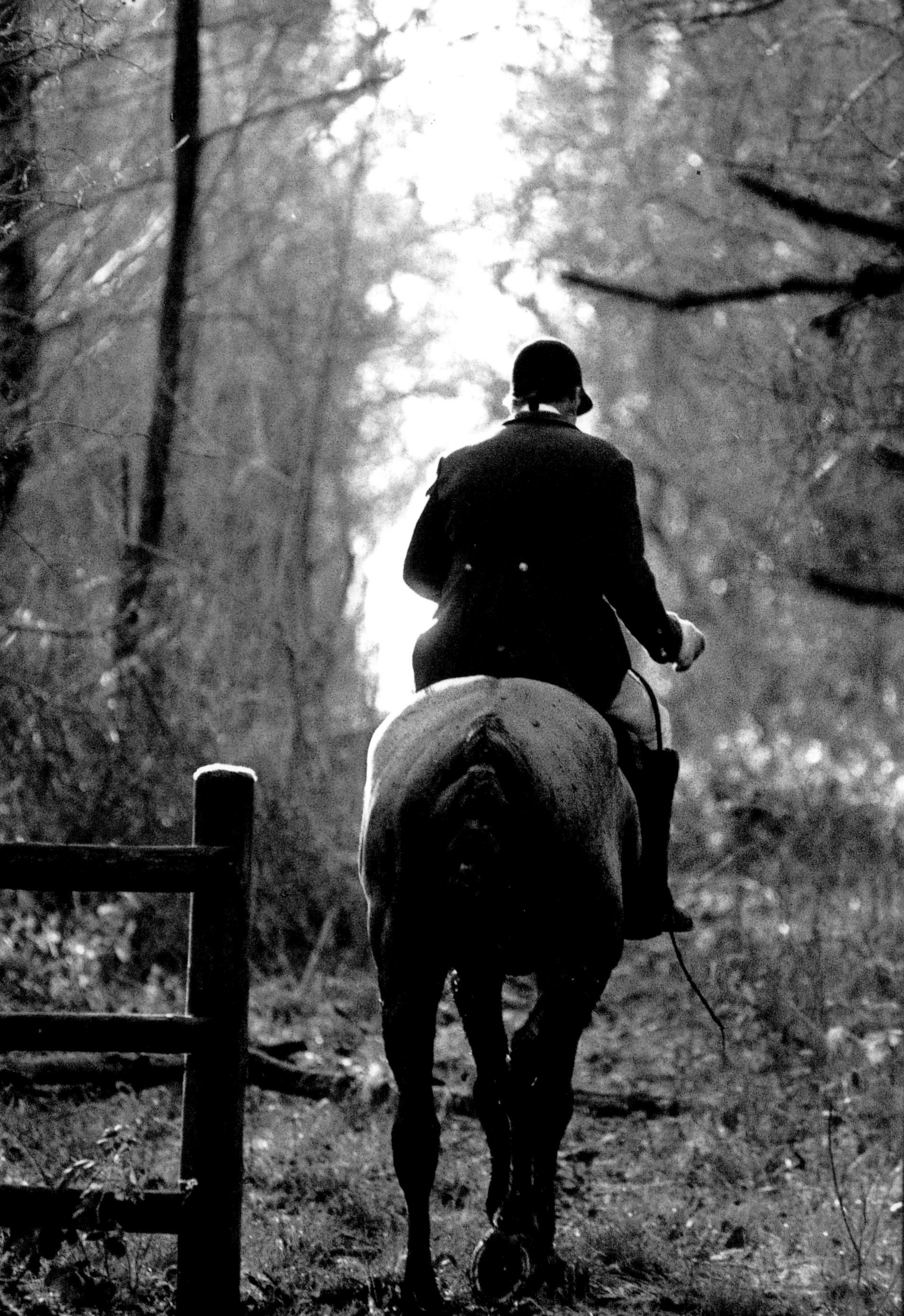

A rider of the VWH heads for home

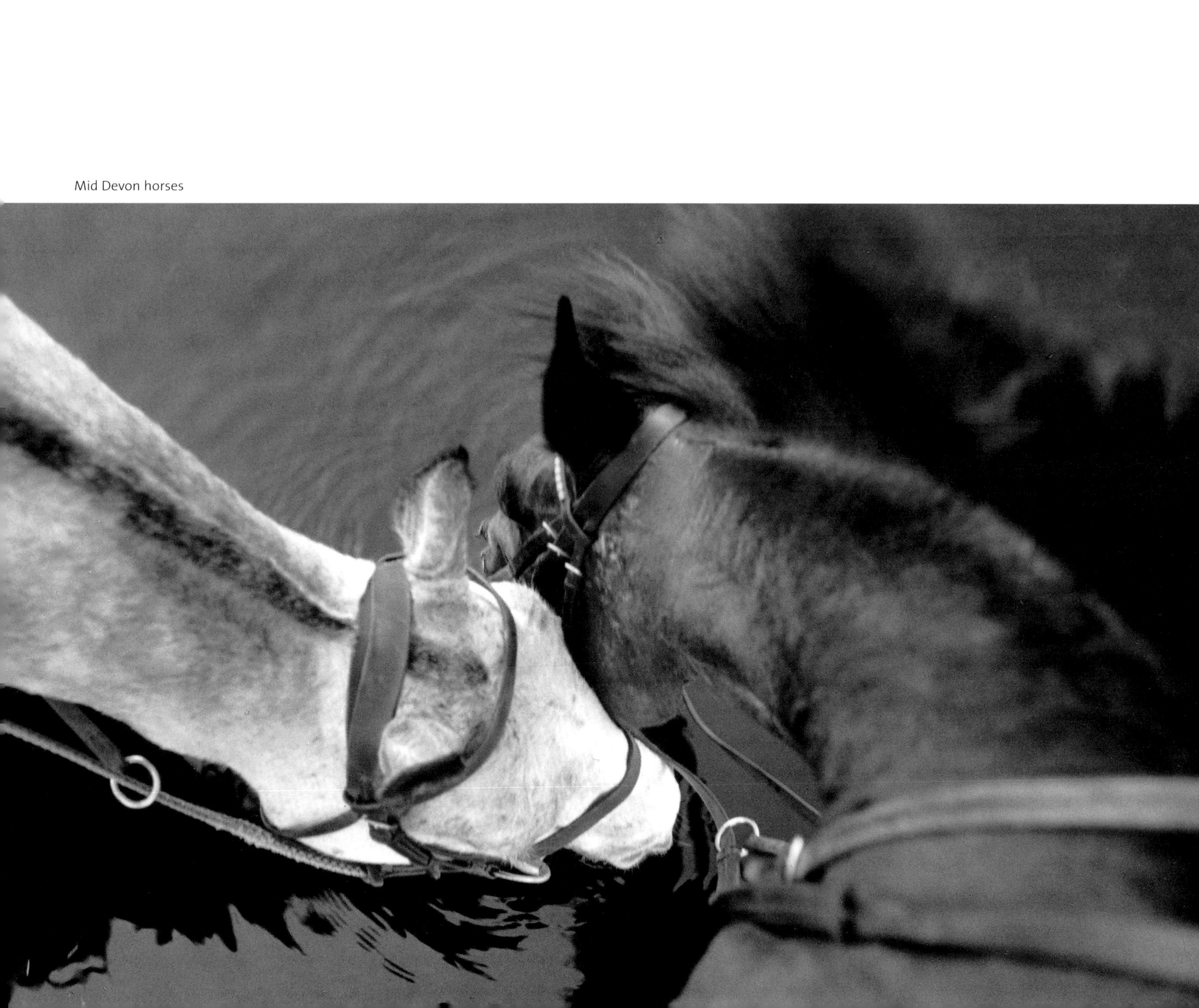

The mounted field of the Buccleuch in the snow

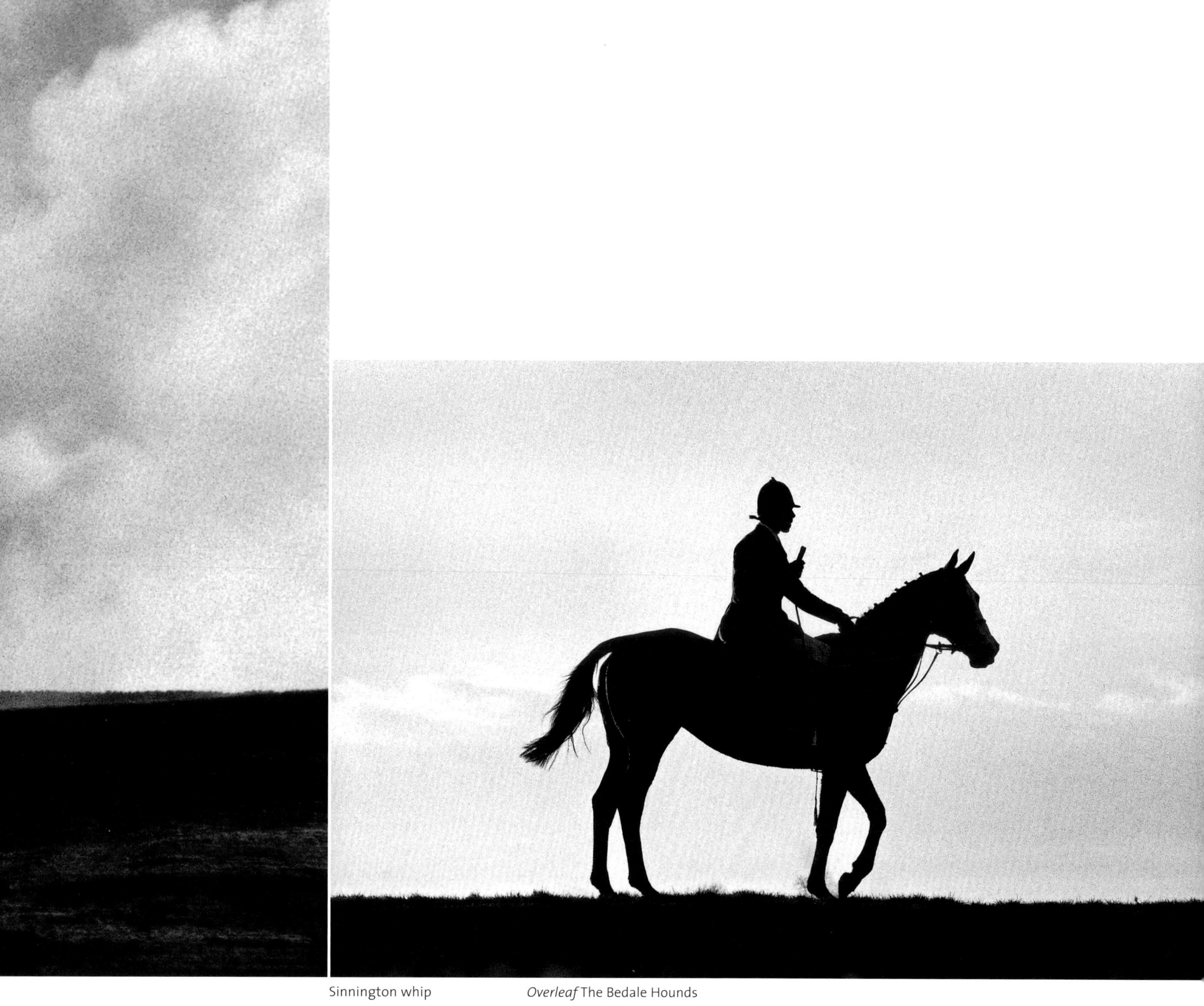

Sinnington whip　　　*Overleaf* The Bedale Hounds

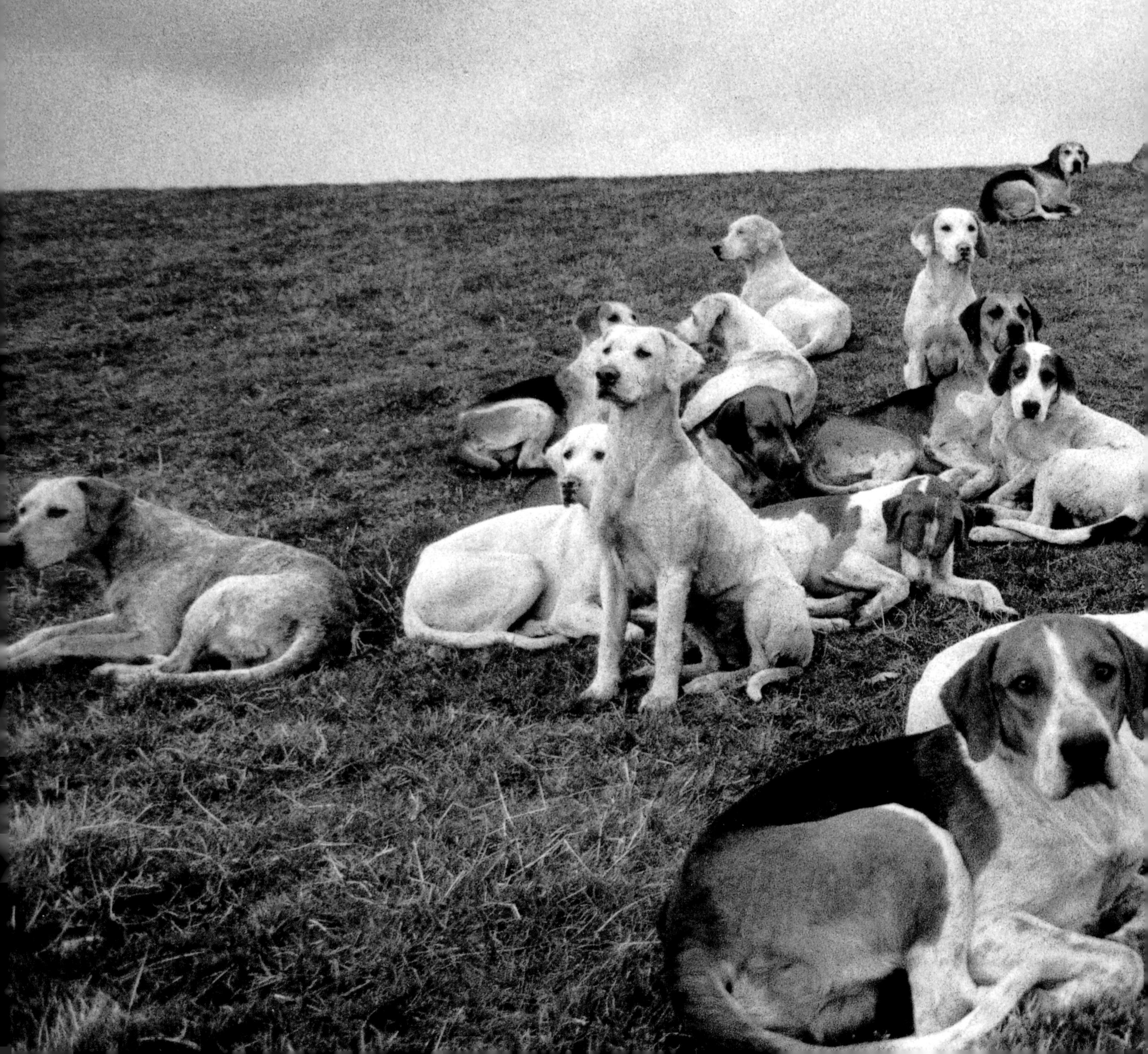

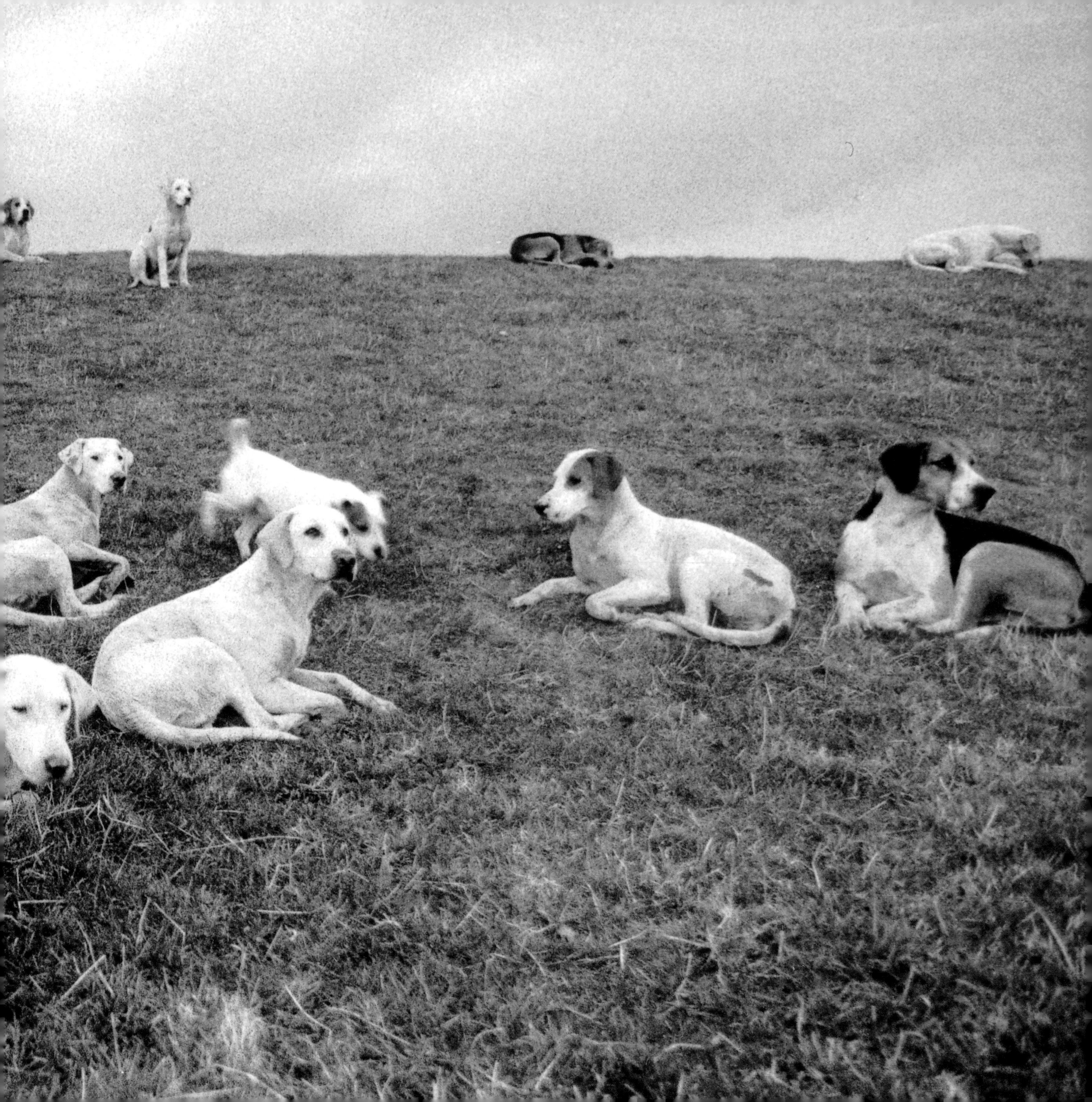

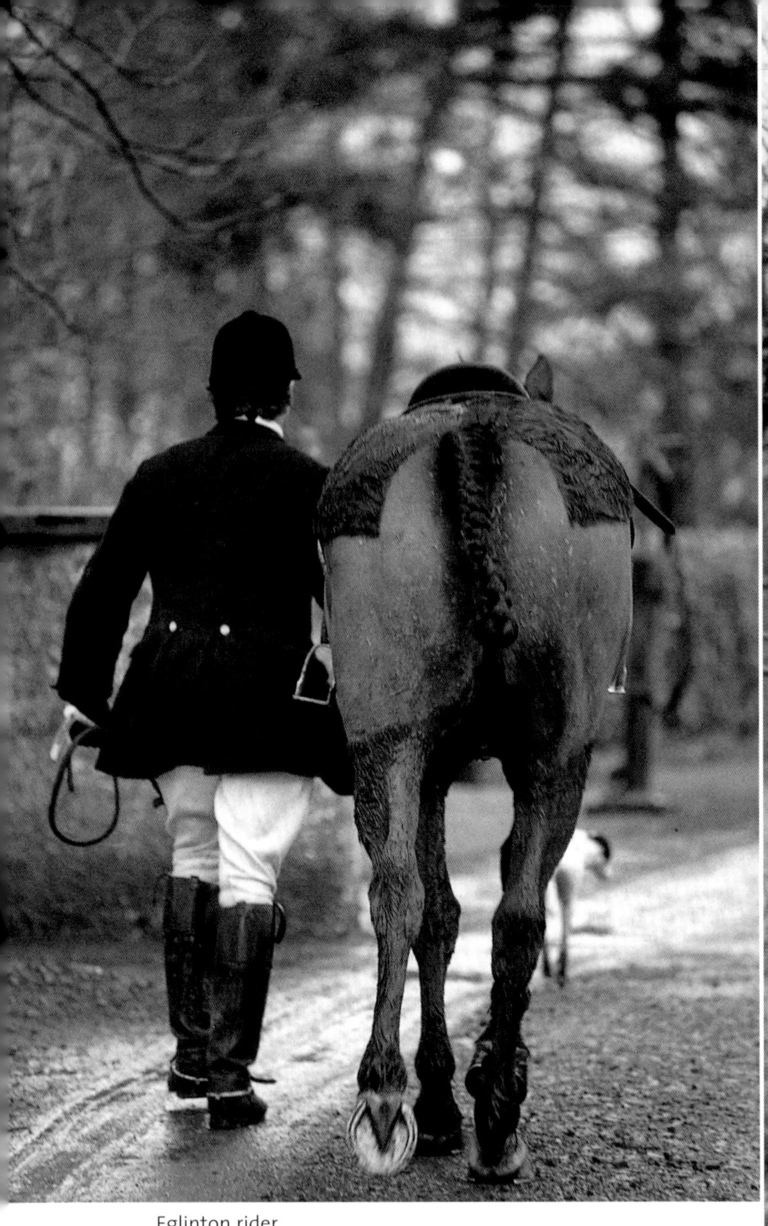

Eglinton rider

Martin Letts, master and ex-huntsman of the College Valley
with his kennel huntsman, Andrew Proe

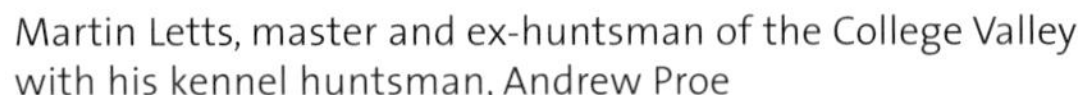

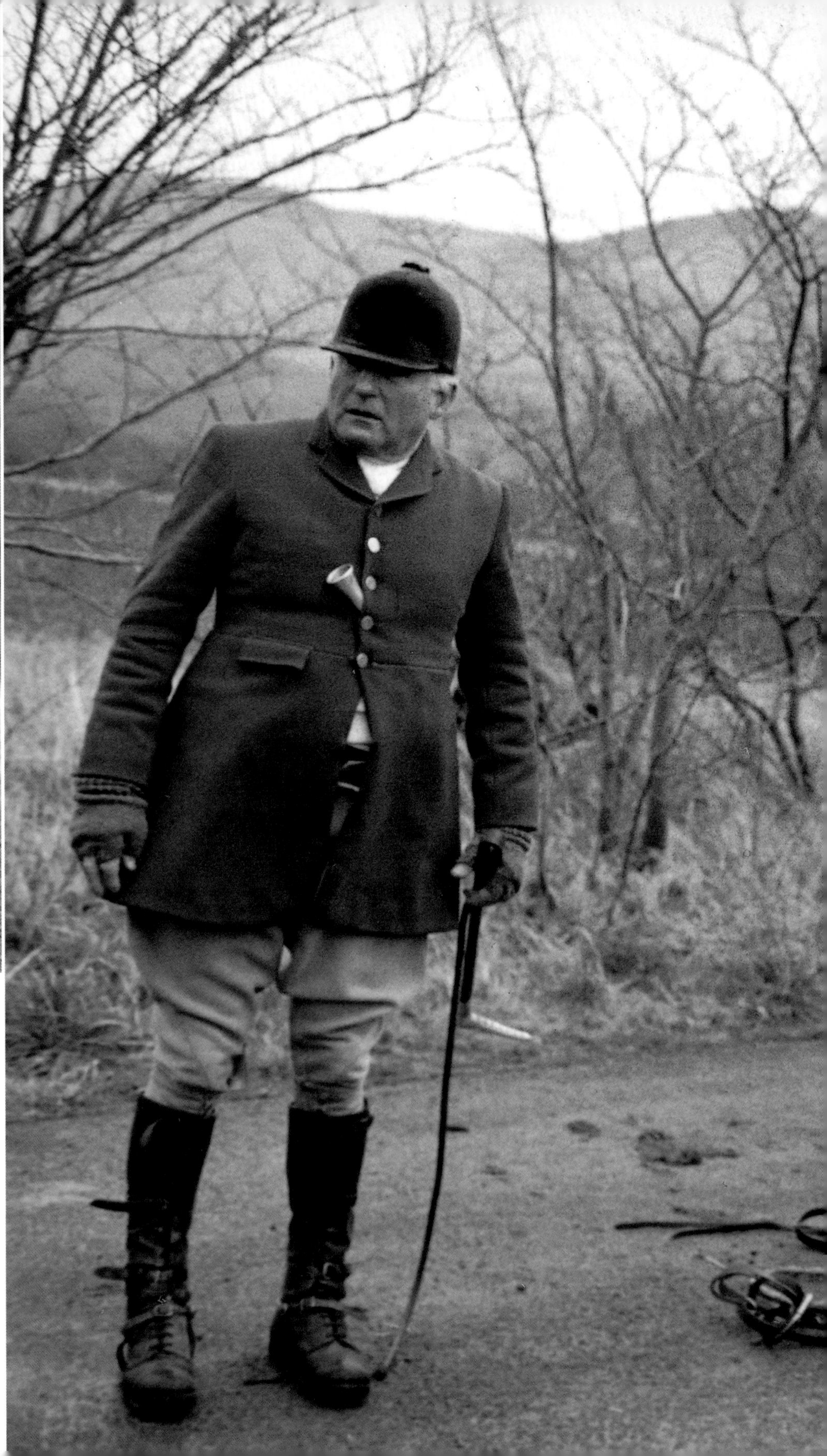

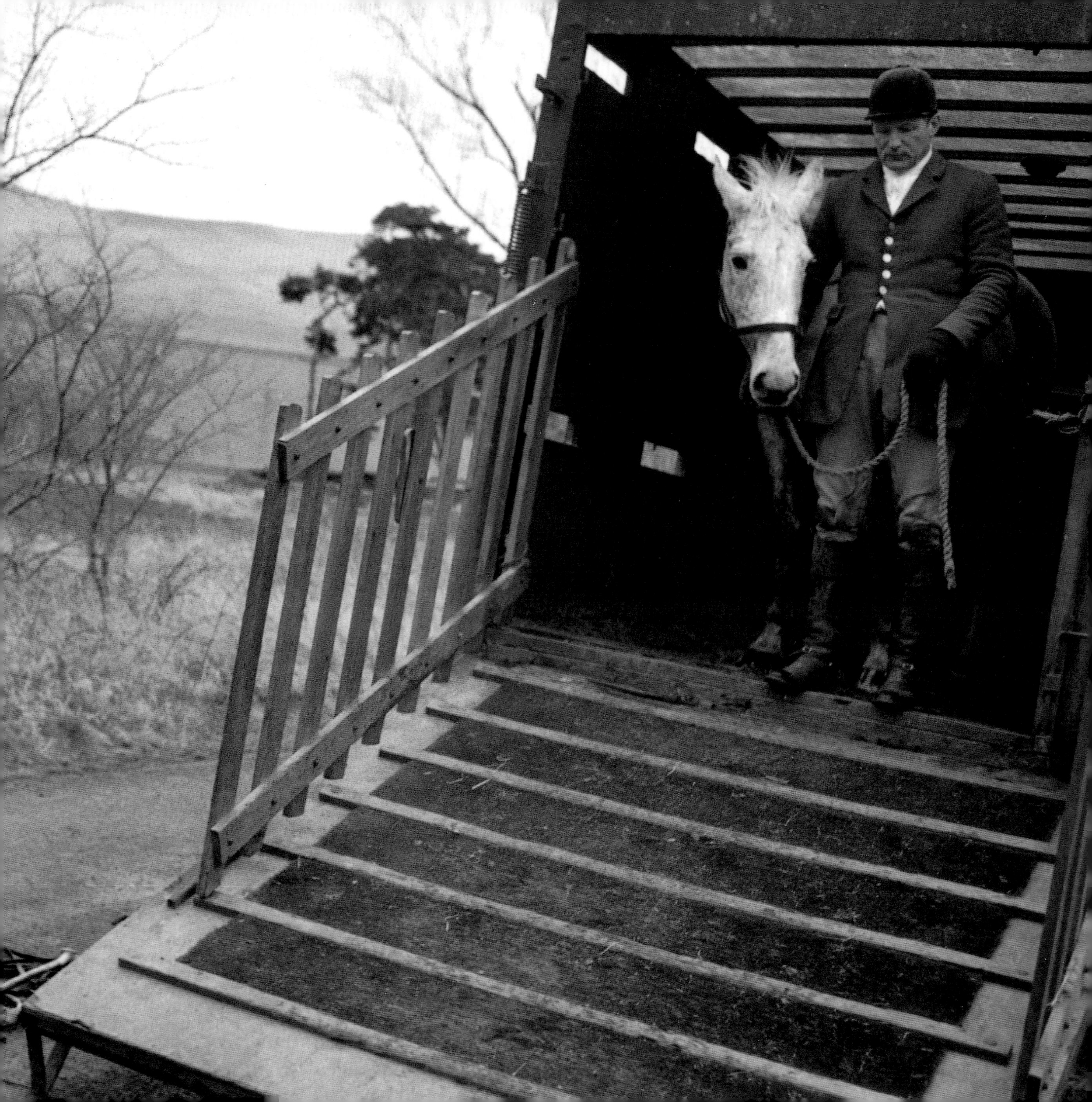

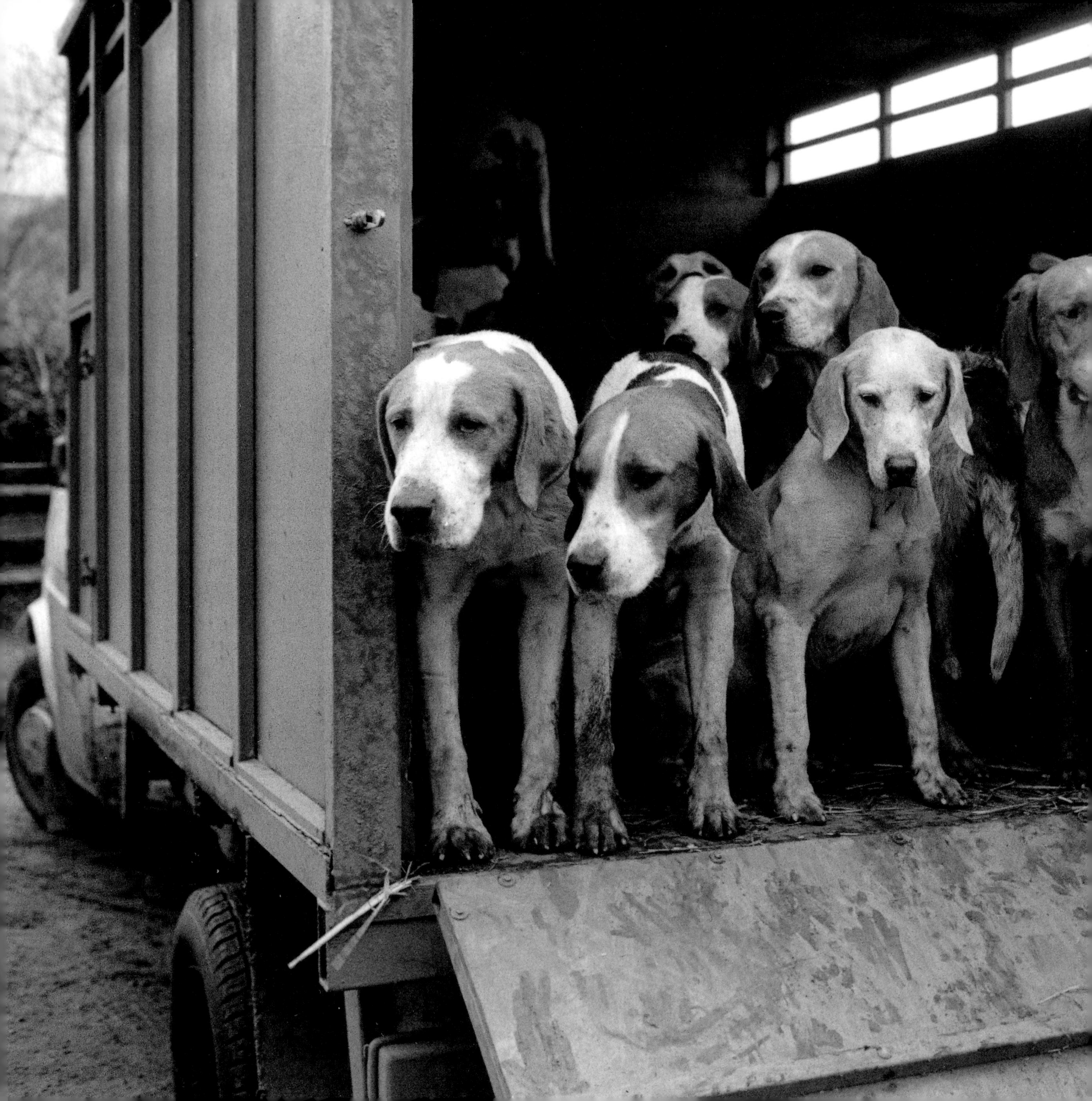

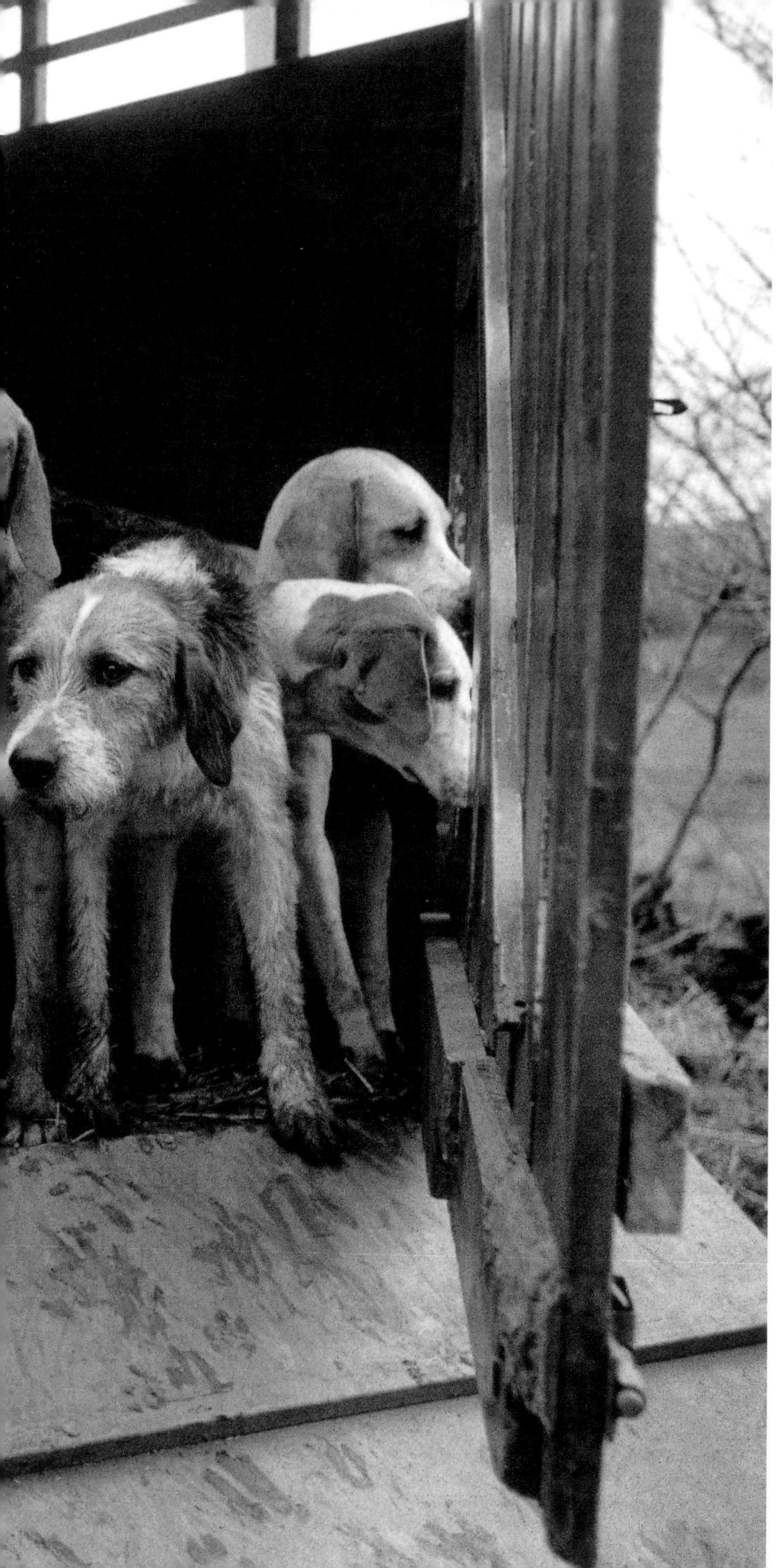

The College Valley hounds waiting to go home

Overleaf
The Blackmore and Sparkford Vale stables

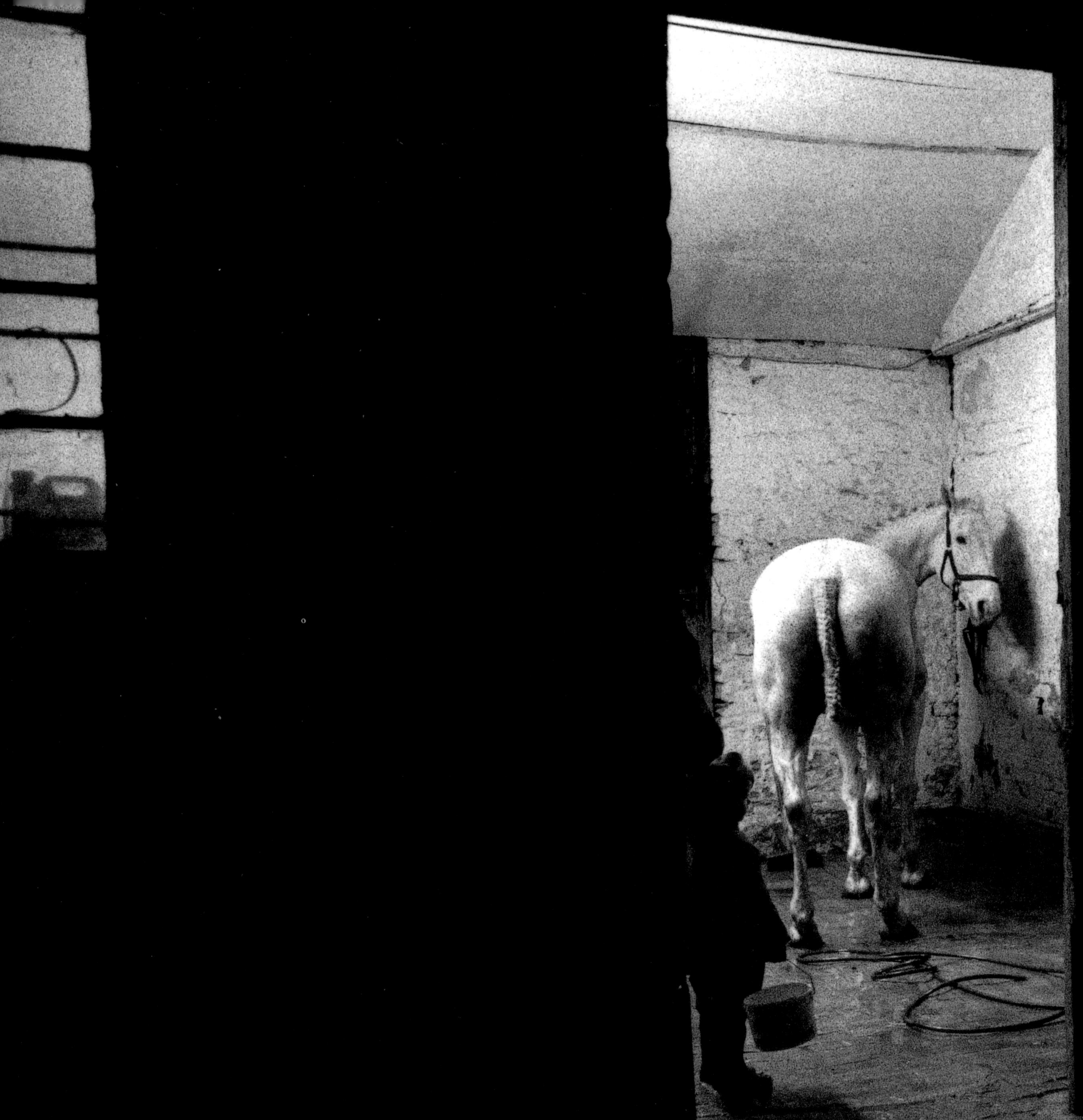

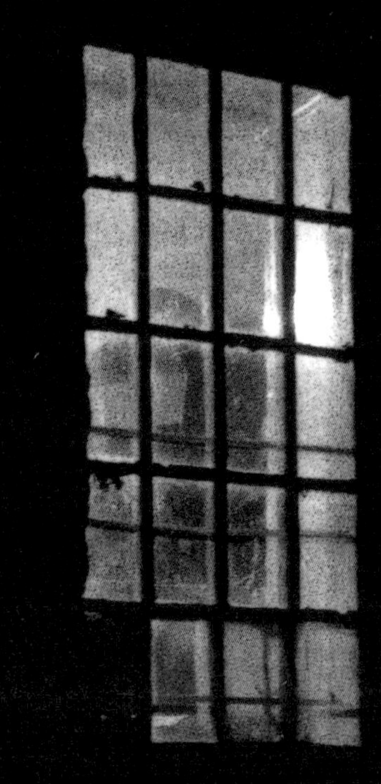
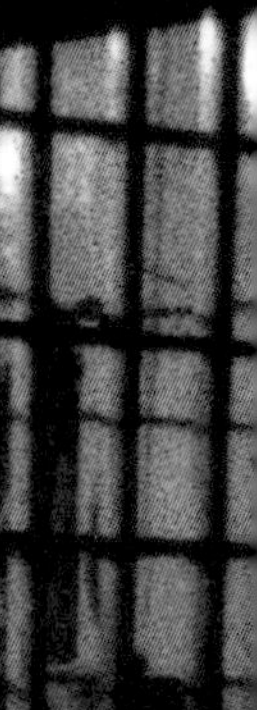

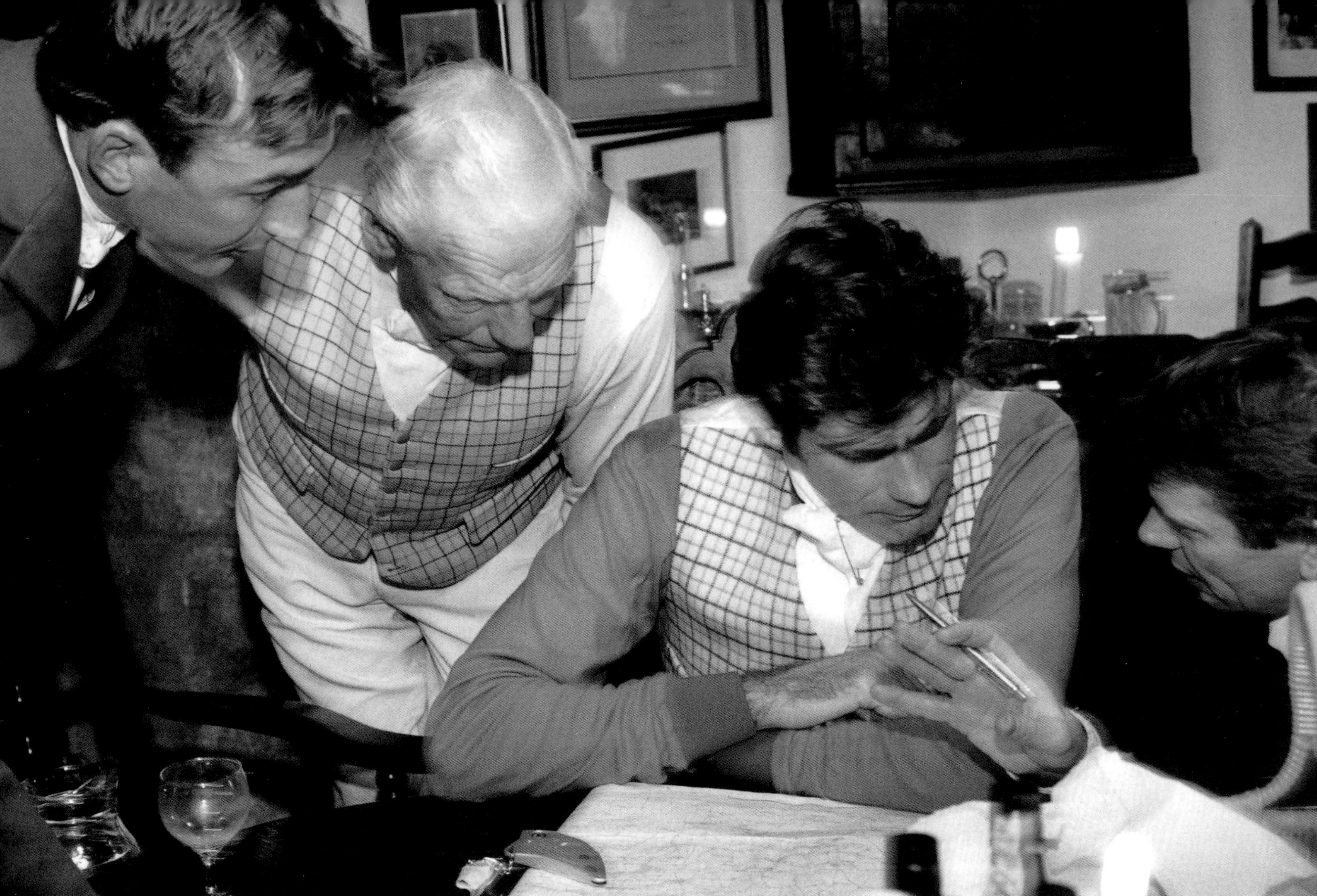

Members of the Tiverton Hunt consult the map

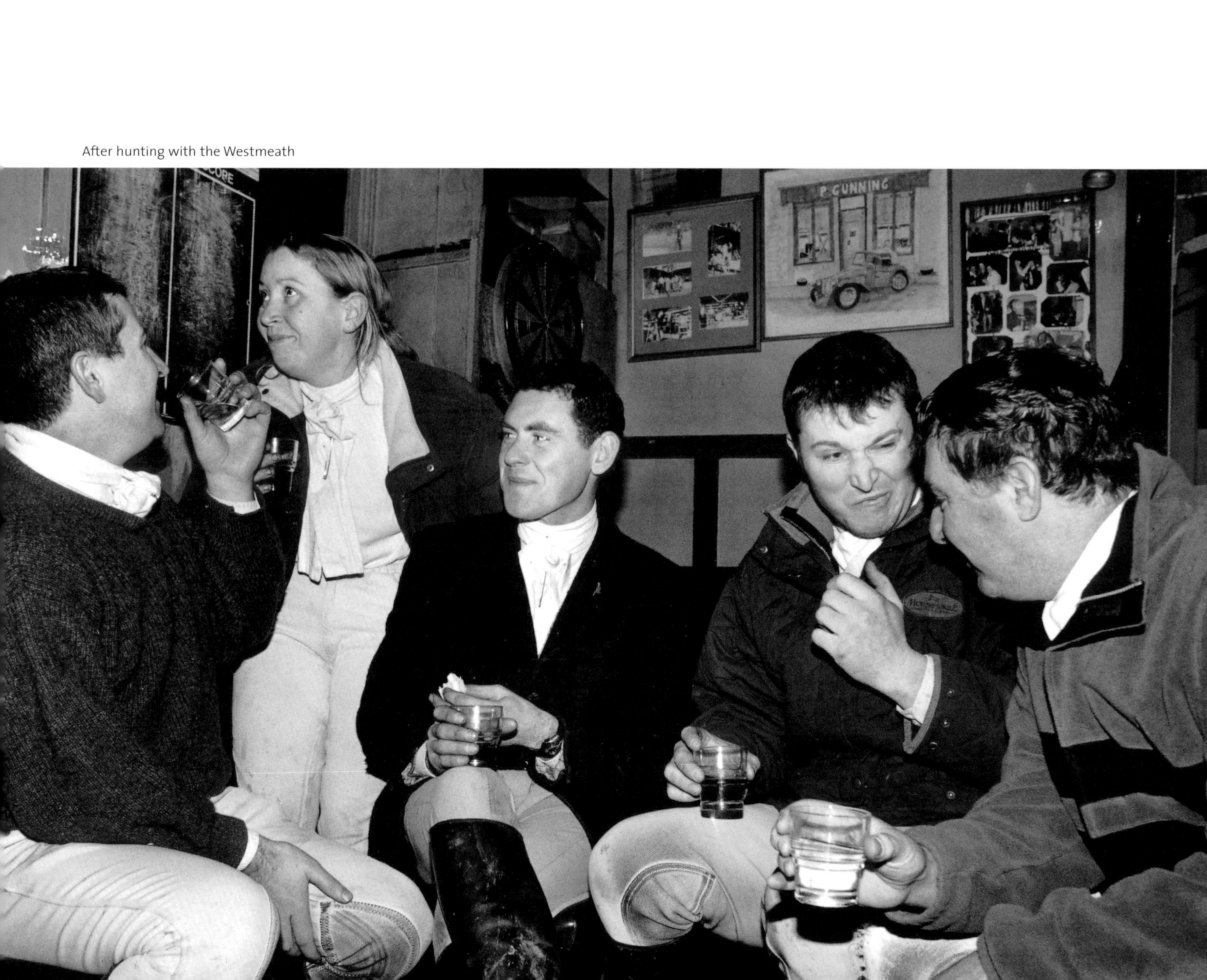

After hunting with the Westmeath

Buccleuch hunt tea

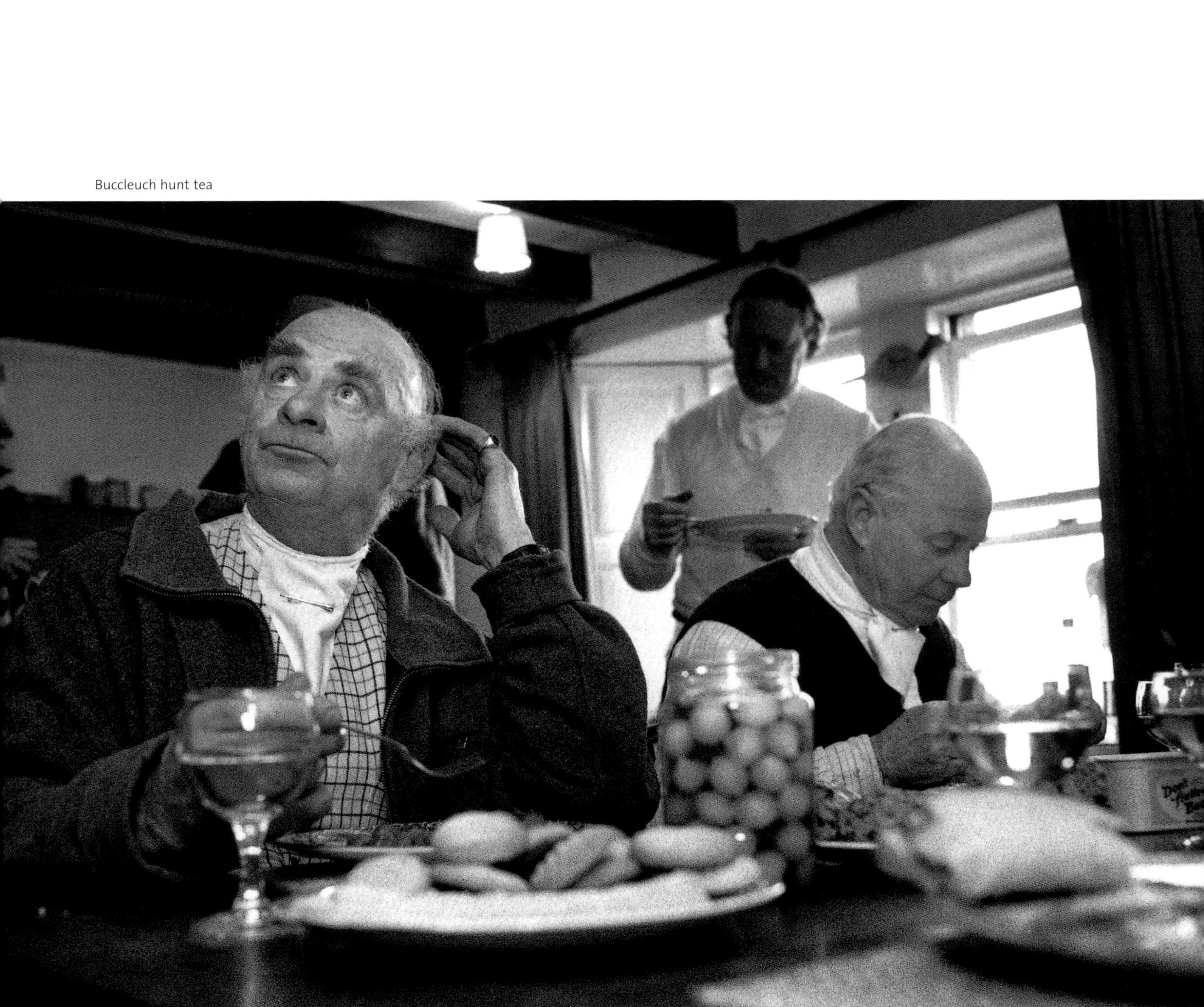

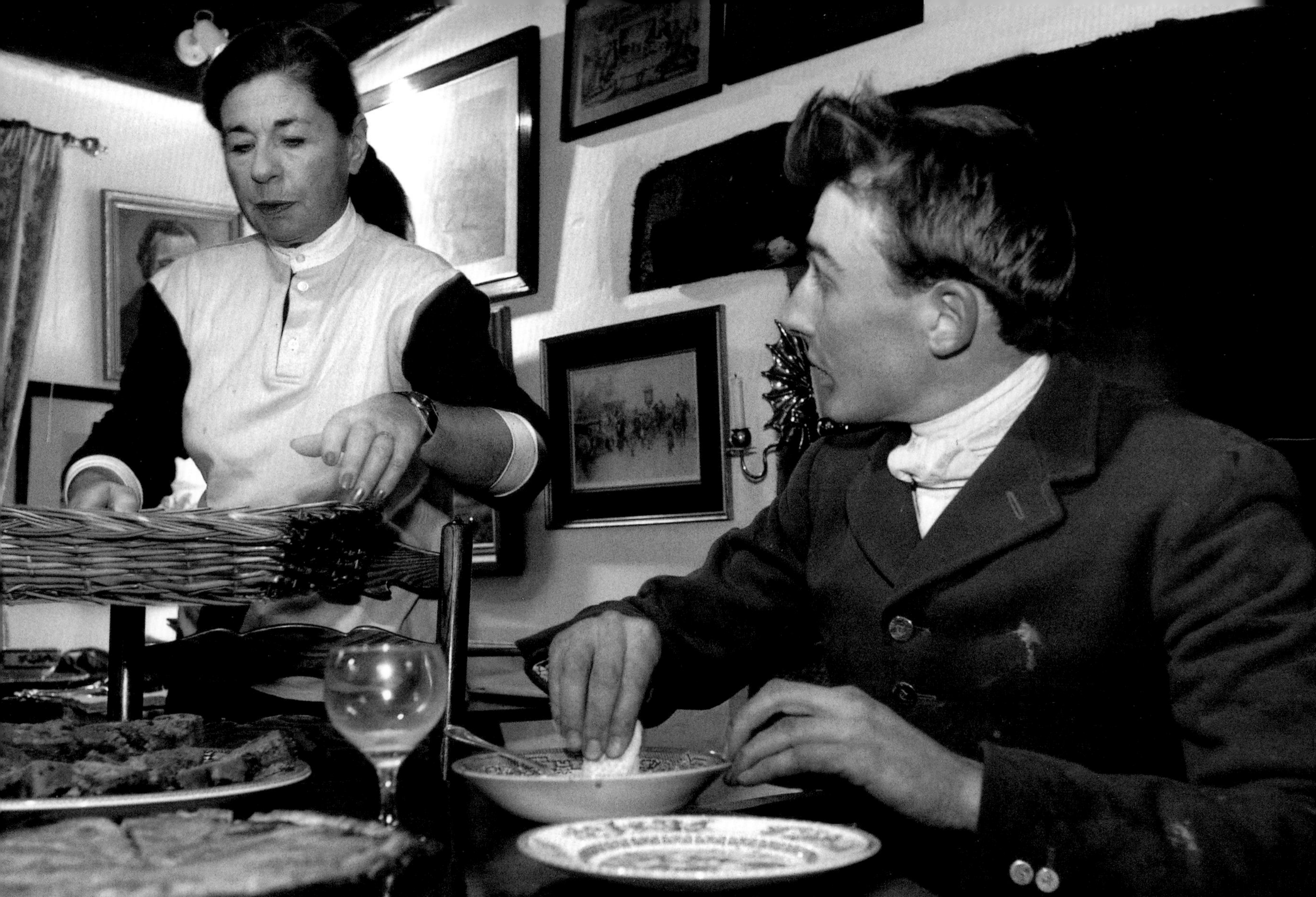

Tiverton hunt tea

The Portraits

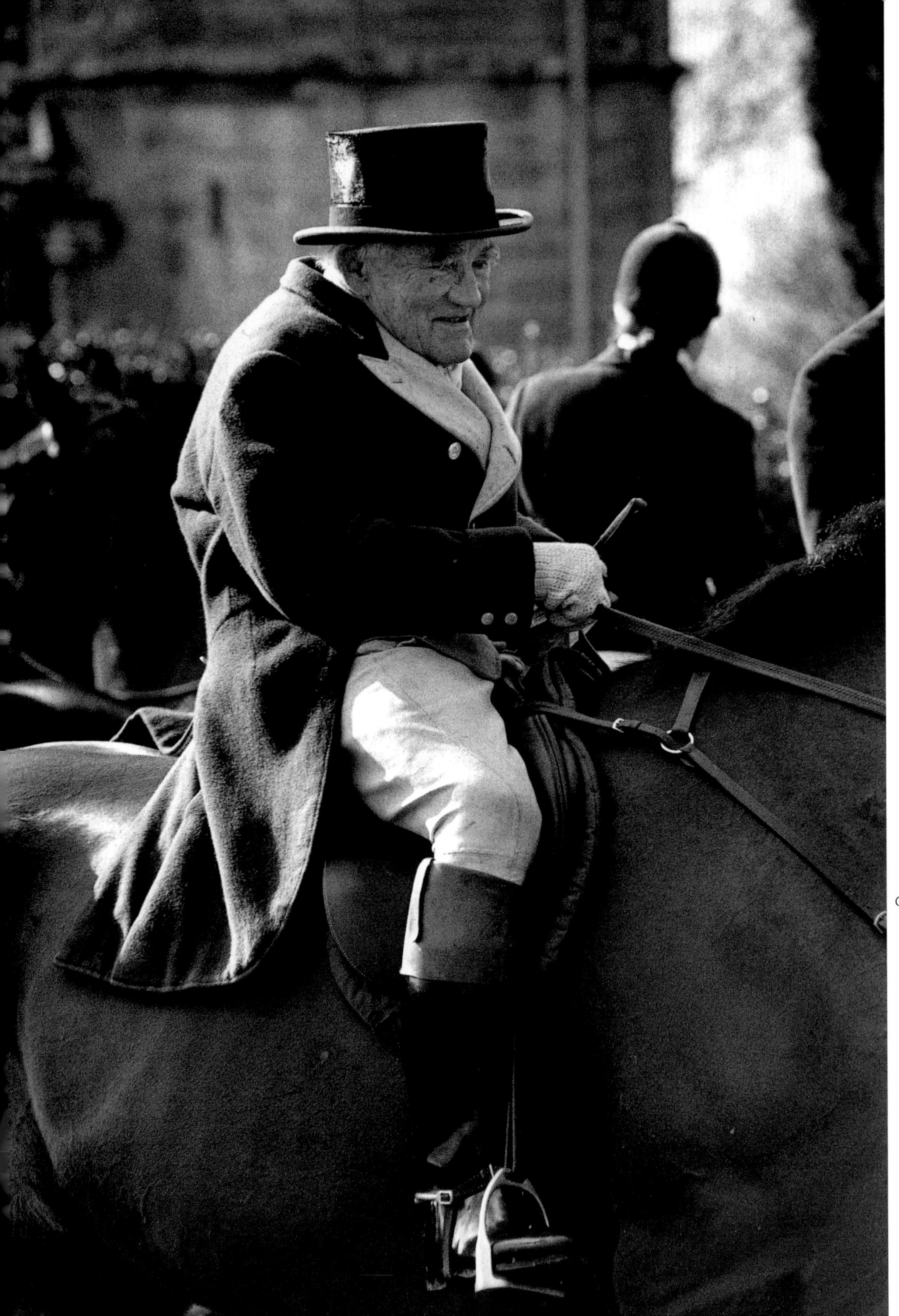

George Saloschin, Beaufort

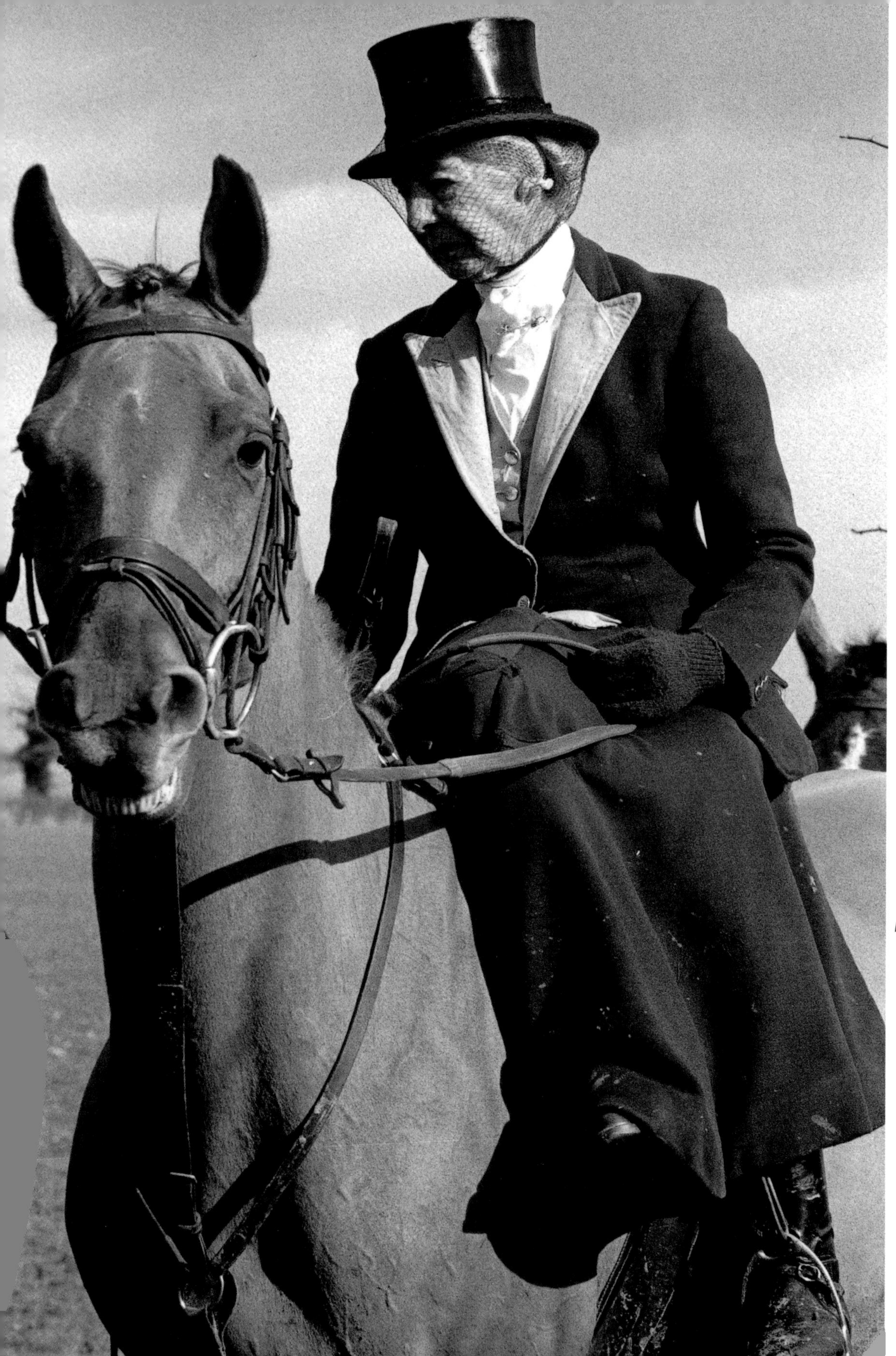

Mrs Elizabeth Pope, Beaufort

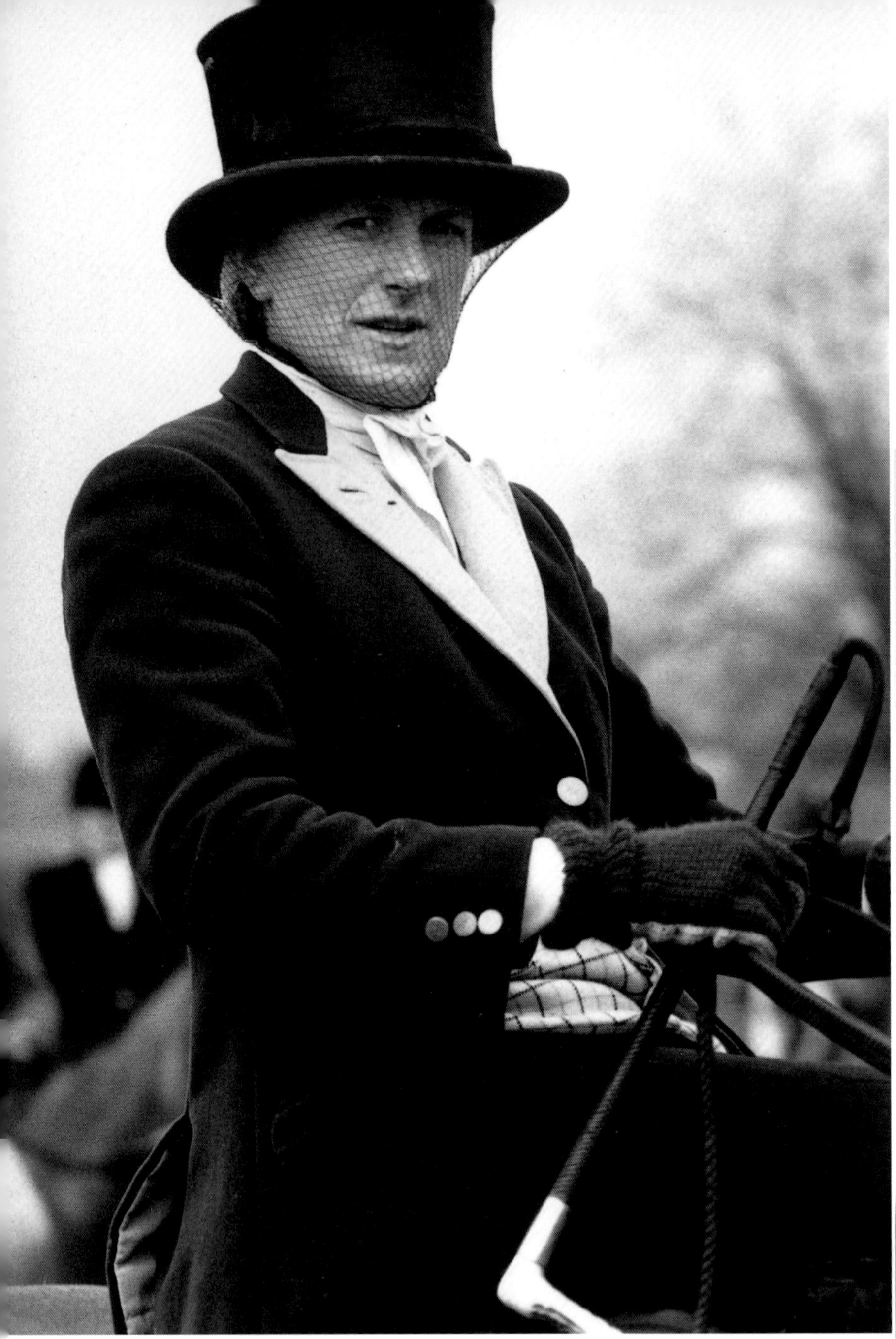

Jonny Sumption, Tiverton

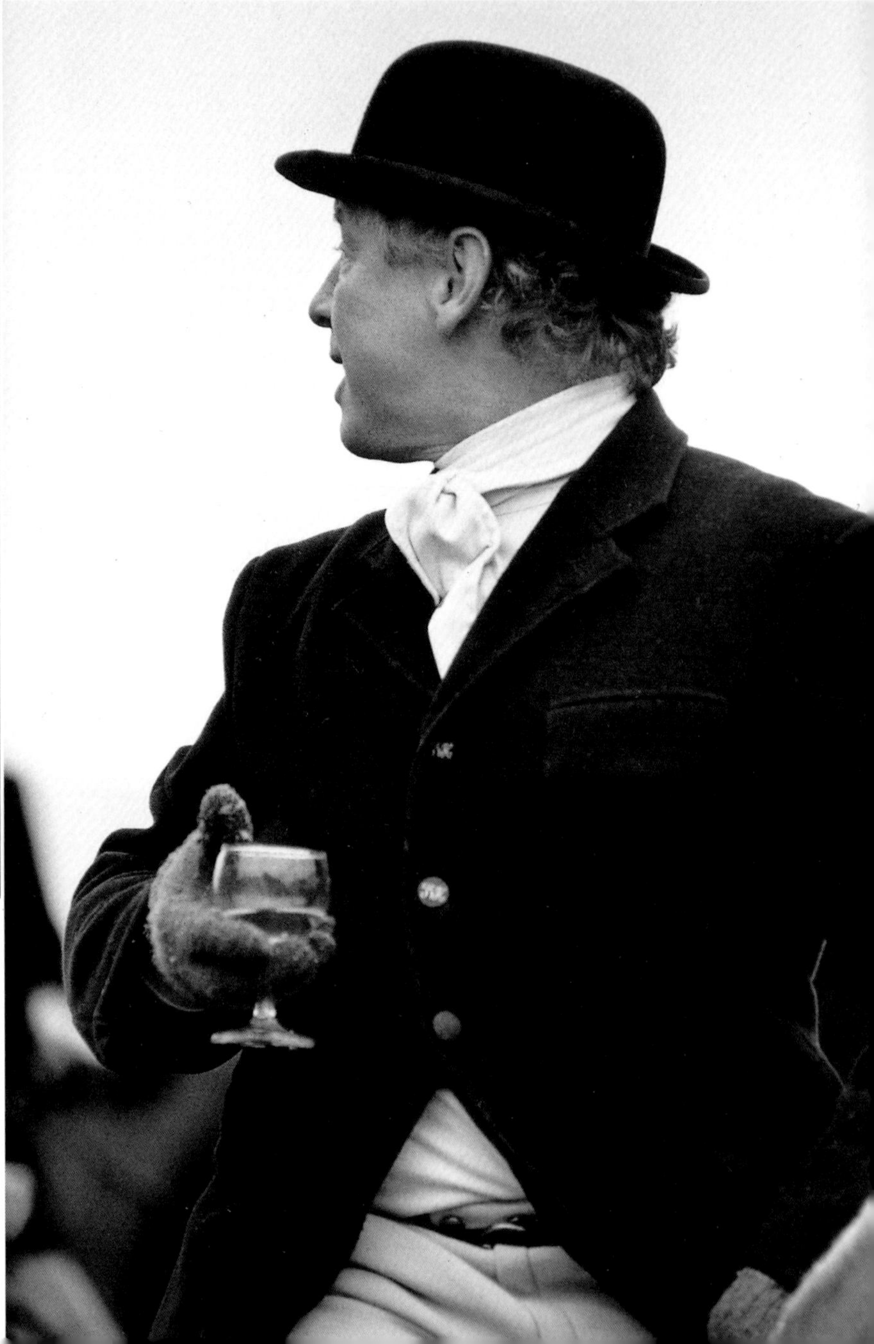

Carol Wilson, Beaufort

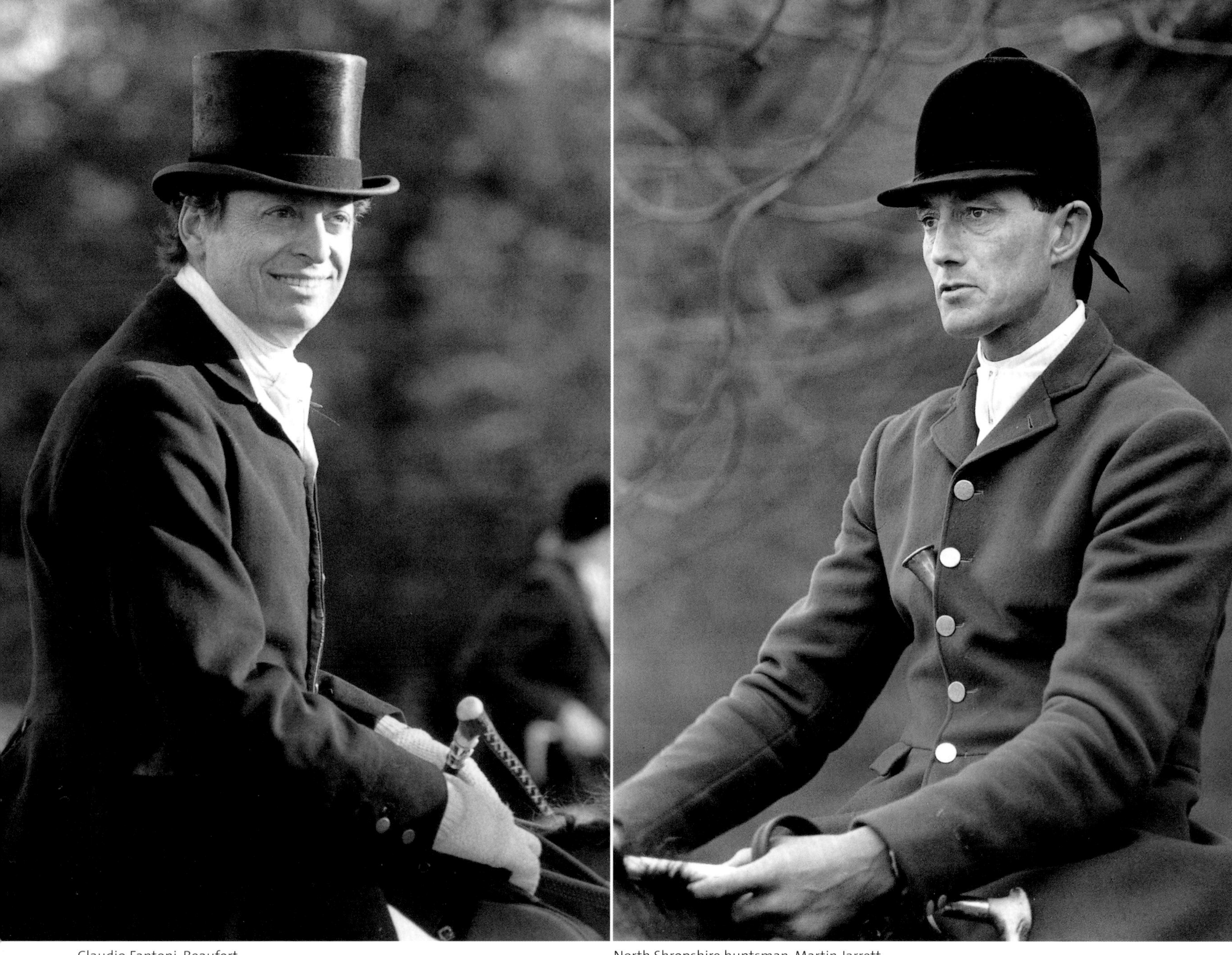

Claudio Fantoni, Beaufort

North Shropshire huntsman, Martin Jarrett

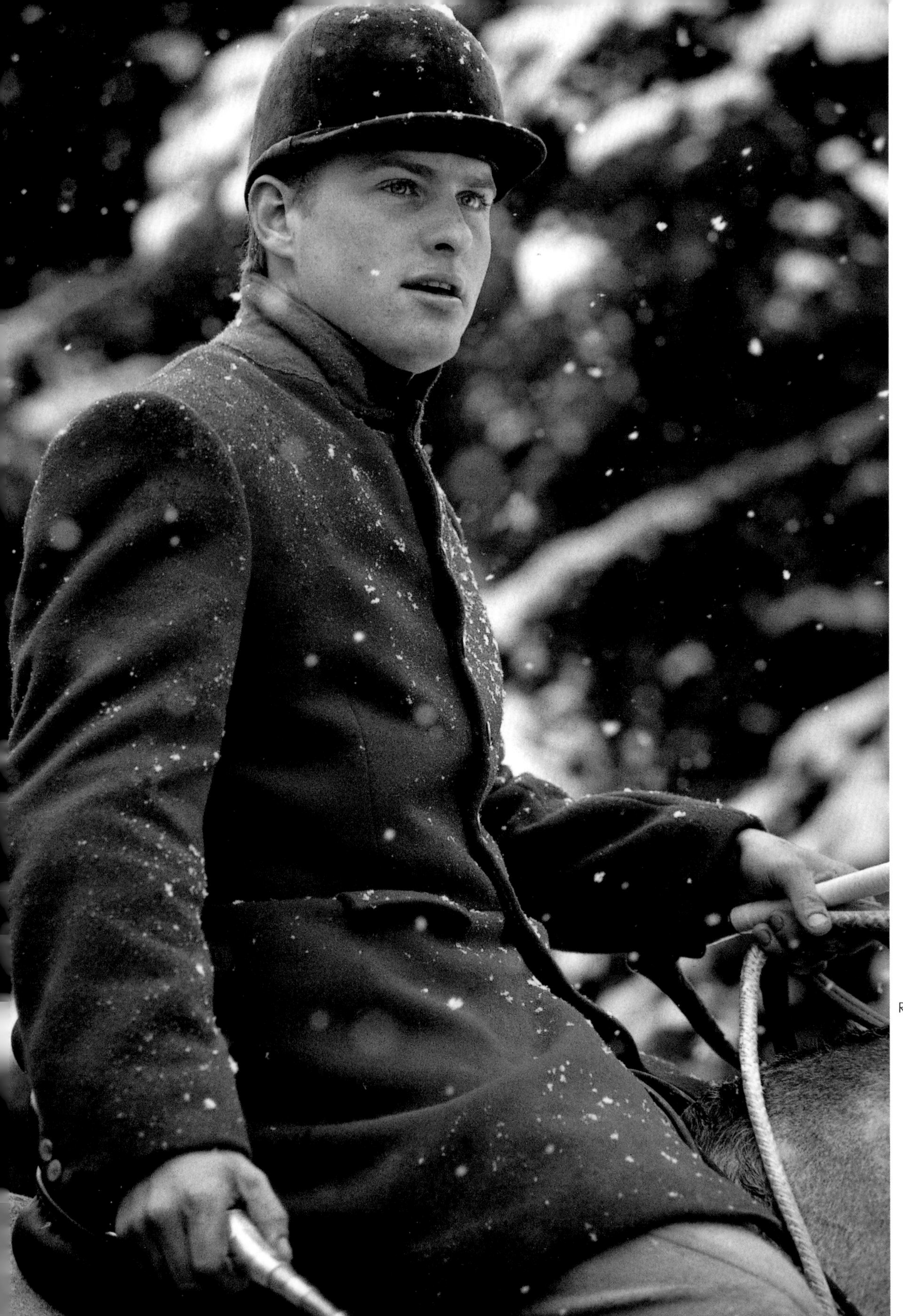

Rory Innes, ex huntsman of the Jedforest

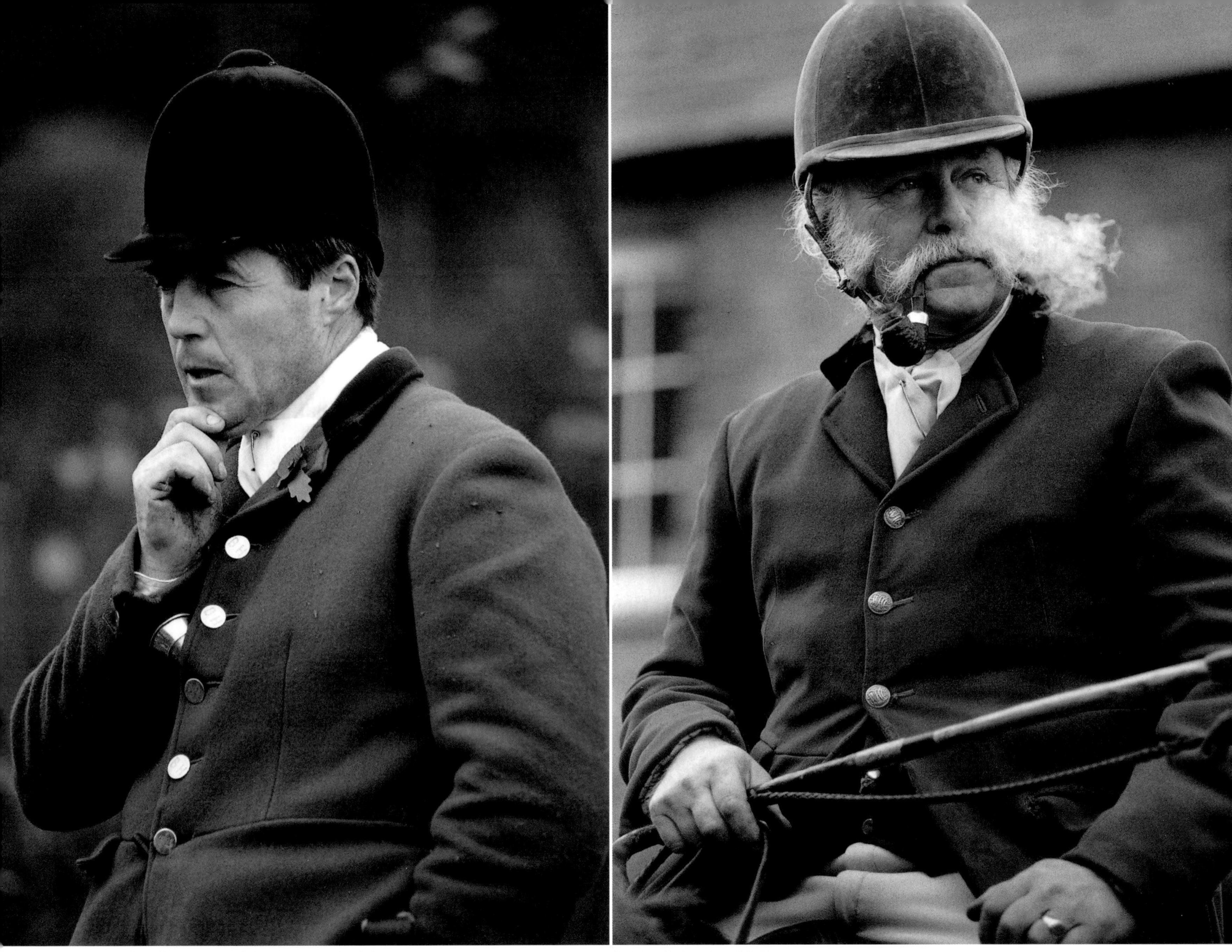

Ian Hawkins, huntsman of the Brecon and Talybont

Dr John Perks, Warwickshire

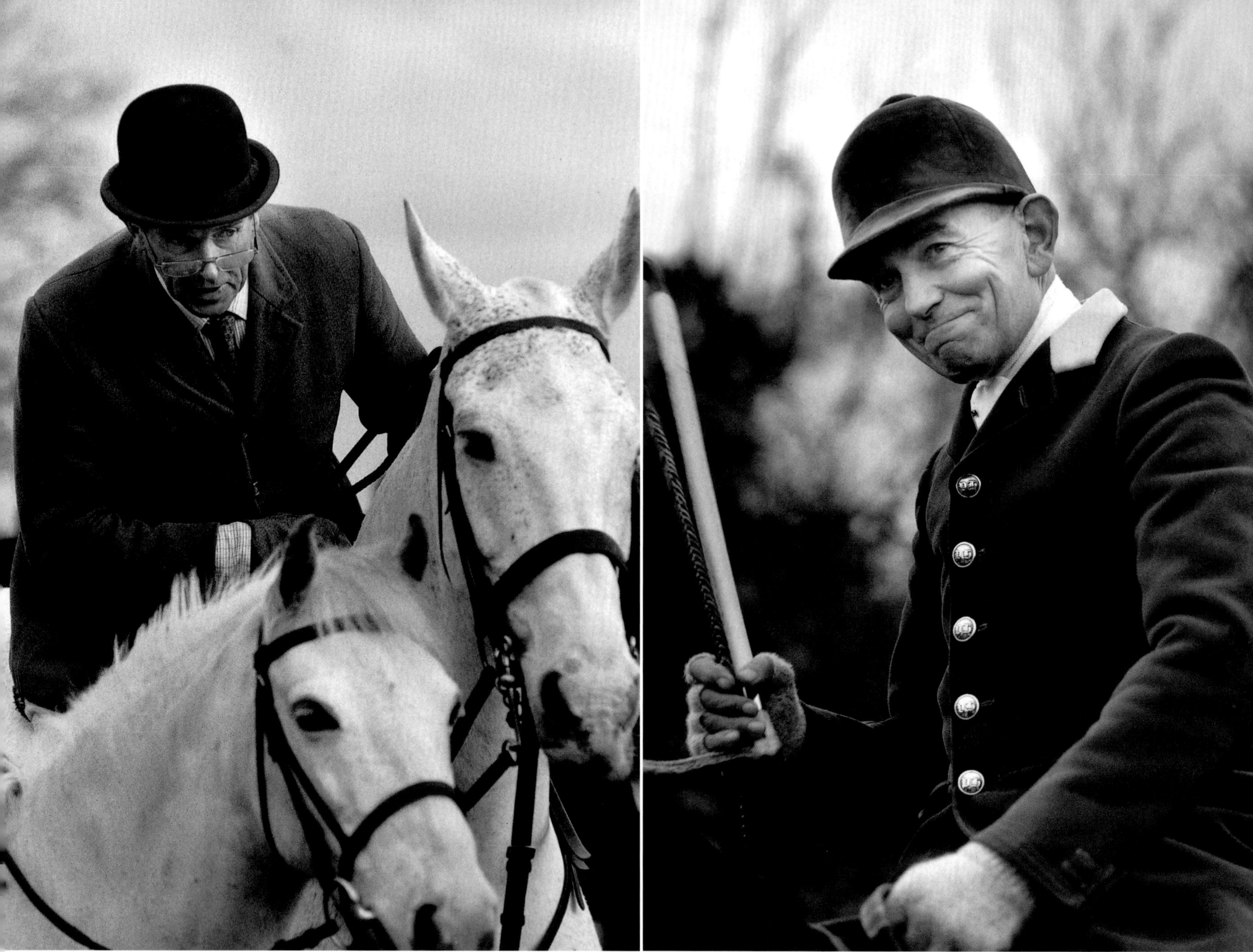

Robin Abel Smith, Quorn

Colin Stephenson, amateur whip of the Pytchley

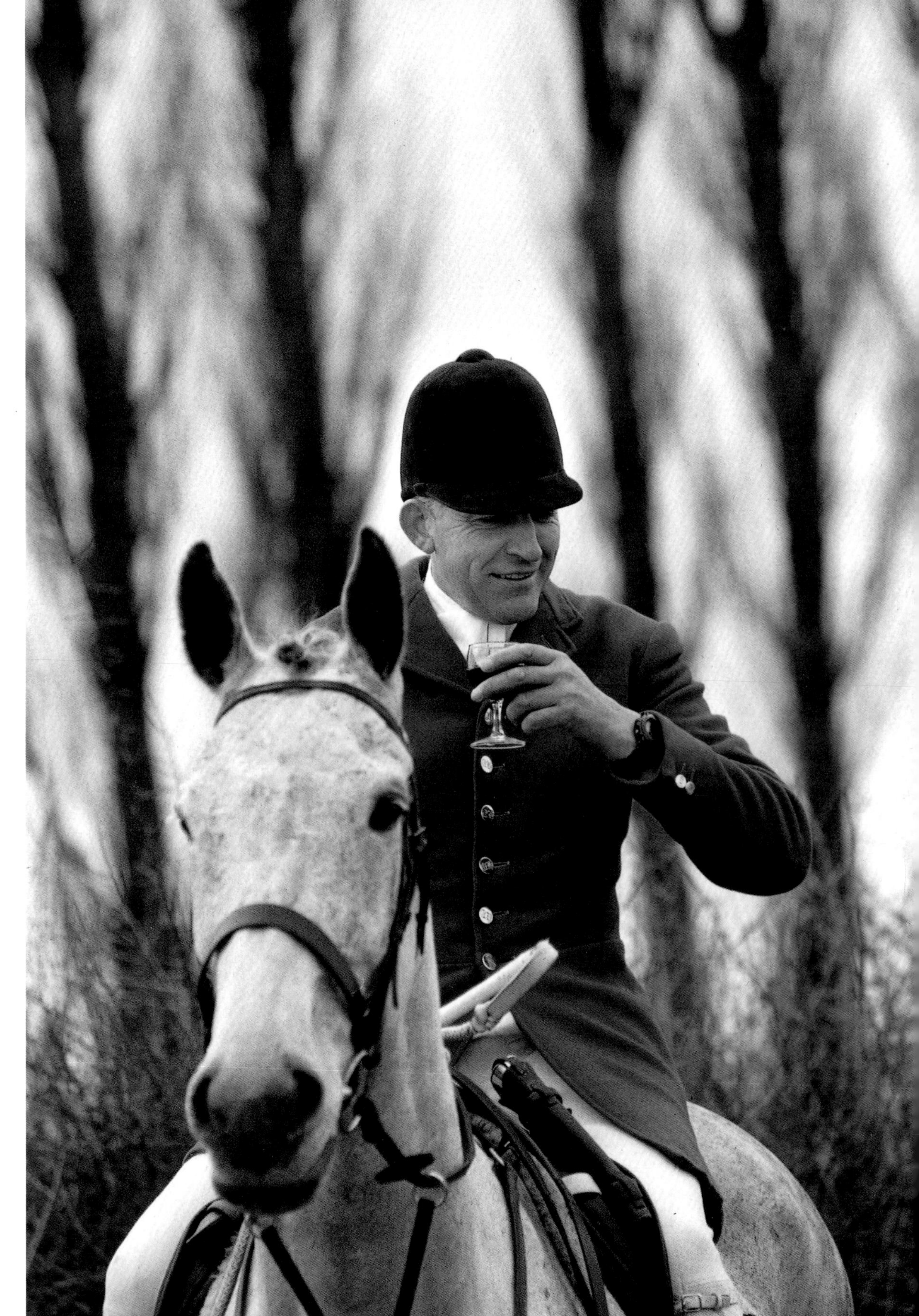

Quorn huntsman, Peter Collins

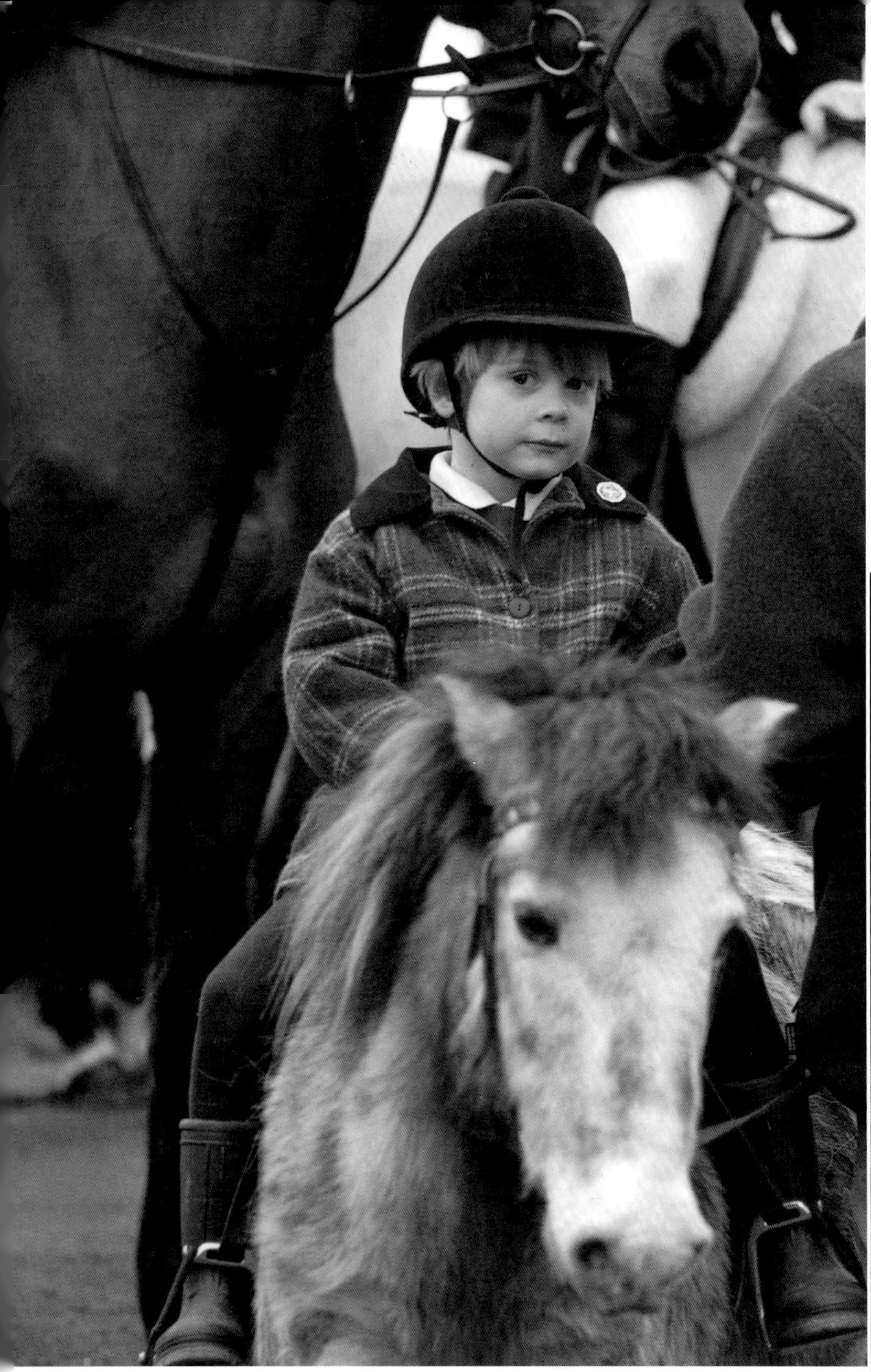

Hamish, Dumfries

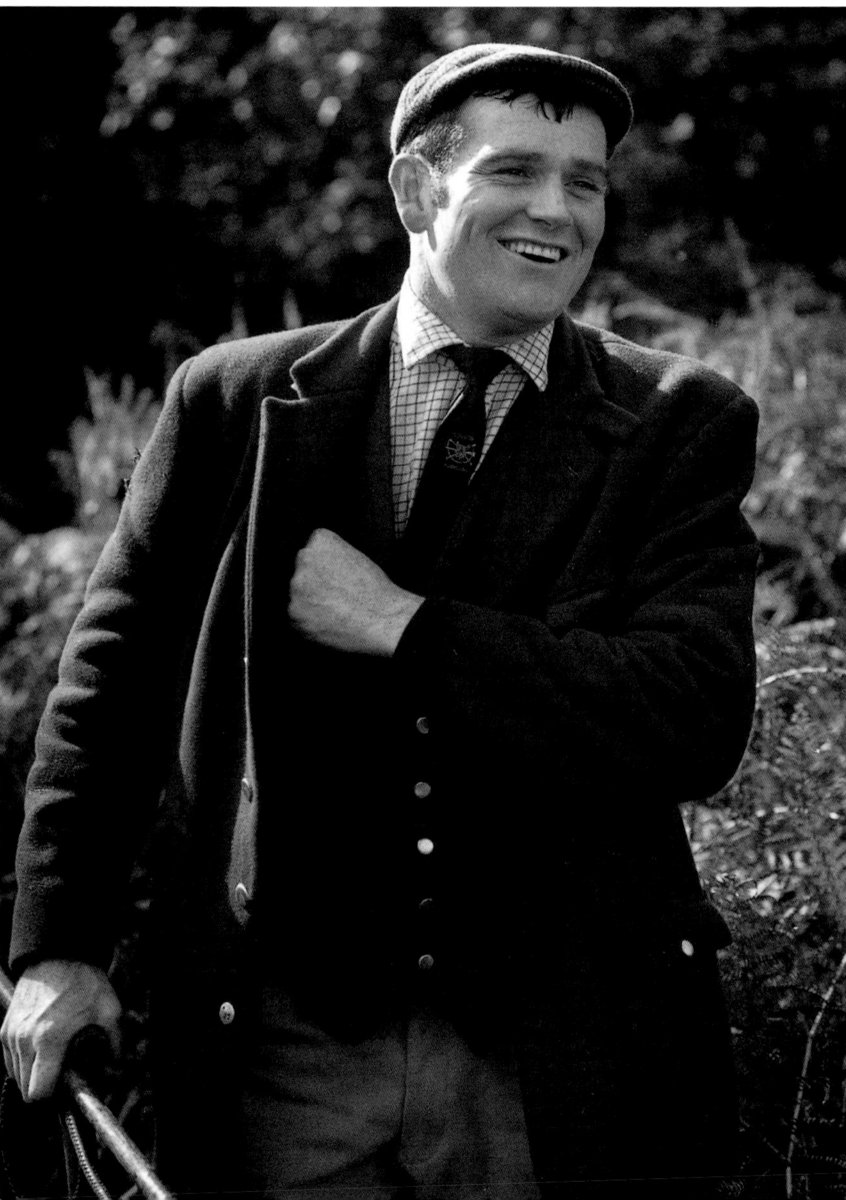

Mike Nicholson, Coniston huntsman

Rev Mulholland, Beaufort

Roger Dancer, Heythrop

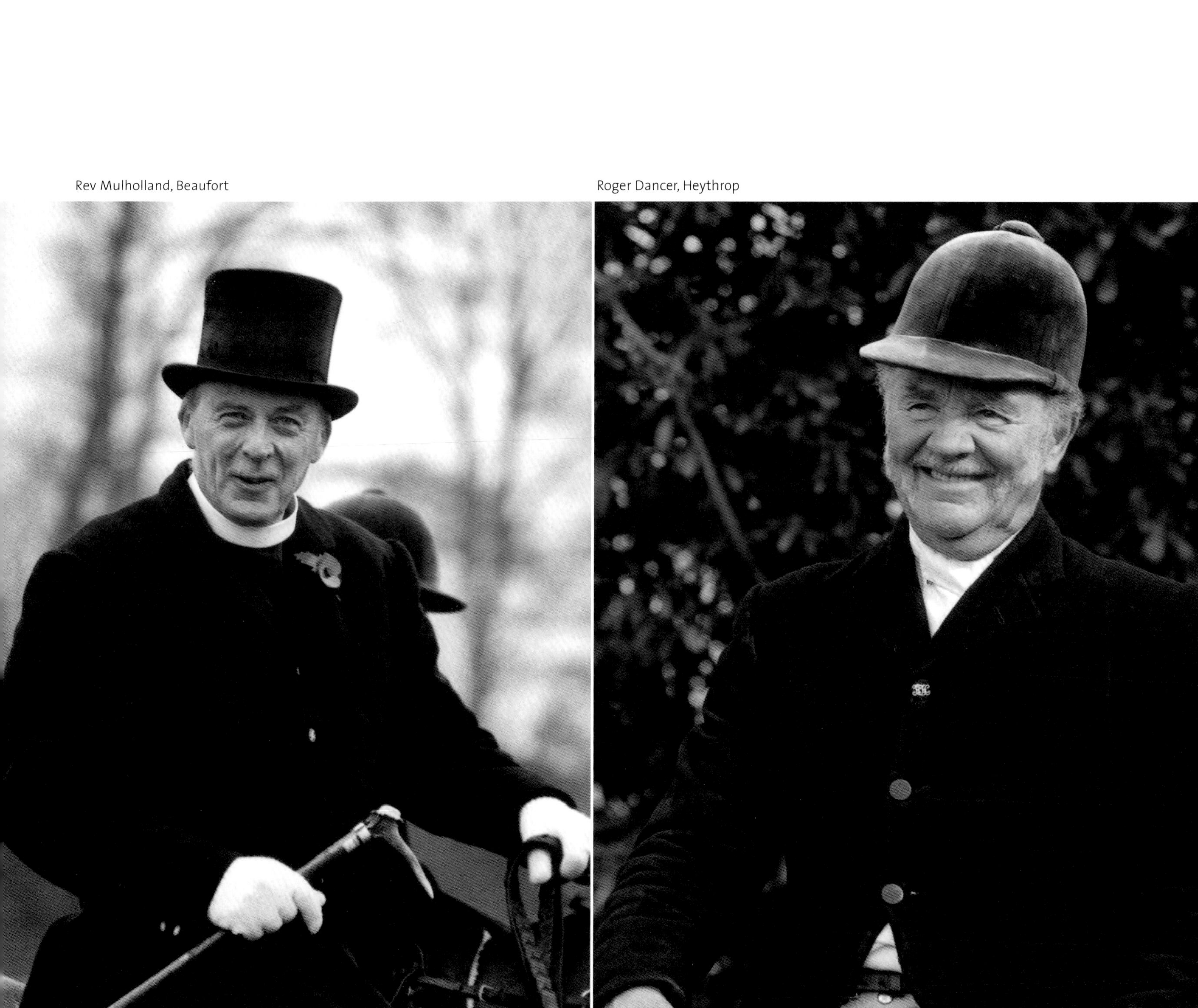

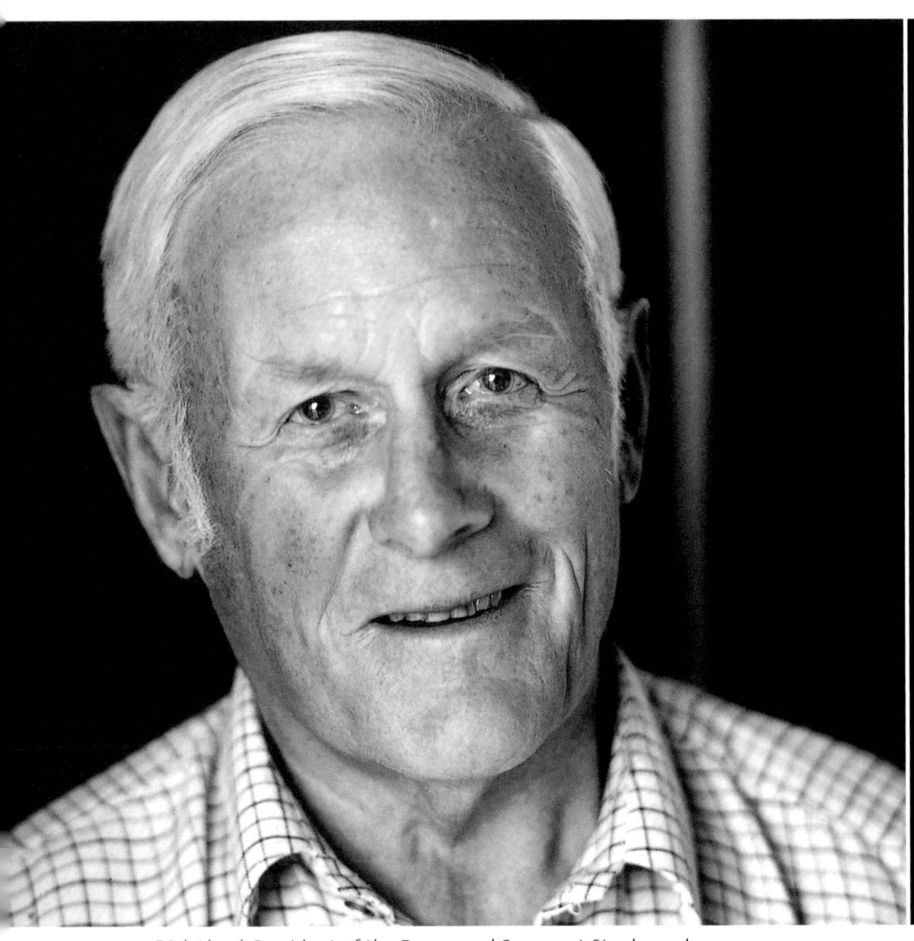

Dick Lloyd, President of the Devon and Somerset Staghounds

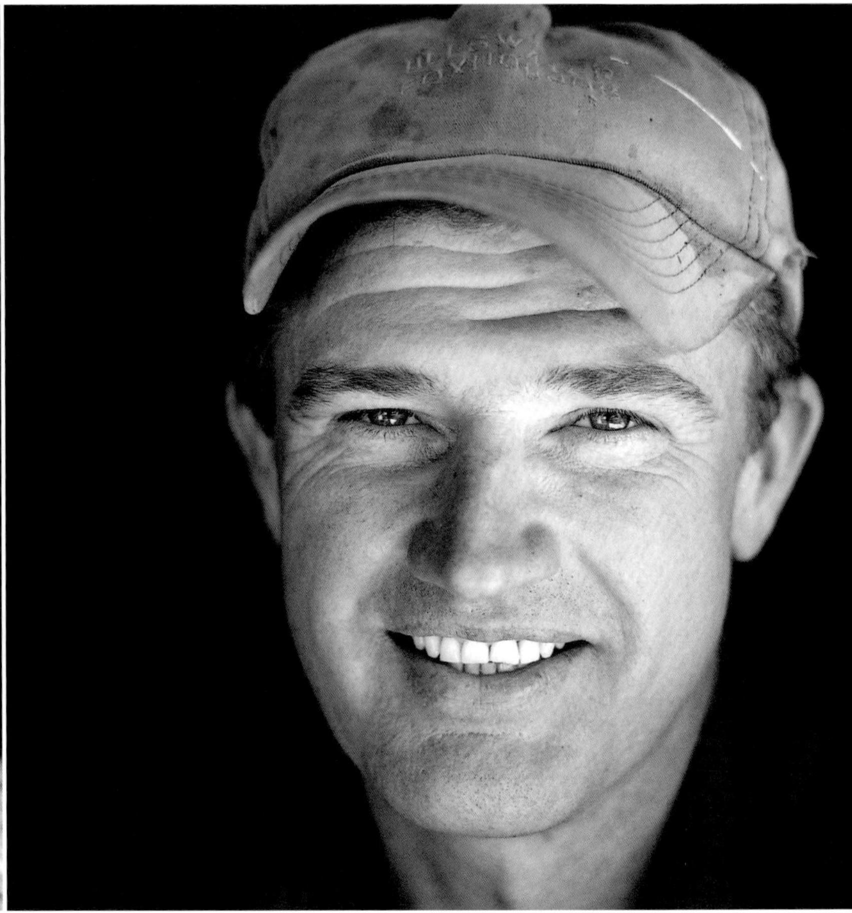

John Harrison, Ullswater huntsman

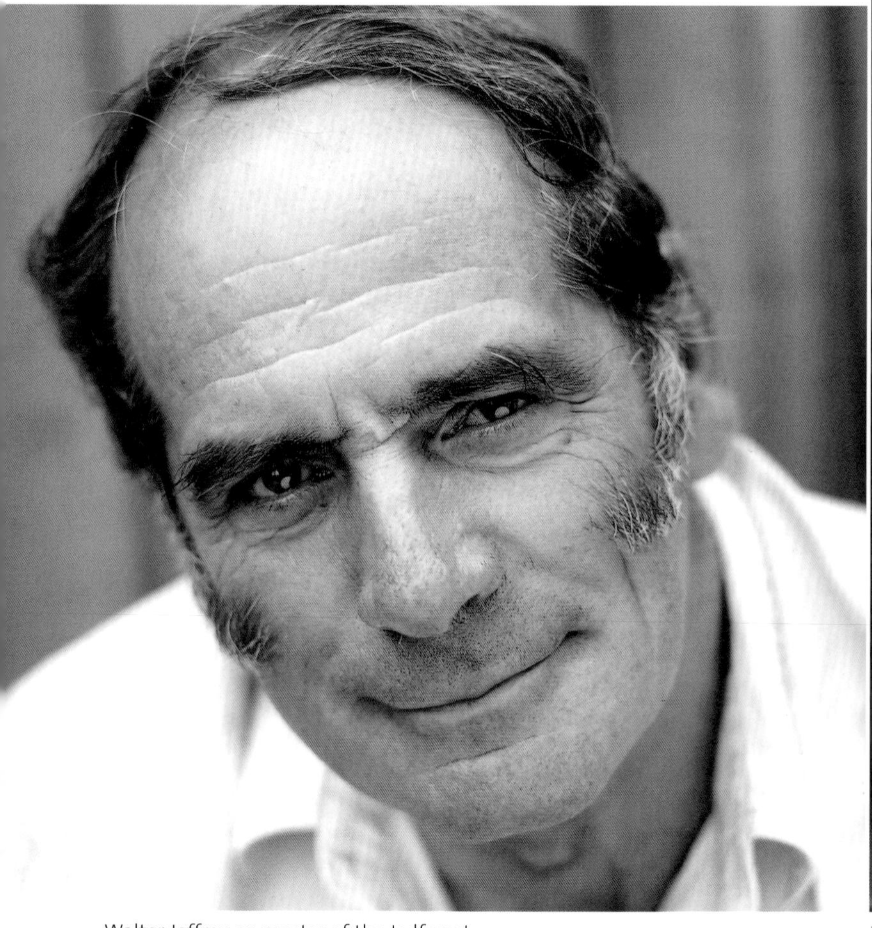

Walter Jeffrey, ex master of the Jedforest

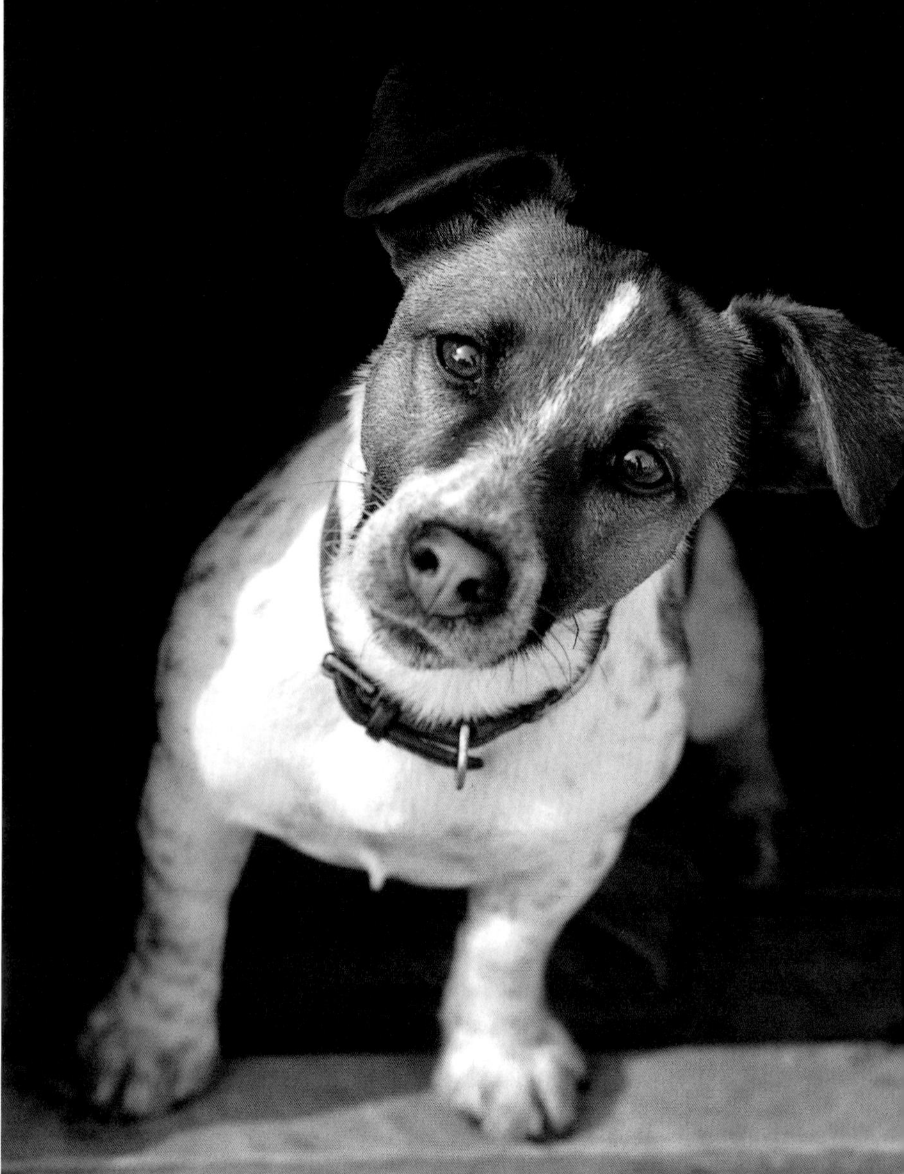

Nell

Kit Dwerryhouse, former head groom at the Quorn

Paul Whitehead, huntsman of the Lunesdale

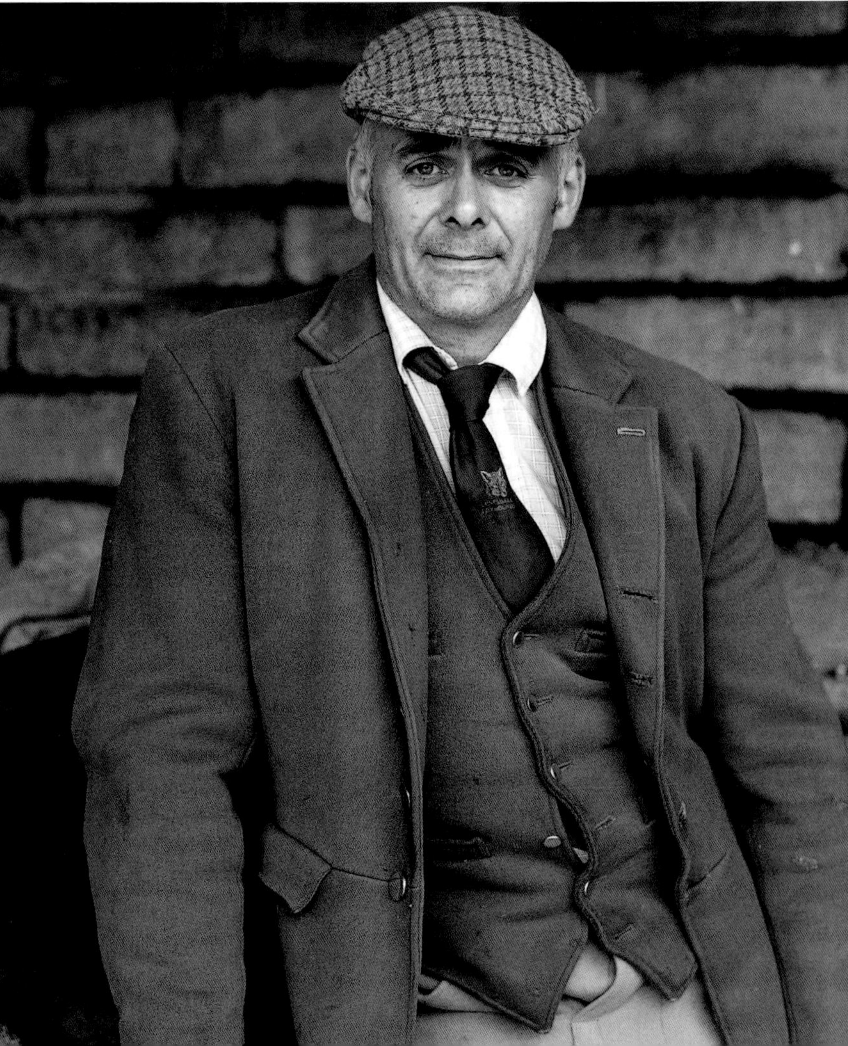

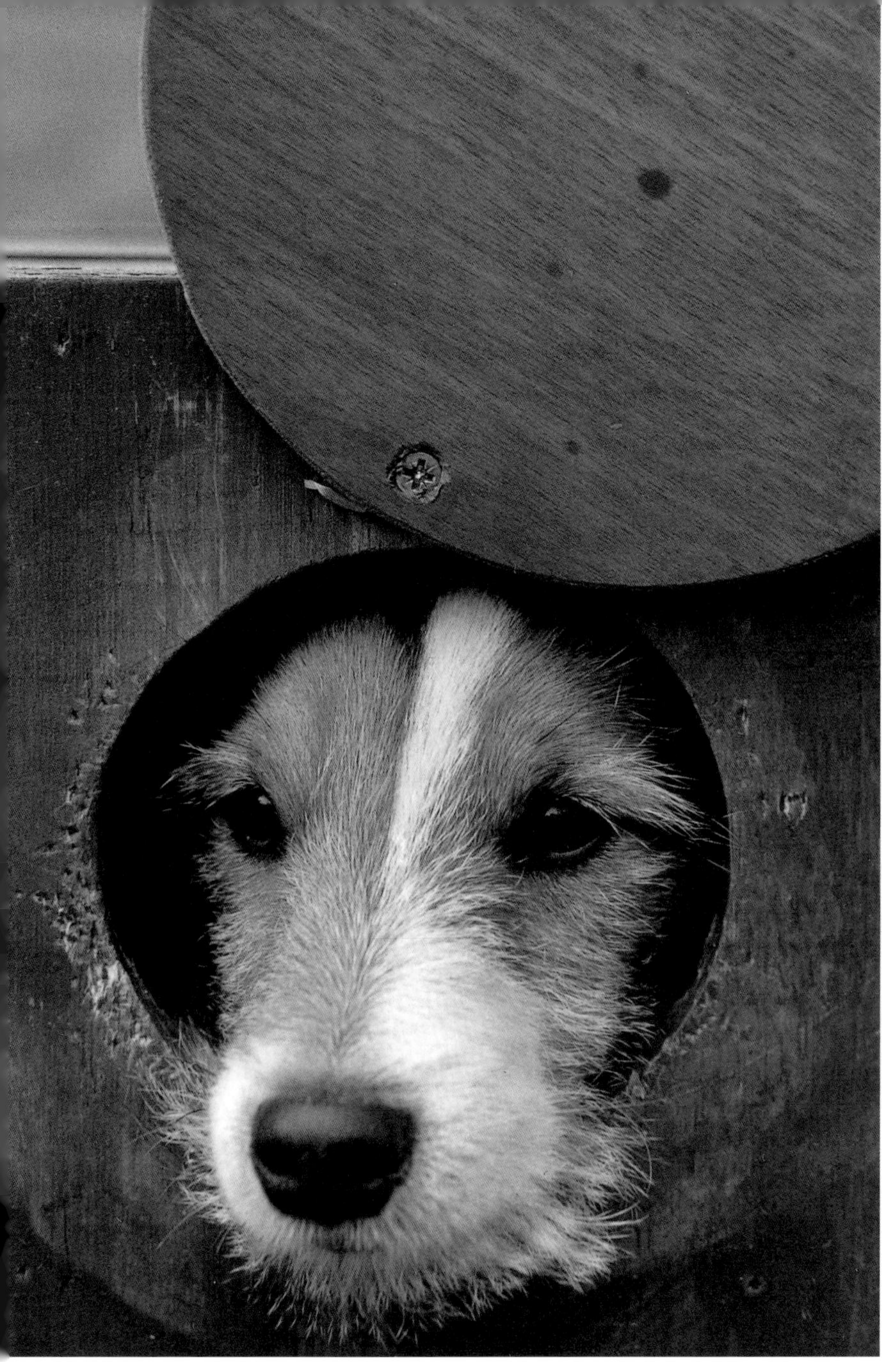

Atherstone terrier

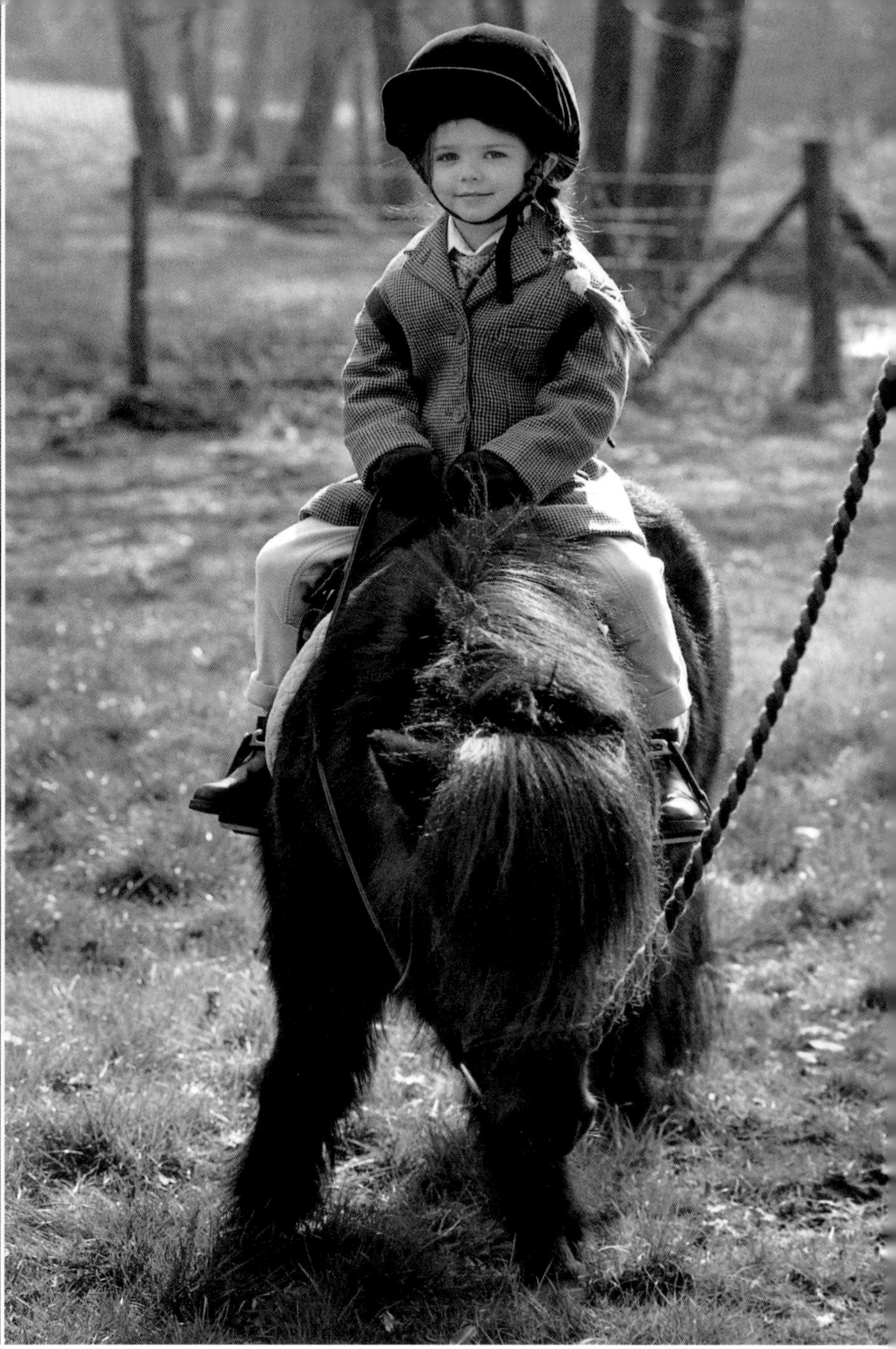

Alice Edmonds, Mid Devon

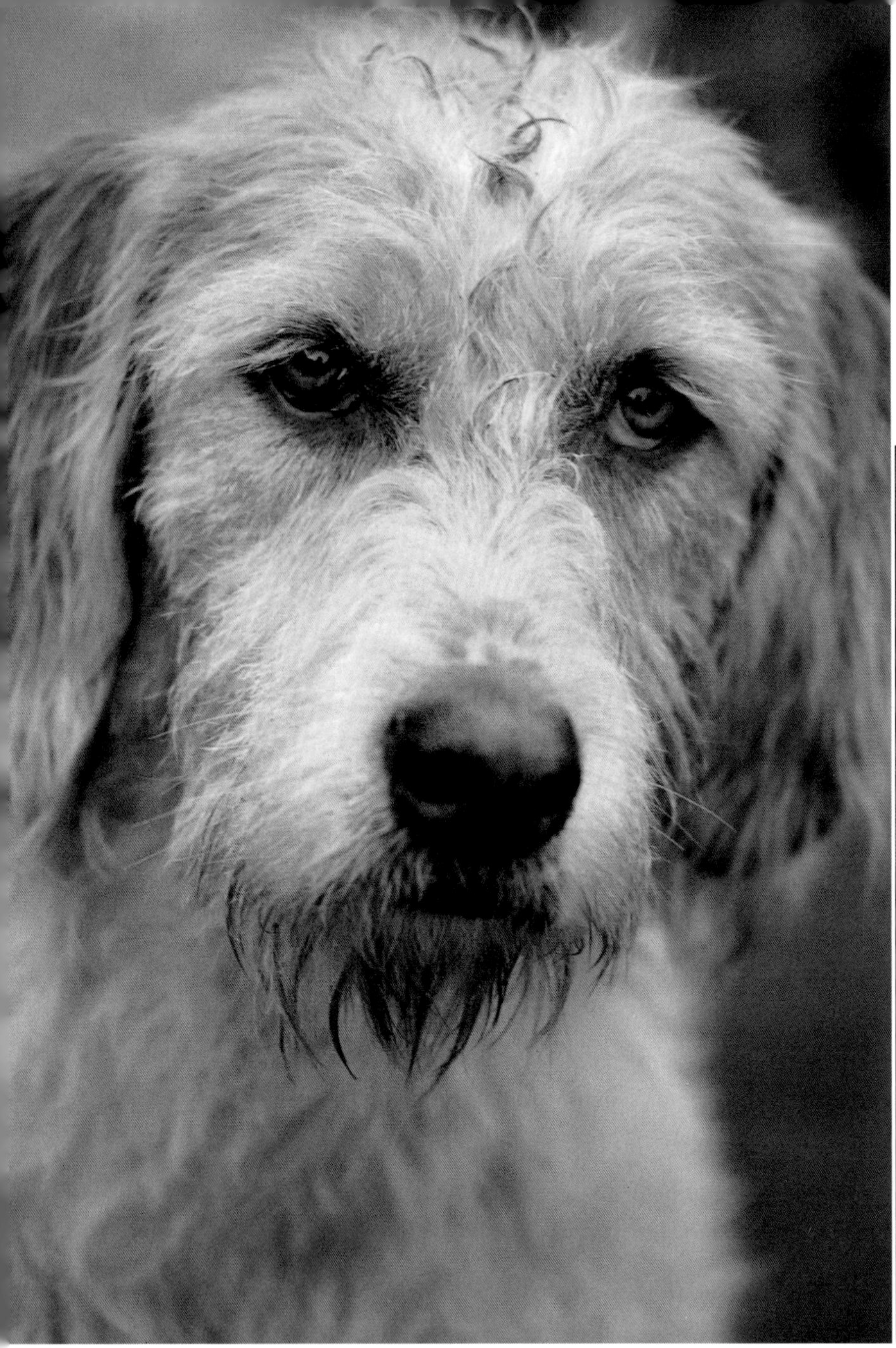

Brecon hound

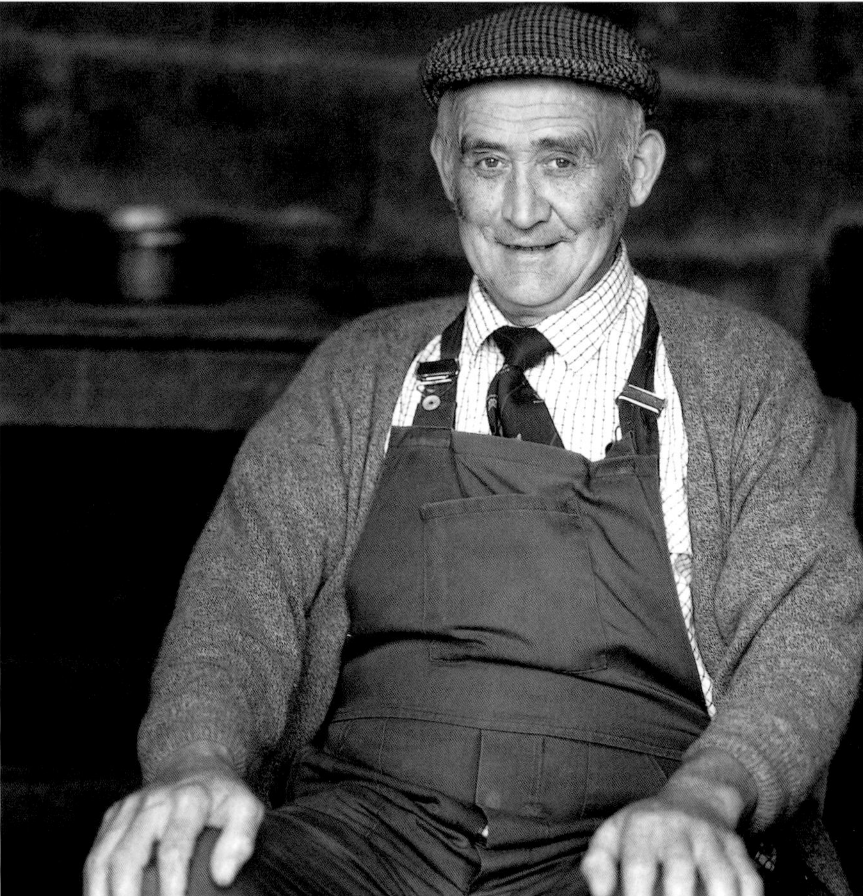

Pritch Bland, huntsman of the Melbreak

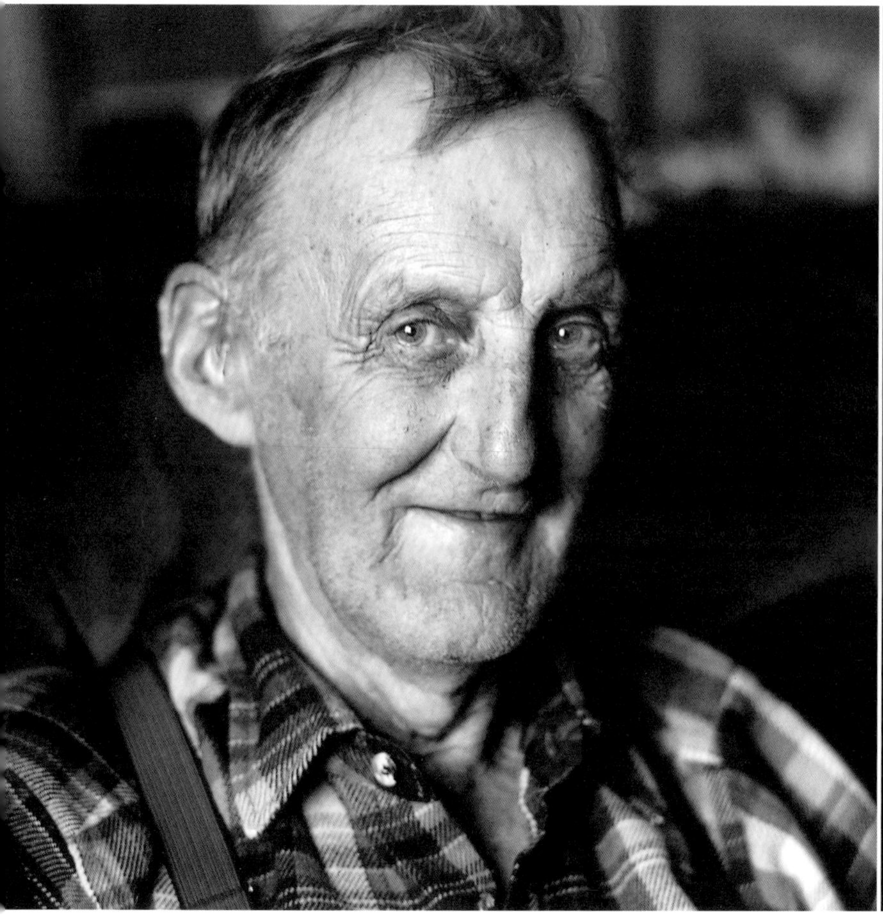

Tommy Graves, Coniston

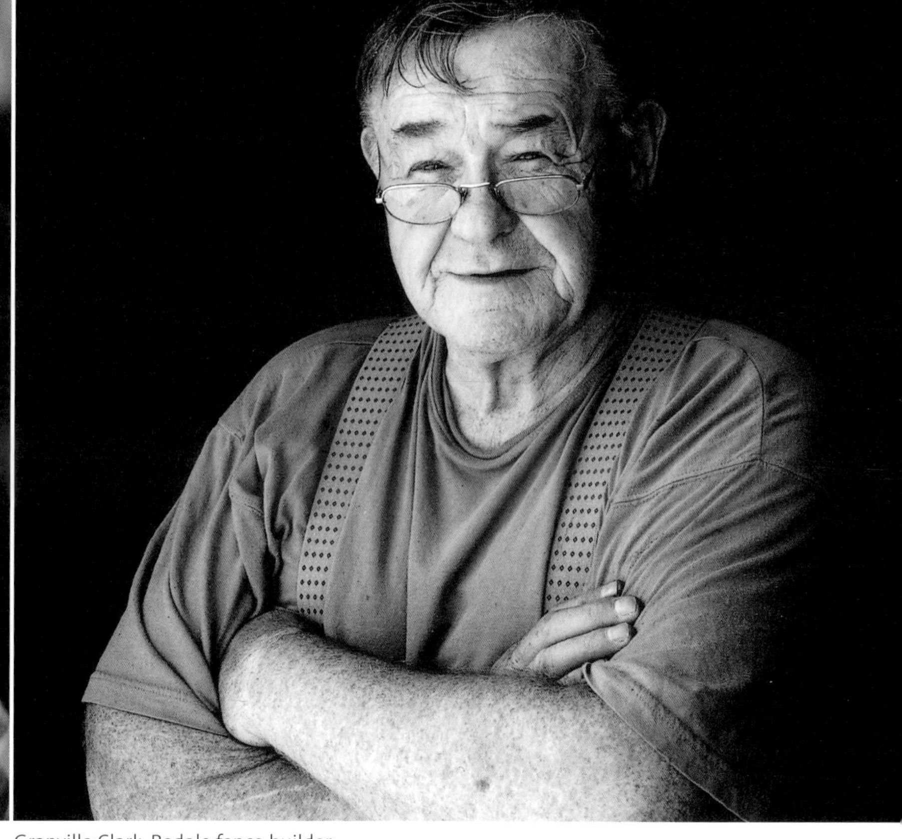

Granville Clark, Bedale fence builder

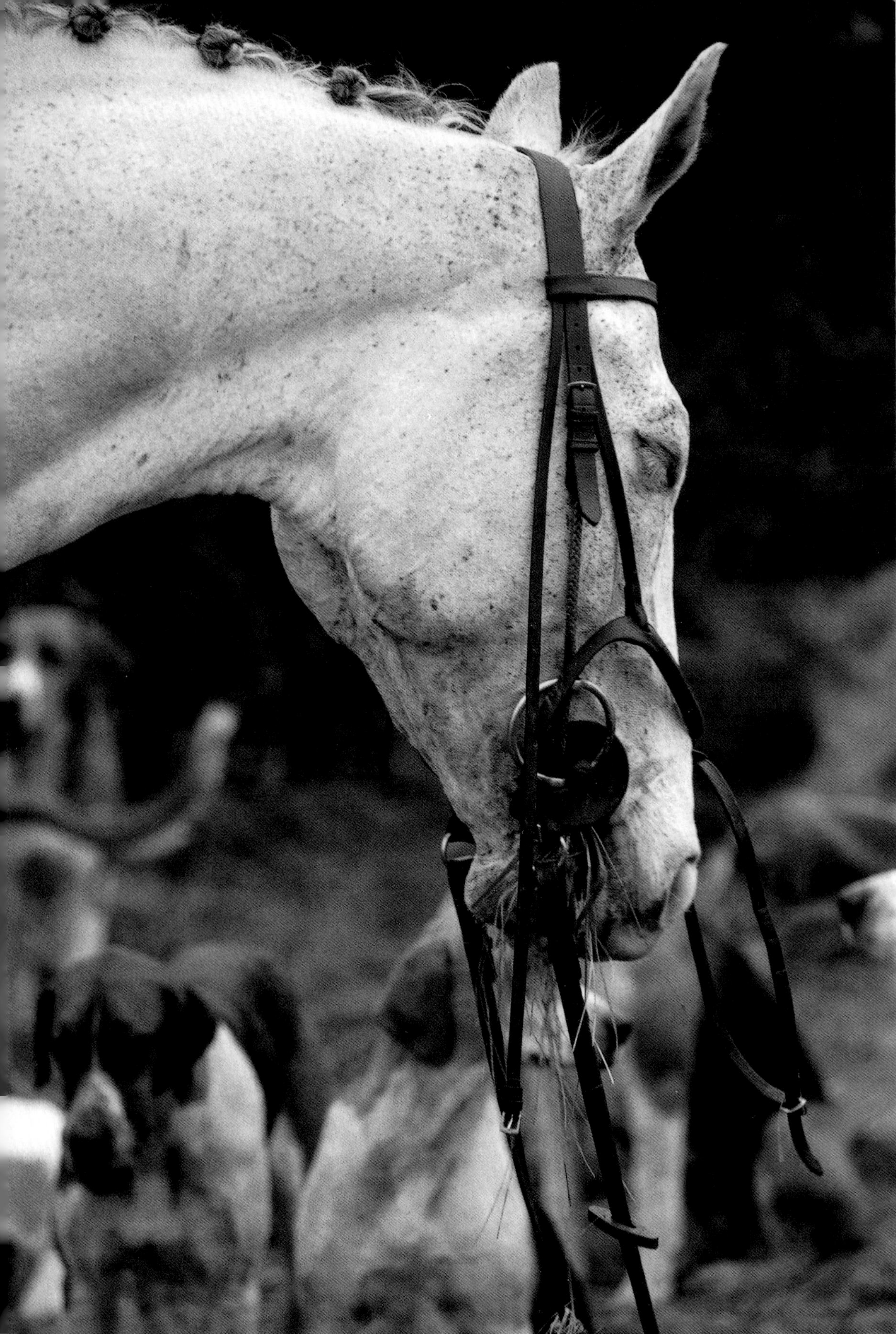

Belvoir hunt horse

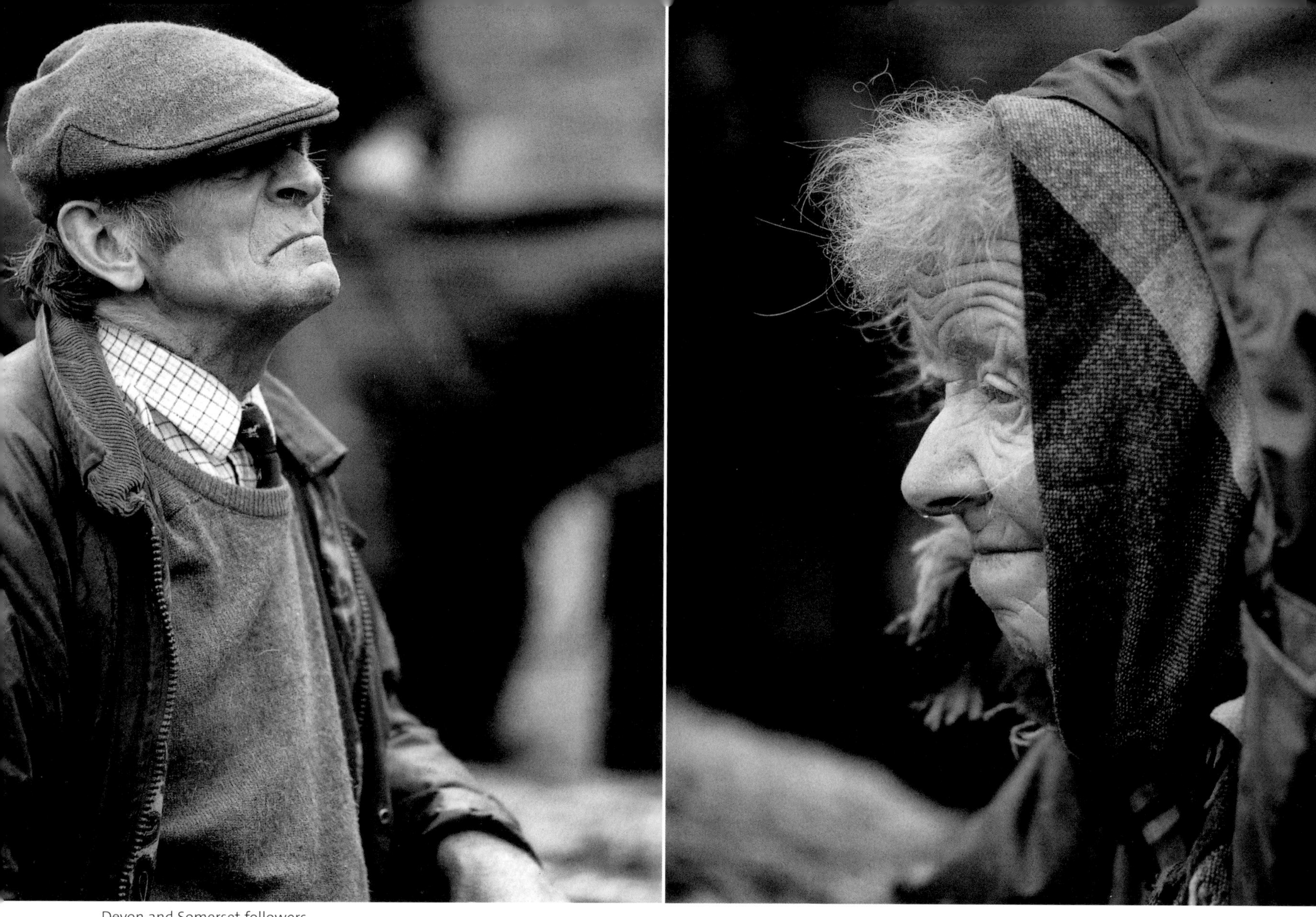

Devon and Somerset followers

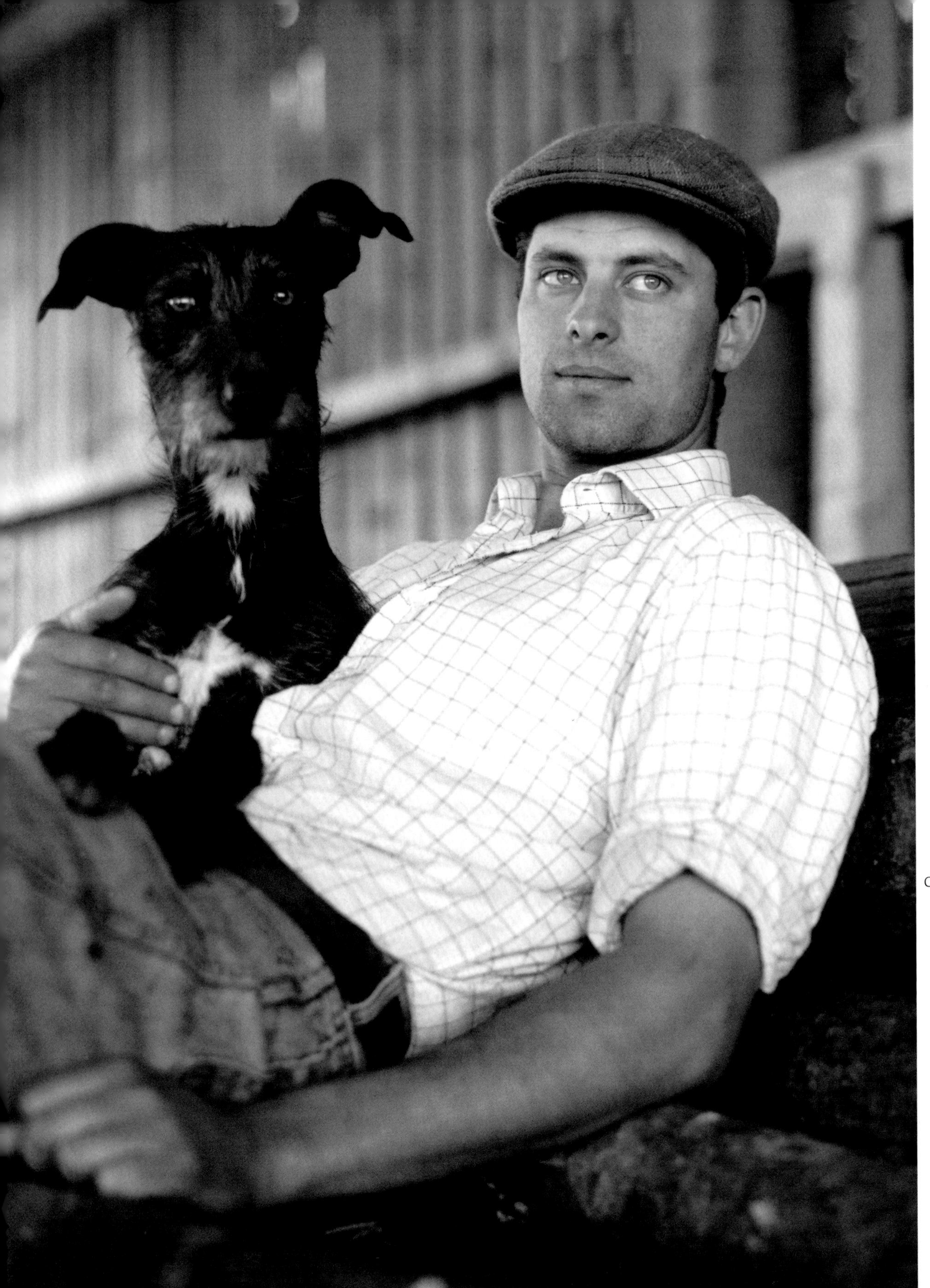

Charlie Frampton, Bedale huntsman

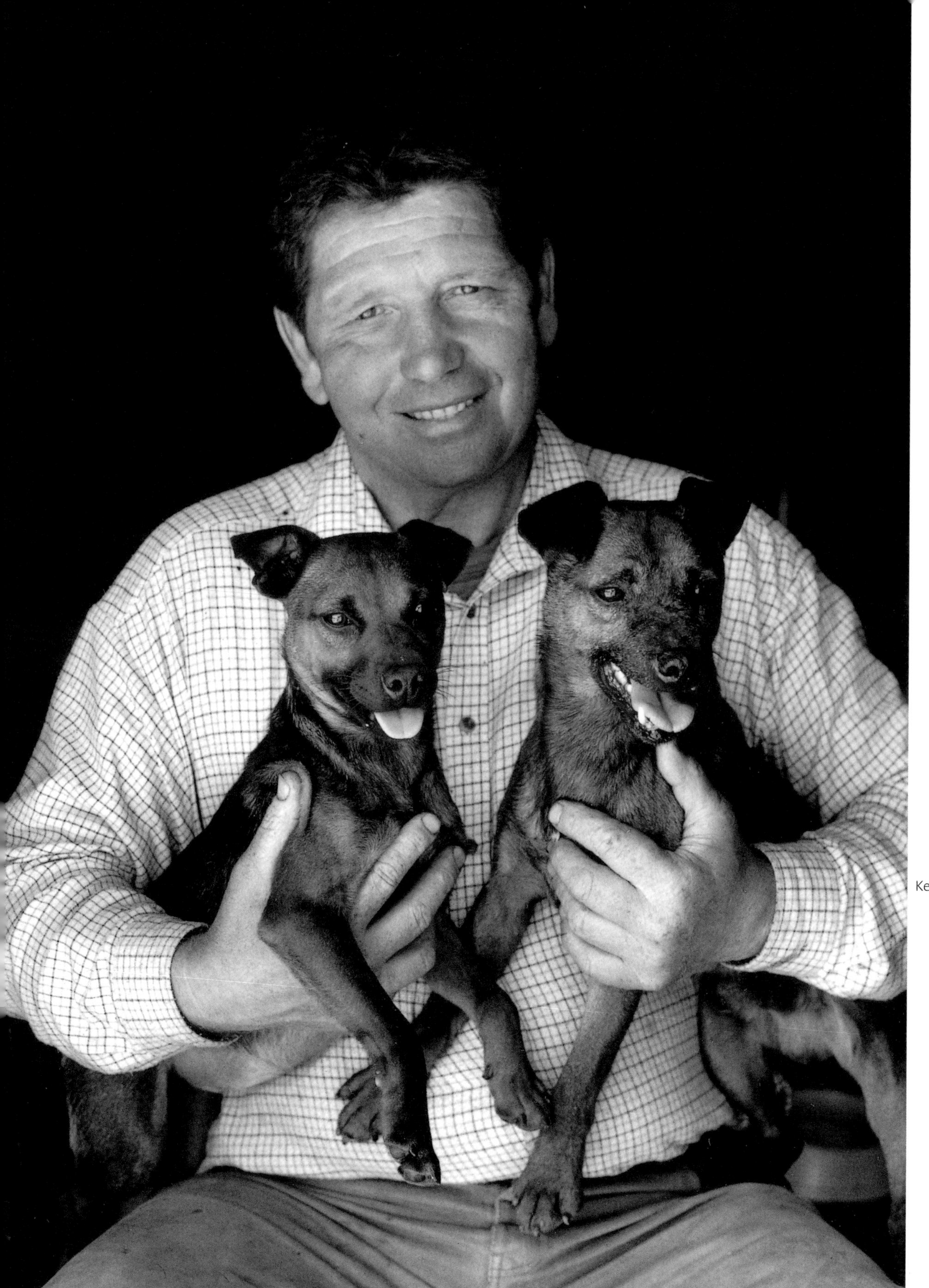

Kevin Newcombe, Bedale terrierman

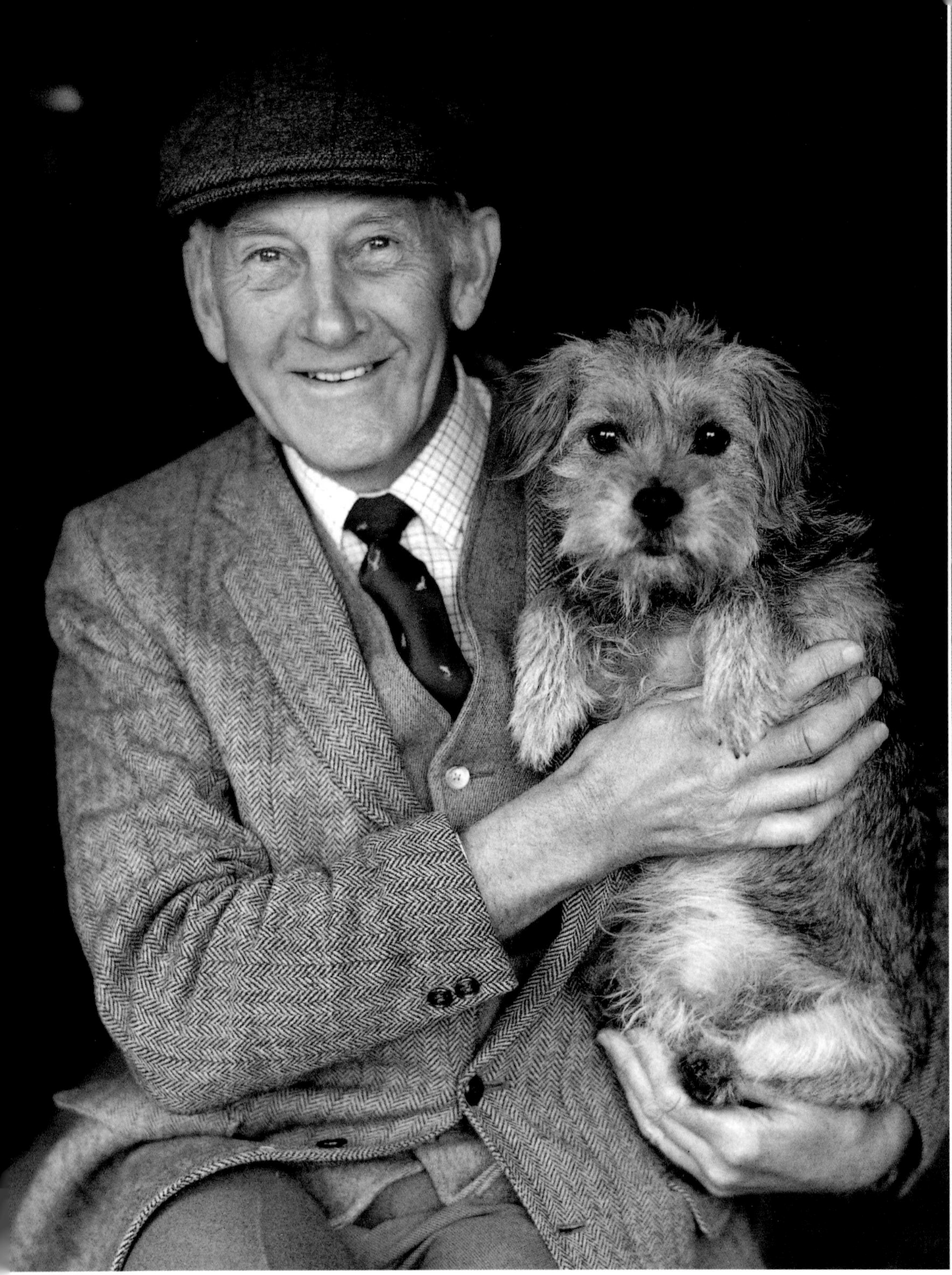

Stan Mattinson, former huntsman of the Coniston

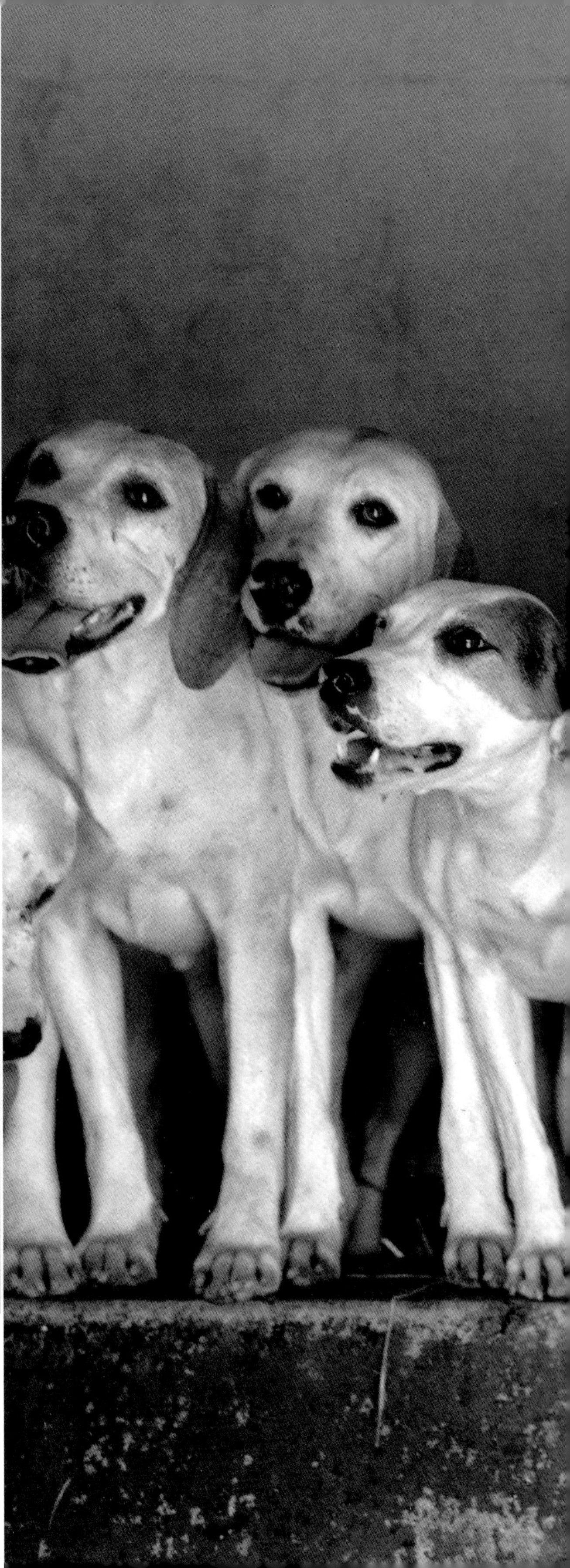

Maurice Bell, huntsman of the Wensleydale

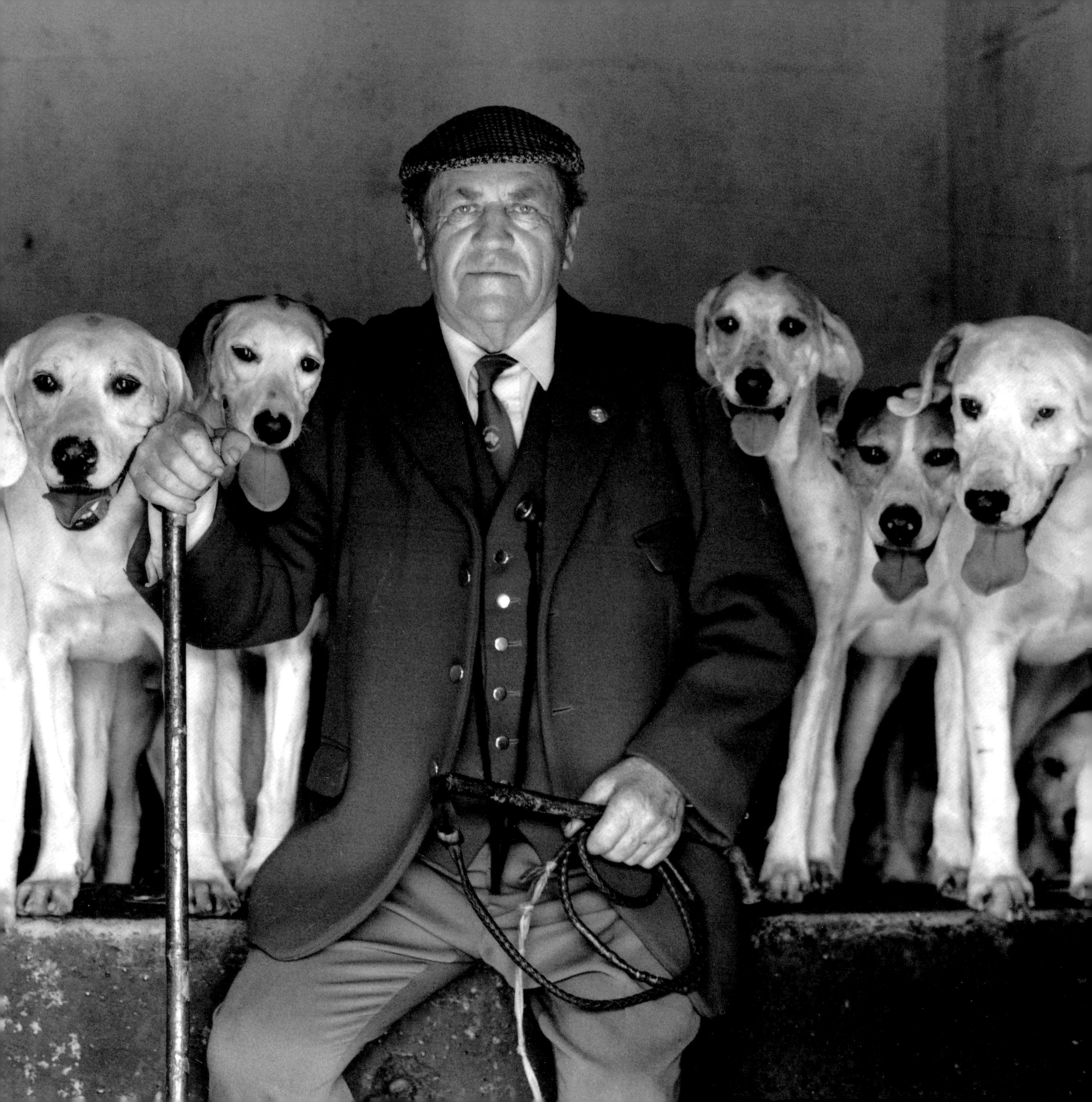

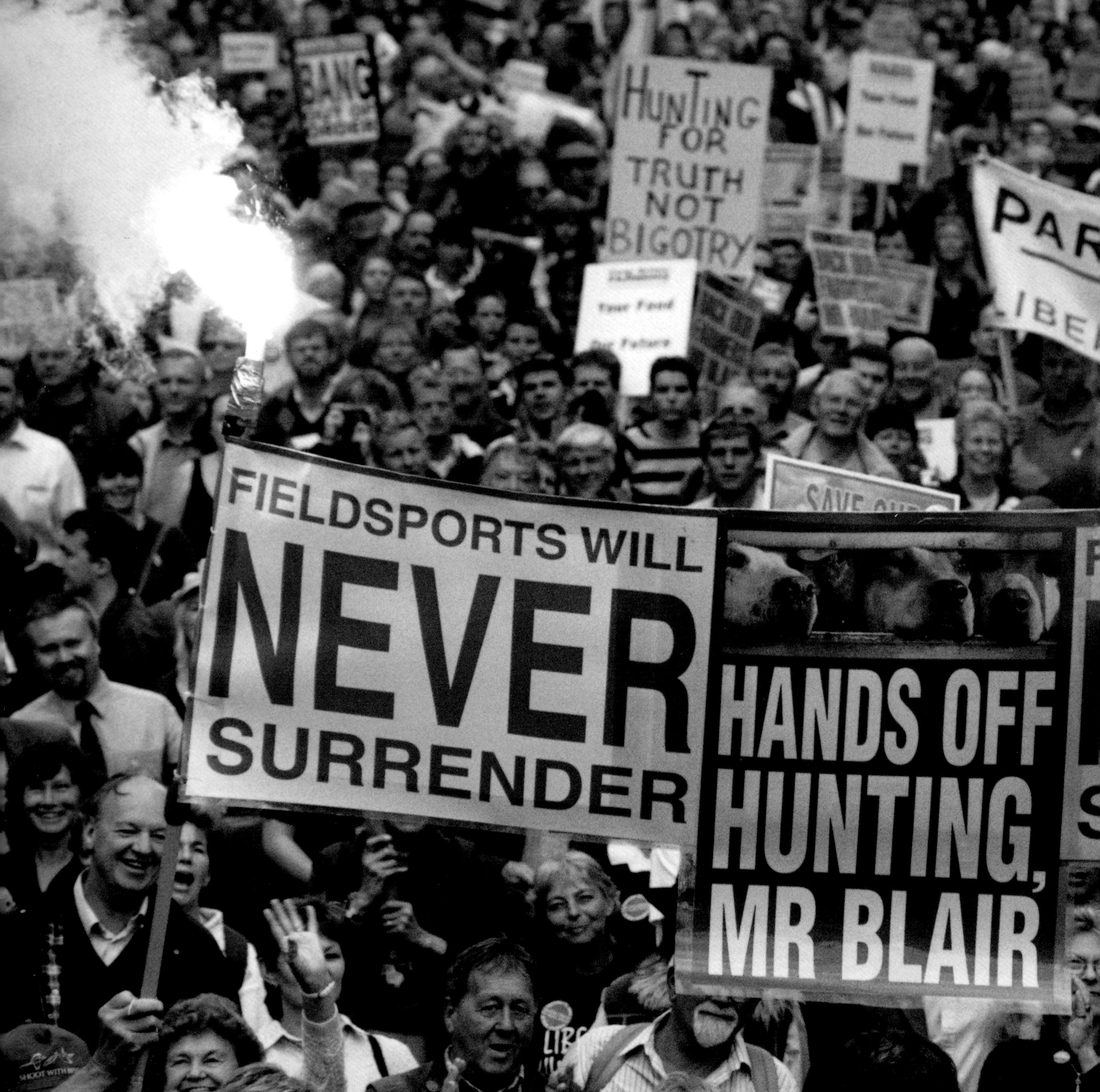

HUNTING FOR TRUTH NOT BIGOTRY
PAR
LIBE
Your Food
Our Future
SAVE OUR
FIELDSPORTS WILL NEVER SURRENDER
HANDS OFF HUNTING, MR BLAIR
LIBE
SHOOT WITH

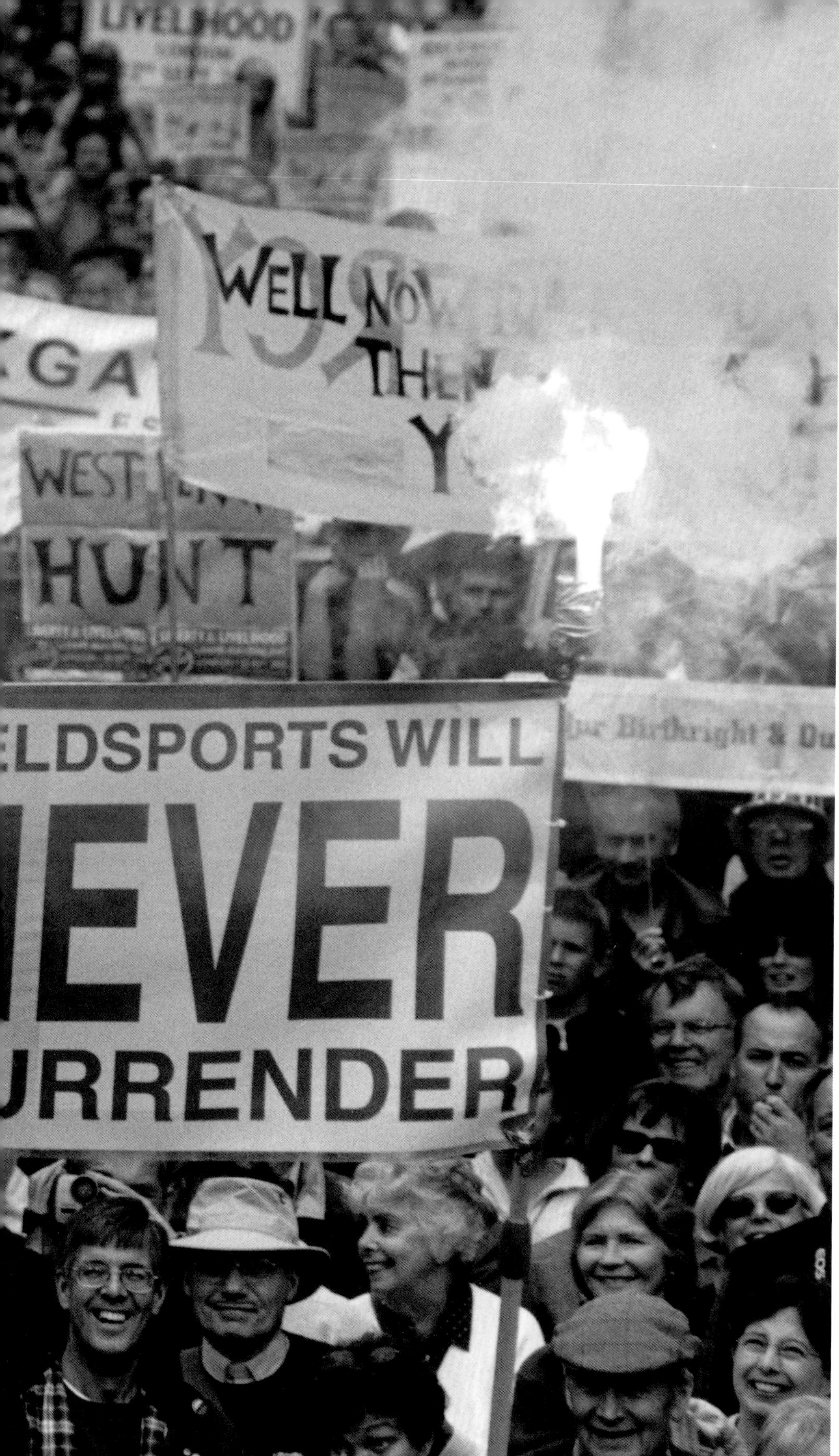

The Liberty and Livelihood March 22nd September 2002

Hunts in Britain and Ireland

* Indicates hunts visited for photography

Foxhounds England and Wales
Aber Valley
Albrighton
Albrighton Woodland
Ashford Valley
* Atherstone
* Avon Vale
Axe Vale
* Badsworth and Bramham Moor
Banwen Miners
* Barlow
* Duke of Beaufort's
* Bedale
* Belvoir (Duke of Rutland's)
* Berkeley (Earl of)
Old Berkshire
* Bewcastle
* Bicester with Whaddon Chase
Bilsdale
* Blackmore and Sparkford Vale
Blankney
* Blencathra
* Border
Braes of Derwent
* Brecon and Talybont
Brockelsby
Burton
Caerphilly and District
Cambridgeshire with Enfield
   Chace
Carmarthenshire
Cattistock
* Cheshire
Cheshire Forest
Chiddingfold, Leconfield and
   Cowdray
Cleveland
Clifton-on-Teme
* College Valley/North
   Northumberland

* Coniston
East Cornwall
North Cornwall
South Cornwall
Cotley
* Cotswold
* North Cotswold
Cotswold Vale Farmers'
* Cottesmore
Crawley and Horsham
Croome and West Warwickshire
Cumberland
* Cumberland Farmers'
Curre and LLangibby
Cury
Cwrt y Cadno Farmers'
Dartmoor
* David Davies
Derwent
East Devon
* Mid Devon
South Devon
South Dorset
Dulverton Farmers'
* Dulverton (West)
South Durham
Dwyryd
Eggesford
* Eryri
Eskdale and Ennerdale
Essex
East Essex
Essex Farmers' and Union
Essex and Suffolk
* Exmoor
Farndale
* Fernie
Fitzwilliam (Milton)
Flint and Denbigh
Four Burrow

Gelligaer Farmers'
Glaisdale
Glamorgan
* Goathland
Gogerddan
* Golden Valley
Grafton
Grove and Rufford
Hampshire (HH)
Haydon
North Herefordshire
South Herefordshire
* Heythrop
High Peak
Holcombe
Holderness
Hursley Hambledon
* Hurworth
Irfon and Towy
Isle of White
East Kent
Lamerton
* Ledbury
North Ledbury
Llandeilo Farmers'
Llangeinor
Llanwnnen and District Farmers'
North Lonsdale
Ludlow
* Lunesdale Foxhounds Limited
* Melbreak
Mendip Farmers'
* Meynell and South Staffordshire
* Middleton
Monmouthshire
* Morpeth
* Nantcol Valley
New Forest
West Norfolk
South Notts

Oakley
Pembrokeshire
South Pembrokeshire
Pendle Forest and Craven
Pennine
North Pennine
Pentyrch
Percy
* West Percy
Portman
Puckeridge
* Pytchley
Woodland Pytchley
Quorn
Radnorshire and West
   Herefordshire
Royal Artillery (Salisbury Plain)
* Saltersgate Farmers'
Seavington
* Sennybridge Farmers'
* North Shropshire
South Shropshire
Silverton
* Sinnington
West Somerset
West Somerset Vale
Southdown & Eridge
South Wold
Spooner's and West Dartmoor
Staffordshire Moorland
North Staffordshire
* Staintondale
Stevenstone
Suffolk
Old Surrey, Burstow and
   West Kent
Surrey Union
East Sussex and Romney Marsh
Tanatside
Taunton Vale

Tedworth
Teme Valley
Tetcott
South Tetcott
Thurlow
* Tiverton
Tivyside
Torrington Farmers'
* Towy and Cothi
Tredegar Farmers' Hunt Club
North Tyne
* Tynedale
* Ullswater
* United
Vale of Aylesbury with Garth
    and South Berks
Vale of Clettwr
* VWH
* Vine and Craven
* Warwickshire
* Wensleydale
Western
West Street Tickham
* West of Yore
Wheatland
* Sir Watkin Williams-Wynn's
Wilton
South and West Wilts
Worcestershire
York and Ainsty (North)
York and Ainsty (South)
Ystrad Taf Fechan
* Zetland

Foxhounds Scotland
* Berwickshire
* Duke of Buccleuch's
* Dumfriesshire
* Eglinton
* Fife

* Jedforest
* Kincardineshire
* Lanarkshire and Renfrewshire
* Lauderdale
* Liddesdale

Foxhounds Ireland
Avondhu Hunt Club
Ballymacad
Bree
Brosna
Carbery
West Carbery
Carlow Farmers'
County Clare
East Down
North Down Harriers
* Duhallow
Dungannon
* County Galway ('The Blazers')
East Galway
North Galway
Golden Vale
* Island
Kildare Hunt Club
* Kilkenny
North Kilkenny
Kilmoganny
Laois (Queen's County)
* County Limerick
* Louth
* Macroom
* Meath
Muskerry
Ormond
* Scarteen (The Black and Tans)
* Shillelagh and District Hunt
    Club Limited
South Union
* Tipperary

North Tipperary
United Hunt Club
Waterford
West Waterford
* Westmeath
Wexford
* Wicklow

Harriers England
Aldenham
Axe Vale
Cambridgeshire Harriers
    Hunt Club
Cotley
Dartvale and South Pool
Dunston
Easton
Granta Harriers
High Peak
Holcombe
Minehead
Modbury
North Norfolk
Pendle Forest and Craven
Rockwood
Ross
Taunton Vale
Vale of Lune
Waveney
Weston and Banwell

Harriers Ireland
Abbeyfeale Foot Harriers
Aghabullogue
East Antrim
Mid-Antrim
Bray
County Clare
East Clare
Cloyne Harrier Hunt Club

Coolnakilla
Derrygallon
Donegal
Doneraile Hunt
Dripsey Hunt Club
Drumlin Hounds
South County Dublin
Dungarvan
Fermanagh
Fingal
Galtee
Iveagh
Kill Harriers
Killeady
Killeagh
Killinick
Killultagh, Old Rock and
    Chichester
Kilworth and Araglen
Kingdom Hunt Club
Limerick Harriers
Lismore
County Longford
Mullinavat and District
Newry
Nore Vale
Oriel
Premier
County Roscommon
Route
County Sligo
Stonehall Harrier Hunt Club
Streamstown Harriers
Tara
Tynan and Armagh
South Tyrone Hunt
Upton
Westmeath
South Westmeath
Woodstone

Beagles England and Wales

Airedale
Ampleforth
Old Berkeley
Black Combe and District
Blean
Bleasdale
Bolebroke
Brighton and Storrington
Britannia
North Bucks
Catterick
Cheshire
Chilmark and Clifton Foot
Christchurch and Farley Hill
Claro
Clinkard Meon Valley
Colne Valley
Cumbria
North Dartmoor
DNS Beagles
North Devon
Dummer
Ecclesfield
Mr Jonathan Elliott's
Emlyn
Mid-Essex
Eton College
Forest and District
Glyn Celyn
Holme Valley
Hunsley Beacon
Ilminster
Isle of Wight Foot
Marlborough College
Monmouthshire
Newcastle and District
New Forest
Norfolk Beagles Hunt Club

Oakley Foot
Palmer Milburn
Park Beagles Brown Hare
    Conservation Group
Per Ardua
Pevensey Marsh
Pimpernel (Royal Signals)
Pipewell
Purbeck and Bovington
Radley College
Royal Agricultural College
Royal Rock
Sandhurst and Aldershot
Shropshire
West Somerset Beagles
Stoke Hill
Stokesley Farmers'
Stour Valley
Stowe
Surrey and North Sussex
Taw Vale Beagles Hare
    Conservation Group
Trinity Foot and South Herts
Warwickshire
North Warwickshire
Weardale and Tees Valley
Wick and District
Wiltshire and Infantry
WCB – The Wye Beagles
Wyre Forest

Beagles Ireland

Armagh and Richhill Beagle Club
Balgarrett
Ballydine Beagle Club
Ballyvolane
Bride Valley
Castlelyons Foot Beagles
Curragh Foot Beagles
West Down

Goldburn Beagle Hunt Club
Mr Kerr's Beagles
County Louth
Maigue Valley
Maryboro Farmers
Maryboro Midleton
Pallaskenry
Riverstown Foot
Sunnyland Beagles Hunt Club
Tory Foot Beagle Club
Westmeath Foot Beagles
Wexford Foot Beagles Club
Woodrock and Blackwater Valley

Basset Hounds England and Wales

Albany
Black Mountain
De Burgh and North Essex
    Harehounds
Four Shires Basset Hounds
Huckworthy
Leadon Vale
East Lincolnshire Harehounds
Ryeford Chase Griffon Vendeen
Westerby
West Lodge Harehounds

Mink Hounds England and Wales

Aberdeenshire Mink Hounds
Mr Bell's (West Wales) Mink
    Hounds
* Border Counties Mink Hounds
Cheriton Hunt
Mid Cheshire
Culmstock Mink Hounds
* Dalston
Devon and Cornwall Mink Hunt
Dove Valley Mink Hounds
Eastern Counties
Fourshires

Hampshire Mink Hounds
Kent and Sussex Mink Hounds
Lincolnshire Mink Hounds
Norfolk Mink Hounds Hunting Club
Northamptonshire Mink Hounds
* Northern Counties Hunt
Pembrokeshire and
    Carmarthenshire Minkhounds
Three Counties Mink Hounds
Tynedale Mink Hunt
Valley Mink Hounds
Mid Wales and Glamorgan
West Wales
Wealden Mink Hounds
Ytene Mink Hunt

Mink Hounds Ireland

Bride View Mink Hounds
Cork City Mink Hunt

Staghounds England

* Devon and Somerset
* Quantock
Tiverton

Staghounds Ireland

County Down
Ward Union

Photography © 2005 Amanda Lockhart
Text © 2005 Robin Lane Fox
ISBN 1 84159 298 6

Adelphi Publishers
Northburgh House
10 Northburgh Street
London, EC1V 0AT

Printed and bound in Great Britain by
Butler and Tanner

Sales information: Random House UK
020 7840 8463
Orders to: Grantham Book Services
01476 541 000

A limited edition of images are available for
sale from www.amandalockhart.co.uk

'Better in early youth and strength
The race for life to run,
Than poisoned like a noxious rat,
Or slain by felon gun.

'Better by wily sleight and turn
The eager hound to foil,
Than slaughtered by each baser churl,
Who yet shall till the soil.

'For not upon these hills alone,
The doom of sport shall fall;
O'er the broad face of England creeps,
The shadow on the wall.

'The years roll on, old manners change,
Old customs lose their sway;
New fashions rule; the grandsire's garb
Moves ridicule today.

'The woodlands where my race has bred,
Unto the axe shall yield;
Hedgerow and copse shall cease to shade
The ever-widening field.

'The manly sports of England
Shall vanish one by one;
The manly blood of England
In weaker veins shall run.

'The furzy down, the moorland heath,
The steam plough shall invade:
Nor park nor manor shall escape –
Common, nor forest glade.

'Degenerate sons of manlier sires
To lower joys shall fall;
The faithless lore of Germany,
The gilded vice of Gaul.

'The sports of their forefathers
To baser tastes shall yield;
The vices of the town displace,
The pleasure of the field.

'For swiftly o'er the level shore
The waves of progress ride;
The ancient landmarks one by one
Shall sink beneath the tide.

'Time-honoured creeds and ancient faith
The Altar and the Crown,
Lordship's hereditary right,
Before the tide go down.

'Base churls shall mock the mighty names,
Writ on the roll of time;
Religion shall be held a jest,
And loyalty a crime.

'No word of prayer, no hymn of praise
Sound in the village school:
The people's education
Utilitarians rule.

'In England's ancient pulpits
Lay orators shall preach
New creeds, and free religions
Self-made apostles teach.

'The peasants to their daily tasks
In surly silence fall;
No kindly hospitalities
In farmhouse or in hall.

'Nor harvest feast nor Christmastide
Shall farm or manor hold;
Science alone can plenty give,
The only god is Gold.

'The homes where love and peace should
dwell
Fierce politics shall vex,
And unsexed woman shall strive to prove
Herself the coarser sex.

'Mechanics in their workshops
Affairs of state decide;
Honour and truth – old-fashioned words –
The noisy mob deride.

'The statesmen that should rule the realm
Coarse demagogues displace;
The glory of a thousand years
Shall end in foul disgrace.
'The honour of old England,
Cotton shall buy and sell,
And hardware manufacturers
Cry "Peace! – lo! all is well."

'Trade shall be held the only good,
And gain the sole device;
The statesman's maxim shall be peace,
And peace at any price.

'Her army and her navy
Britain shall cast aside;
Soldiers and ships are costly things,
Defence an empty pride.

'The German and the Muscovite
Shall rule the narrow seas;
Old England's flag shall cease to float
In triumph on the breeze.

'The footsteps of the invader
Then England's shore shall know,
While home-bred traitors give the hand
To England's every foe.

'Disarmed before the foreigner,
The knee shall humbly bend,
And yield the treasures that she lacked
The wisdom to defend.

'But not for aye – yet once again,
When purged by fire and sword,
The land her freedom shall regain
To manlier thoughts restored.

'Taught wisdom by disaster,
England shall learn to know
That trade is not the only gain
Heaven gives to man below.